THE INTIMATE LIFE OF L.M. MC

Who ultimately is L.M. Montgomery, and why was there such an obsession with secrecy, hiding, and encoding in her life and fiction? Delving into the life of Canada's most enigmatic writer, *The Intimate Life of L.M. Montgomery* addresses these questions. The eleven essays illuminate Montgomery's personal writings and photographic self-portraits and probe the ways in which she actively shaped her life as a work of art. This is the first book to investigate both these writings – which include thousands of pages in journals, a memoir, correspondence, and scrapbooks – and her photography.

Using theories of autobiography and life writing, the essays explore the author's flair for the dramatic and her exuberance in costuming, as well as the personal facts behind some of her fiction, including the beloved *Anne of Green Gables*. Focusing on topics such as sexuality, depression, marriage, ageing, illness, and writing, the essays strip away the layers of art and artifice that disguised Montgomery's most intensely guarded secrets, including details of her affair with Herman Leard, her marriage with Ewan Macdonald, and her friendships with Nora Lefurgey and Isabel Anderson. The book also includes rare photographs taken by Montgomery and others, many of which have not previously appeared in print.

One of the highlights of *The Intimate Life of L.M. Montgomery* is the inclusion of a secret diary that Montgomery wrote with Lefurgey in 1903. This amusing document is a rare find, for Montgomery's teasing banter presents us with a new voice that is distinct from the sombre tone of her journals. Published here for the first time, more than one hundred years after its composition, this diary is a welcome addition to the literature on this important figure.

This volume fills in many of the blanks surrounding Montgomery's personal life. Engaging and erudite, it is a boon for scholars and Montgomery fans alike.

IRENE GAMMEL is a professor of English and Canada Research Chair in Modern Literature and Culture at Ryerson University.

'Myself in 1902' – self-portrait taken by L.M. Montgomery in her Cavendish room. (L.M. Montgomery Collection, Archival and Special Collections, University of Guelph Library.)

The Intimate Life of L.M. Montgomery

Edited by Irene Gammel

UNIVERSITY OF TORONTO PRESS
Toronto Buffalo London

© University of Toronto Press Incorporated 2005
Toronto Buffalo London
Printed in Canada

Reprinted 2005

ISBN 0-8020-8924-0 (cloth)
ISBN 0-8020-8676-4 (paper)

Printed on acid-free paper

Library and Archives Canada Cataloguing in Publication

The intimate life of L.M. Montgomery / edited by Irene Gammel.

Includes bibliographical references.
ISBN 0-8020-8924-0 (bound)   ISBN 0-8020-8676-4 (pbk.)

1. Montgomery, L.M. (Lucy Maud), 1874–1942.   2. Montgomery,
L.M. (Lucy Maud), 1874–1942 – Friends and associates.   3. Novelists,
Canadian (English) – 20th century – Biography.   I. Gammel, Irene

PS8526.O55Z686 2005   C813′.52   C2004-904536-9

University of Toronto Press acknowledges the financial assistance
to its publishing program of the Canada Council for the Arts and the
Ontario Arts Council.

This book has been published with the help of a grant from the Canadian
Federation for the Humanities and Social Sciences, through the Aid to
Scholarly Publications Programme, using funds provided by the Social
Sciences and Humanities Research Council of Canada.

University of Toronto Press acknowledges the financial support for
its publishing activities of the Government of Canada through the
Book Publishing Industry Development Program (BPIDP).

Contents

Acknowledgments

I would like to thank the contributors, whose enthusiasm in engaging the topic, each other's texts, and the editorial comments has made this collaboration and book a pleasure to work on. In particular, I would like to thank Jennifer Litster for unstinting help with proofreading the diary annotations, and Mary Beth Cavert for sharing her wealth of researched materials. I am also grateful to others who are not contributors but have had a significant hand in shaping this book: J. Paul Boudreau, for his exuberantly creative – and always inspirational – input and for procuring important illustrations and helping trace Montgomery's steps in Lower Bedeque; Patricia Srebrnik, for her outstanding help with the editing of several chapters, a task that involved significant time commitments and painstaking attention to scholarly detail; and Donya Beaton, for her passion in visualizing Montgomery, as she spent countless hours in restoring old photographs and daguerreotypes.

There is a favourite memory with each book I have worked on, an emotional kernel that creates momentum and excitement and permeates the shape of the entire book. A central memory concerns the spring and summer of 2003. Exactly one hundred years after Montgomery and Nora Lefurgey composed the secret diary featured in this book, Jennie Macneill and I followed the traces of the people who populate this diary. In numerous telephone calls, we joked that we were chasing the Cavendish beaux, as our hunt gained momentum and revealed tantalizing clues. With her kind eyes and her uncompromising dedication to preserving the Montgomery homestead, Jennie Macneill knew some of the beaux personally, and could relate stories of Robert MacKenzie and others. She also provided a plethora of photos from which the book benefited immensely. The chase after another beau, James Alexander

Stewart, led me to Ruth Gallant in Ontario, a woman whose vibrancy and enthusiasm were equally infectious, who had an almost encyclopedic knowledge of James, Garfield, and Annie Stewart, all mentioned in the diary. Ruth Gallant generously provided photographs and daguerreotypes, some over one hundred years old. Another emotional touchstone was Bette Campbell, who gave permission to publish the Nora Lefurgey part of the collaborative diary, and provided photographs of Nora as well. I had written to Bette's husband, Edmund Jr, Nora's son. Bette Campbell wrote back to say that her husband had passed away two years earlier and that receiving my letter addressed to him had mystified her; it was like a sign from beyond the grave. She had vibrant memories of Nora, whom she admired and adored, and she relayed fondly how Nora and her husband, Ned, lived in British Columbia, where Ned was a manager in a copper mine in 1912, and where their son Edmund was born in 1914. Thus each search has its own story and its unique set of memories, as many people have provided invaluable help with or permission for photographs and archival materials, including Marilyn Bell (Prince Edward Island Archives); Elizabeth Boswall, Mary E. Campbell, M. Coles, Lou Daley, and Elizabeth Deblois (L.M. Montgomery Institute); and Elizabeth Epperly, Paul Hansen, Janet Haslem, Simon Lloyd, Nancy MacFarlane, Anne Nichols, Jim Nichols, Mary McDonald-Rissanen, and Anastasia Rogers (Archives of Ontario).

Special thanks go to the team at the University of Guelph Archives; to Lorne Bruce, for expert help with and permission for the diary; and to Ellen Morrison and Darlene Wiltsie for always patient and swift help with the diary and with illustrations for the book.

Special thanks also go to the L.M. Montgomery Institute (LMMI) at the University of Prince Edward Island – and its director Elizabeth Deblois – for its involvement in and support of this collection as the host of the International L.M. Montgomery and Life Writing Symposium (see Introduction for details) and for providing financial support through Aliant Telecom; as well as to Elizabeth Epperly and Mary Rubio, for their involvement in the publication of this book. The book was originally to be published by Canadian Children's Literature Press, in collaboration with LMMI, but in a twist of fortune it now appears under the imprint of University of Toronto Press. It was Elizabeth Epperly who first suggested that I publish the diary.

I am grateful to the Social Sciences and Humanities Research Council of Canada for providing, as it were, the lifeline for this project, with generous grants for research travel and time release. I am grateful to the

Aid to Scholarly Publications Programme for a publication subsidy. To Richard Kurial, Dean of Arts at the University of Prince Edward Island, I am grateful for both his enthusiastic support of this project and the provision of the important research space which greatly benefited this book. I am also grateful for the support of the Centre for Comparative Literature at the University of Toronto during my stay as Visiting Scholar in the winter term of 2004.

I would like to thank the team at University of Toronto Press, led by acquisitions editor Siobhan McMenemy, who extended professional help and guiding vision throughout this project. I want to thank Siobhan especially for her patience and support on so many fronts. I am also indebted to the anonymous readers for their support and for their cogent, insightful, and detailed comments and suggestions, which have all found their way into the book and have helped correct errors. Others have provided feedback on aspects of this book and will find their traces in it, including Lisa LaFramboise, Jane Magrath, and Gail Mansur. I am very grateful to our copy editor, Ken Lewis, whose keen sense of stylistic elegance and meticulous attention to fine detail allowed us to catch many errors and to present the highest quality manuscript. I wish to thank Frances Mundy for her excellent care in shepherding the book through the production process. For professional assistance with this book, I wish to thank my team of fine student assistants, in particular, Chandra Gordon and Maria O'Brien.

Finally, I wish to thank the students in my 2002 L.M. Montgomery course at the University of Prince Edward Island, for passionately engaging Montgomery and life writing, and for discussing their personal impressions and family memories of this famous Island author. I dedicate this book to the memory of Nora Lefurgey, whose sharp wit and elfin smile made her one of Montgomery's closest confidantes.

Permissions

Material written by L.M. Montgomery is excerpted with the permission of Ruth Macdonald and David Macdonald, trustee, who are the heirs of L.M. Montgomery.

L.M. Montgomery and Nora Lefurgey's diary is taken from volume 2 of the unpublished typescript journal of L.M. Montgomery, located in the University of Guelph Library and is reproduced with the permission of the L.M. Montgomery Collection, Archival and Special Collections, University of Guelph Library, the heirs of L.M. Montgomery, and Bette Campbell.

The Alpine Path and *The Poetry of L.M. Montgomery* are published by Fitzhenry & Whiteside Ltd.

L.M. Montgomery's Ehpraim Weber: Letters, 1916–1941 is published by MLR Editions.

Excerpts from L.M. Montgomery's Island scrapbooks are reproduced with the permission of the L.M. Montgomery Birthplace Foundation and the heirs of L.M. Montgomery.

L.M. Montgomery, Emily of New Moon, and *The Blue Castle* are trademarks of Heirs of L.M. Montgomery Inc. and are used with permission.

Anne of Green Gables, characters, names, and related indicia are trademarks and/or Canadian official marks of the Anne of Green Gables Licensing Authority Inc., which is owned by the heirs of L.M. Montgomery and the Province of Prince Edward Island and are used with permission.

Excerpts from *The Selected Journals of L.M. Montgomery,* volumes I, II, III, and IV © 1985, 1987, 1992, 1998, University of Guelph, edited by Mary Rubio and Elizabeth Waterston, and published by Oxford

University Press, are reproduced with the permission of Mary Rubio, Elizabeth Waterston, and the University of Guelph, courtesy of the L.M. Montgomery Collection, Archival and Special Collections, University of Guelph Libraries.
'Untangling the Web: L.M. Montgomery's Later Journals and Fiction, 1929–1939' © Mary Rubio and Elizabeth Waterston.

Abbreviations

AAGG	*The Annotated Anne of Green Gables*
AGG	*Anne of Green Gables*
AIs	*Anne of the Island*
AP	*The Alpine Path*
BC	*The Blue Castle*
EC	*Emily Climbs*
ENM	*Emily of New Moon*
GGL	*Green Gables Letters*
GR	*The Golden Road*
MDMM	*My Dear Mr. M.*
MEW	*L.M. Montgomery's Ephraim Weber*
SJ	*The Selected Journals of L.M. Montgomery*
UJ	Unpublished Journals
USB	Unpublished Scrapbooks

'My downstairs bedroom, which Nora and I shared,' detail, showing their co-written diary on top of the bookshelf. (L.M. Montgomery Collection, Archival and Special Collections, University of Guelph Archives.)

THE INTIMATE LIFE OF L.M. MONTGOMERY

Introduction

Life Writing as Masquerade: The Many Faces of L.M. Montgomery

Irene Gammel

> You are a will-o'-the-wisp, elusive, exclusive, impulsively flitting here and there, leaving a trail of exotic sweetness that haunts one with a mad desire.
>
> Isabel Anderson to L.M. Montgomery, 8 February 1932, *SJ*, 4:165

There is a well-known self-portrait of Montgomery (see frontispiece) in which she is posing in front of her books in her bedroom in Cavendish, fashionably dressed in a fur-trimmed coat, a parasol in her gloved hand and a hat with a polka-dot veil obscuring her face.[1] Her exuberance in costuming is emblematic, revealing but also simultaneously veiling her face. This veil recurs in many photographs and journal entries. Inevitably we ask ourselves, Who is the enigmatic L.M. Montgomery behind the veil? And why was there such an obsession with secrecy, hiding, and encoding in her life and fiction? This book proposes to tackle these questions.

The Intimate Life of L.M. Montgomery is a book of essays about Montgomery's life writing as a relatively unexplored but crucially important field within Montgomery studies. Besides photographs and other records, Montgomery left thousands of pages of intimately personal writings in journals, memoirs, correspondence, and scrapbooks.[2] Keenly aware of her international status as the beloved author of *Anne of Green Gables*, she indicated clearly that in her personal writings she consciously and carefully crafted her life, for posterity, as a literary and artistic artefact. Thus, on 16 April 1922, she noted in her journal: 'This journal is a faithful record of one human being's life and so should have a certain literary value' (*SJ* 3:51). While Betty Jane Wylie has called her an 'addicted diarist' (22), the posthumous publication of the journals has had the effect of the proverbial bombshell. Readers were shocked to learn that their beloved Montgomery had never loved her husband, had hated her social duties as minister's wife, and in fact, had scorned many of the people who thought she was their friend. The editors of Montgomery's journals, Mary Rubio and Elizabeth Waterston, have highlighted the journals' literary quality, but they have also questioned the fact that she rewrote them at various times during her life, while omitting important events, and had a habit of recycling journal materials and clippings from scrapbooks in letters and fiction (Introduction, *SJ*, 3:xxvii; see also Drain 7–18).[3] Just how reliable is the story of her life after several revisions? What ultimately is the relationship between the public celebrity author and the private woman?

The essays collected in the present volume undertake a systematic examination of Montgomery's shaping of her life story by delving into not only her published and unpublished journals, letters, and scrapbooks, but also her photographic self-portraits and her fiction. They both draw upon recent theoretical approaches to indicate Montgomery's sophistication as an avid autobiographer, and contribute to theories of life writing by considering such issues as identity construction, role-playing, and aesthetic and narrative strategies; the tension between the public and the private self, and between revealing and concealing the self; the relationship between photograph and text; the relationship between fiction and life writing. This book is ultimately part of a concerted international effort to unveil the intimate life of Canada's most enigmatic literary icon.

Performing the Self

Women have traditionally written in the personal forms of letters and diaries, but only recently has this writing been accepted as writing. 'This diary writing does not really count as writing,' wrote Virginia Woolf on 20 January 1919 in her diary, while Anaïs Nin also laboured to find acceptance for her diaries within the literary genre. It has taken the past two decades for scholars to document that life writing is not a passive mirroring of self, but a forum for self-invention and self-discovery, for the articulation of female agency, and for both resisting and re-inscribing social conventions.[4] Since Montgomery shaped her life writing – including her visual self-portraits – as a self-consciously literary and artistic genre, theories of autobiography and life writing are crucial in examining the extent to which she managed to achieve a sense of agency for herself in composing her self-portraits in journals, letters, autobiography, and photography, and the extent to which her life writing reflects her profound entrapment in social conventions.

Montgomery had a flair for the dramatic, and one common thread in this collection is the focus on role-playing and theatricality in Montgomery's life writing. Scholars have linked life writing to performance, in which the writer assumes different roles, performs acts, and stages a variety of selves.[5] These performance theories help us to examine Montgomery's self-dramatizing in the journals, with particular reference to costuming: she dons different dresses as she dons different selves. 'Myself I wore a widow's dress and veil,' she wrote in January 1927 in describing a concert for which 'all the performers – wore old-time costumes – big sleeves – bustles – crinolines – bonnets, veils' (*SJ* 3:325) (fig. I.1). Montgomery took delight in what twenty-first-century critics would recognize as 'masquerade.' As Amelia Jones remarks in 'Performing the Other as Self': 'Masquerade [is] the production of the self as exacerbatedly the thing most expected – but marking this thing as fake,' a mode of self-production which would become increasingly common in popular culture by the 1980s (74). Montgomery performed herself in the images most expected of women of her time, the bride posing in her wedding trousseau, the demure author of simple girls' fiction, the minister's wife and loving mother (see fig. I.2), producing socially pleasing visual selves in photography (often inserted in her journals) and verbal self-portraits in journals, letters, and memoirs. Yet she always juxtaposed these expected images of herself with subversive self-portraits: the dissatisfied wife, for example, who 'was never in love with Ewan' (*SJ* 2:206), the neurotic lover of Herman Leard, the depressive sufferer, the career woman and celebrity author. In examining the literary and artistic work behind these autobiographical personae, this volume also extends the insights of such foundational biographical studies as Francis Bolger's *The Years before 'Anne,'* Mollie Gillen's *The Wheel of Things*, Mary Rubio and Elizabeth Waterston's *Writing a Life*, and Genevieve Wiggins's *L.M. Montgomery*. This book also extends the work begun by Alexandra Heilbron in *Remembering Lucy Maud Montgomery*, in collecting the memories of people who knew Montgomery personally. These memories enable us to trace the gaps in her journals.

Since the publication of the first volume of the journals in 1985, readers of Montgomery's journals have routinely noted that she fails to

I.1 'Myself I wore a widow's dress and veil' – L.M. Montgomery (centre) in costume at a concert party in January 1927. (Acc. 2330.38-6. Public Archives and Records Office of Prince Edward Island.)

I.2   Playing the roles most expected – minister's wife and mother: Maud with Stuart, Ewan, and Chester. Postcard inscribed: 'With greetings from the Manse.' 1925. (Acc. 2330.38-7. Public Archives and Records Office of Prince Edward Island.)

tell the entire truth, leaving strategic gaps, although one might also point out the opposite: she was remarkably frank, considering that she grew up in Victorian times and in rural Prince Edward Island. In the *Encyclopedia of Life Writing*, Rachel Cottam has noted that the diarist who writes for an audience is often considered 'insincere and thus not considered to be writing a "proper" diary' (Cottam 269). Yet diary scholars have made a forceful case for the diary as a 'a publicly oriented, artistically conceived genre,' as Elizabeth Podnieks writes in the introduction to a special issue of the journal *A/B: Auto/Biography Studies* entitled *Private Lives / Public Texts: Women's Literary Diaries and Journals* (2). Also, in '"I Write for Myself and Strangers": Private Diaries as Public Documents,' Lynn Bloom has helped us to distinguish between the private and the public diary, the first written for private consumption and the latter written and revised for publication (23–37).[6] Montgomery's use of the term 'journal' signals the specific subcategory of the public diary. Using a key strategy of what I term retrospective disclosure, she recorded some of the intimate or unsettling events in her life – not on the day they occurred – but weeks, months, and even years later. Such aesthetic working out of her intimate life requires theorizing both with respect to its literary function and its autobiographical truth value. My own collection of essays, *Confessional Politics: Women's Sexual Self-Representations in Life Writing and Popular Media* (1999), has begun this task by documenting that the woman writer always negotiates the extent and the form of her intimate disclosures, sometimes simultaneously courting and sidestepping the reader's voyeuristic gaze. Women show remarkable awareness of both the risks and the empowerment involved in disclosing intimate subject matter. Some writers use hybrid genres such as confessional fiction or autobiographical fiction, for fictionalizing strategies present a protective screen for intimately personal writing (Saint-Martin 28–46). Moreover, the use of aesthetic forms is a way of ordering and disclosing traumatic experiences (Cooke 65–80). These theories will be helpful in examining Montgomery's literary crafting of her life story.

This book also takes its place within an impressive flourishing of scholarship on Montgomery. Over the last two decades, scholars have documented the high literary quality of Montgomery's romance fiction by examining her sophisticated intertextual engagement with the British romantics. They have noted her social criticism and use of satire as a way of complicating and subverting the simplicity of the convention-driven domestic romance genre. They have acknowledged her enormous contributions to girls', children's, and women's literature. They have also documented that Montgomery was not an innocent or simple writer, but was profoundly implicated in the nation-building efforts of the young Confederation.[7]

Two of my own books have advanced the field in situating Montgomery within the larger cultural field. *Making Avonlea: L.M. Montgomery and Popular Culture* (2002), a book of essays, has investigated Montgomery's international popular culture industry, including spin-off novels, films, musicals, dolls, and other merchandise, ultimately documenting Montgomery's remarkable ability to reach and influence a mass audience around the globe. *L.M. Montgomery and Canadian Culture* (1999), a collection of essays I co-edited with Elizabeth Epperly, highlighted Montgomery's Canadianness and revealed the extent to which 'Anne' has become a Canadian cultural icon, similar to the Mountie, exported into the world as a synecdoche for Canada itself. *The Intimate Life of L.M. Montgomery* presents the third volume in this series, and it is the first book devoted to the life writing of L.M. Montgomery, Canada's most enduring celebrity author.

The Secret Diary of L.M. Montgomery and Nora Lefurgey

The *pièce de resistance* of this book is the publication of a co-authored diary written by L.M. Montgomery and her friend Nora Lefurgey from January to June 1903, when Nora was boarding at the old Macneill homestead. This text – featured in the first chapter – is a rare find for at least two reasons: first, Montgomery's teasing banter presents a new voice that is distinctly different from that of the journals; and second, the diary has remained buried in Montgomery's typescript journal housed at the University of Guelph Archives. It is virtually unknown to readers and scholars and is introduced here for the first time. I learned about this text at the International L.M. Montgomery and Life Writing Symposium in 2002, when Jennifer Litster presented a paper entitled 'The Secret Diary of Maud Montgomery.' When I received the first sample pages sent to me by the University of Guelph Archives, I was quickly captivated by its focus on boys and boy talk and its allusive talk about garters and other 'unmentionable' items of clothing. For today's reader, this diary anticipates and parodies the voyeuristic pleasures of a *Bachelorette* reality television show. We meet the male 'heroes' who were the objects of Montgomery's and Nora Lefurgey's merciless flirting and teasing; there are as well some fleeting, yet revealing, references to the real beaux in Montgomery's life, Ewan Macdonald and Edwin Simpson. What is striking in this newly discovered diary is that Montgomery was engaged in hilarious jest at virtually the same time that she poured her darkest depression and gloom into her private journal. The same woman who would crack hilarious jokes in her co-authored diary on 19 April 1903 had recorded her misery just a week earlier, on 12 April, in her journal: 'I am tired of existence. Life has been a sorry business for me these past five years' (*SJ* 1:287). The spectrum of personae coexisting in the same person is remarkable. We are left with baffling contradictions, yet also with a sense that laughter was the escape and cure-all that helped her manage the shadows of depression discussed by Janice Fiamengo in chapter 6. The diary's collaborative structure, too, is unique.

Montgomery writes in her journals on 12 April 1903: 'When Nora came here we started for sport's sake a sort of co-operative diary, she writing it one day and I the next.' She adds, '... we set out to make it as laughable as possible. I think we have succeeded' (*SJ* 1:287). Although the original diary is lost, I found a tantalizing glimpse of the diary in a photograph identified by Montgomery as 'My downstairs bedroom which Nora and I shared' (see p. xiv). The diary is perched on top of her bookshelf, its dark cover attractively decorated in yellow or golden ink, with the title DIARY running diagonally across the top. Two interlocking hearts in the centre, above the year 1903 in the lower right corner, speak to the close friendship of the two women whose hearts were set on romance and revel. Today this diary is a belated treasure and pleasure for lovers of Montgomery's fiction.

Nora Lefurgey (1880–1977), too, requires a brief introduction. Born in Prince Edward Island, of proud Huguenot-French heritage, Nora was a schoolteacher in New Glasgow, Cavendish, and North St Eleanors. Her father was a parliamentary reporter in Ottawa and likely kindled Nora's writing ambitions. More daring and adventurous than Montgomery, Nora inspired her friend to new levels of outrageousness that she might not have achieved on her own. The friendship was energized by their wild chasing of Cavendish and Bay View beaux. Their mock competition for James Alexander Stewart's affections triangulated and intensified the friendship. Nora was Montgomery's androgynous complement, a woman who loved to don pants for outdoor activities (see fig. 3.2). When I contacted Nora's daughter-in-law, Bette Campbell, in search of photographs, her enthusiasm was palpable, as she described Nora as the quintessential modern woman: Nora smoked cigarettes, she was an avid equestrian, and she was simultaneously glamorous and refined. Bette Campbell described Nora in this way: 'She was just five feet, five inches tall but seemed much taller as she had a long back and very straight spine. She had these piercing brown eyes which just "nailed" one!'[8] Nora Lefurgey and Montgomery shared an impressive forty-year friendship, albeit with some lengthy interruptions. Its dynamics are played out in the diary with an immediacy not found in Montgomery's journals. Here we gain a fuller picture of the autobiographical dimensions of the 'bosom-friendship' that would energize her fiction.

A photo entitled 'Secrets' (see fig. 1.1) – it was taken in 1903 – perhaps best encapsulates the close friendship. Maud Montgomery and Nora Lefurgey pose in front of the Cavendish house in their summer dresses: Maud in white, Nora in dark. Montgomery stands confidently facing the camera, her right arm poised on her waist. Nora is the active partner in a playfully staged scene of intimacy, as she snuggles up to Maud's body, puts her arm around her waist, and lays her cheek on Maud's, pretending to whisper secrets in her ear. It's one of the rare photos that show Montgomery in close bodily contact with a friend, a scene of exuberantly staged female intimacy – a scene also in which Montgomery – laughing, with her eyes half-closed – looks remarkably relaxed, happy, and unselfconscious, as if she had momentarily forgotten about the camera. The photo sums up the playful dynamics of the secret diary as an intimately charged collaboration. The couple's implied secrets, namely, the considerable pleasure found in their sometimes cruel teasing of the male bachelors, convey a unique picture of female bonding. The findings of several essays in this book suggest that Montgomery was sexually repressed, and that a great deal of her erotic life was lived in the realm of fantasy and fiction. Her close friendships with women, including Nora Lefurgey and Frede Campbell, echo the pattern of the passionate yet largely non-physical female friendships described by Lillian Faderman in her classic work, *Surpassing the Love of Men*. Montgomery's romantic friendships with women were emotionally intense and gratifying, with no evidence of the angst or guilt that characterized her romantic friendships with men, although Montgomery did express intense sexual panic in March 1930 after an adoring fan confessed her desire to 'lie "spoon fashion" all through the long night' and to cover Montgomery 'with kisses' (*SJ* 4:34).

As for the editorial principles followed in preparing the diary for publication, many months of research were devoted to annotating and illustrating the text to help the reader understand the jokes, allusions, and courtship complexities (see also my discussion of the illustrations below). Readers will find relevant information in footnotes. With the original handwritten diary no longer extant, the text reproduced in its entirety is the typescript prepared by Montgomery (see fig. 1.8, p. 66), and the ellipses shown are all hers. The typescript has the advantage of remarkable clarity and legibility. The two diarists took pleasure in misspelling words for comic effect, as when Nora spells Maud's name as Maude, with an *e*, to signal a nickname of sorts, and these deliberate changes of orthography have been left intact. To avoid reader confusion, though, the few genuine typographical errors have been quietly corrected, and occasionally missing punctuation, such as a full stop or the end of a parenthesis, has been quietly inserted. Occasional errors in the dates have been quietly corrected on the basis of internal evidence and with the help of a 1903 calendar. Montgomery's occasional hand-written corrections of typographical errors have been quietly inserted. Explanatory footnotes were added only where they were needed to avoid reader confusion. Words and phrases that Montgomery's type-script underlines for emphasis are rendered in italics. The same editorial principle of quietly correcting for ease of reading potentially confusing spelling errors also applies to the manuscript materials reproduced in some of the critical essays in this volume.

The diary is followed by eleven biographical and biocritical essays that examine Montgomery's self-imaging, as well as theorizing general issues of life writing. The book is divided into four parts of three chapters each. Each part is prefaced by a brief introduction outlining its focus and approach. Part 1, 'Staging the Bad Girl,' presents the diary by L.M. Montgomery and Nora Lefurgey, followed by two essays inter-preting the diary and theorizing its aesthetics and functions. The web of women friendships – Montgomery's relationship with Nora Lefurgey and other women friends, including an effusive and mysterious fan nicknamed Isobel in the journals and identified here as Isabel Anderson – is centrally explored behind the play with boys and beaux. Part 2, 'Confessions and Body Writing,' focuses on Montgomery's daring dis-closing and careful withholding in her journals of intimate information, including information about her sexuality, childbirth, and depression. The intimate body – and Montgomery's encoding of it – are thus the focus of Part 2. Montgomery's sexuality is explored in her intense affair with Herman Leard, an affair that in turn highlights the profound repressions of the author. Her journal accounts of her depressions are discussed as a strategy that helped Montgomery in her self-construc-tion as a writer. Part 3, 'Writing for an Intimate Audience,' further amplifies Montgomery's performance of self by focusing on her inti-mate relationship with her audience in her letters and scrapbooks. In her many years of corresponding with Ephraim Weber, she constructed Weber as her ideal reader, similar to the ideal reader projected into the journals. Even in her scrapbooks, she engaged a community through visual forms. Finally, Part 4, 'Where Life Writing Meets Fiction,' offers biographical and theoretical readings that probe the extent to which fiction becomes a forum for projecting and for working out personal issues. The blurring of the boundary between fact and fiction, truth and artifice, is explored in its full complexity. Mary Rubio and Elizabeth Waterston end the book with an interactive discussion of the later journals and fiction, concluding that for Montgomery all writing was a profoundly personal writing. The four parts of the book indicate focus areas, not rigid boundaries, and issues introduced in the early chapters are amplified in later ones to create a cumulative effect throughout the book. Although the book does not observe a strict chronology, its structure moves from the young to the middle-aged Montgomery, and thus from youthful exuberance and play to more sombre themes of depression, illness, and marital disappointment.

As for the genesis of this book, the collection of essays grows out of the International L.M. Montgomery and Life Writing Symposium, hosted in 2002 by the L.M. Montgomery Institute at the University of Prince Edward Island. The most original papers were selected and expanded, and additional papers were solicited. Contributors subsequently exchanged papers so as to deepen the dialogue and sharpen the focus without, however, relinquishing individual differences of perspective. All essays are published here for the first time. This book does not claim to cover all important aspects of Montgomery's life, but it presents in-depth readings of specific areas of her life and writing that have remained shrouded in mystery. In order to fill some of the gaps in Montgomery's personal writings, the book includes interviews with the descendants of people who knew her personally, thereby adding to a multi-faceted picture of the author.

Finally, a note on the book's pictorial contributions. A great deal of research was devoted to illustrating the diary and the essays, and more than one hundred photos have been accumulated for this project, many from private archives. Thirty-nine have been selected to illustrate the book. The majority of these rare portraits, including a daguerreotype over a century old, have been culled from private collections of descendants. Carefully repaired and restored, they are published here for the first time, and hopefully they will inspire further research. Indeed, photographs are integral to this book, reflecting the fact that L.M. Montgomery, an accomplished photographer herself, left a treasure trove of photographs, including self-portraits. Although some of these have been included in the published journals, many that are held at the University of Guelph Archives are still unpublished. In the twenty-first century, when so much information is visually driven, these photographs may be the most important elements of Montgomery's autobiographic image, albeit not in the sense that they reveal a more authentic or less concealed identity.[9] The photographs, too, are carefully staged and exquisitely shaped, as Laura Higgins so aptly noted in her examination of the photographs of Montgomery's room that are featured in her journals: 'While encouraging us to read the illustrated journals for messages about her self, she warns us that there are many layers of self-construction and concealment to negotiate' (109). Self-portraits, as Amelia Jones has theorized, present a 'visual autobiography' which delivers a particular subject 'through a visual text narrated in the "first" person' (69). Above all, self-portraits help us illuminate the construction of embodied selves. Many of the essays in this collection analyse the ways in which Montgomery's photographic self-images either amplify or contradict the verbal self-images, and thus ultimately contribute to unravelling the many layers of self-construction and concealment.

In offering this book, it is my hope that readers will be able not only to explore new dimensions of the life of Canada's most enduring writer, but also to appreciate the complexity and control of a professional writer who invited her readers into her life and imaged for herself a sympathetic posthumous readership. The hand of the consummate artist is omnipresent in Montgomery's private writings and visual self-representations. This book offers portraits of the journal writer, the correspondent, the photographer, and the autobiographer, while also delving deeply into her private roles as intimate friend, obsessive lover, sufferer of depressions, control freak, and ageing woman. Ultimately, this book reveals the many faces and masks that make up the woman and author we know as L.M. Montgomery – a woman who was, as her friend Isabel Anderson remarked, 'a will-o'-the-wisp, elusive, exclusive.'

NOTES

1 For an intriguing discussion of this photo, see Higgins 109.
2 Montgomery's magnum opus, her journals, covering the years from 1889 to 1942, have appeared under the impeccable editorship of Mary Rubio and Elizabeth Waterston in five volumes of *The Selected Journals* of *L.M. Montgomery* (1985, 1987, 1992, 1998, 2004). Montgomery's autobiography appeared in 1917 in serial publication in *Everywoman's World*, a women's magazine, and was reissued as *The Alpine Path*. Her correspondence has appeared in *My Dear Mr. M.*, edited by Francis Bolger and Elizabeth Epperly; *The Green Gables Letters*, edited by Wilfrid Eggleston; and *L.M. Montgomery's Ephraim Weber: Letters, 1916–1941*, edited by Paul Tiessen and Hildi Tiessen.
3 Earlier scholarship has traced the process of Montgomery's composition

and multiple rewriting of her journals (Turner 93–100); the intrusion of shadows in the journals (Buss, *Mapping* 164–5); and the journals' more nuanced voice for adults, in contrast to the voice of sunshine and optimism in her fiction for young readers (Steffler 72–83). Laura Higgins has discussed Montgomery's many photographs of her room, regularly inserted into the journal, as a spatial metaphor for the construction of her private identity, since the room was 'the one place where she was in control of her identity' (102).

4 On the literary diary, see Elizabeth Podnieks's *Daily Modernism*. Among the plethora of excellent studies on autobiography and life writing, see, for instance, Benstock, ed., *The Private Self*; Egan, *Mirror Talk*; Gilmore, *Autobiographics*; Perreault, *Writing Selves*; Smith, *A Poetics of Women's Autobiography*; Smith and Watson, eds, *Women, Autobiography, Theory*; and Stanton, ed., *The Female Autograph*. Although the term 'life writing' has been critiqued, it is useful in that it comprises a broad spectrum of practices, including autobiography, diary, and memoir, as well as self-portraiture in photographs and performance, all of which are discussed in this collection. For an introduction to this term, see Kadar, ed., *Essays on Life Writing*.

5 On the performative in life writing, see Bruss, *Autobiographical Acts*; Hinz, ed., *Data and Acta: Aspects of Life-Writing*; and Smith and Watson, eds, *Interfaces*.

6 For additional theories of the diary, see Bunkers and Huff, eds, *Inscribing the Daily*, Hogan, 'Engendered Autobiographies'; and Nussbaum, 'Toward Conceptualizing Diary.'

7 On Montgomery's use of subversive satire, see Rubio, 'Subverting.' On her romance writing, see Barry, Doody, and Doody Jones, eds, *AAGG*; Epperly, *Fragrance*; and Wilmshurst, 'Quotations.' For her contributions to girls,' children's, and women's literature, see Gammel, 'Safe Pleasures for Girls'; Kornfeld and Jackson, 'Female Bildungsroman'; MacLulich, 'Portraits'; Nodelman, 'Progressive Utopia'; Poe, 'Whole of the Moon'; and Sorfleet, ed., *L.M. Montgomery*. For the political context of Montgomery's writing, see Devereux, '"Canadian Classic"'; and Fiamengo, 'Popular Landscape.'

8 Bette Campbell, telephone interview with Mary Beth Cavert, 27 August 1995.

9 See Higgins, 'Snapshot Portraits,' and Gammel, 'Mirror Looks,' for a discussion of the autobiographical dimensions of Montgomery's photographic self-portraits; and Epperly, 'The Visual Imagination,' on Montgomery's long fascination with photography. See also Smith and Watson, eds, *Interfaces*, for a rigorous investigation of the visual/verbal matrix of autobiographical writing.

PART 1

STAGING THE BAD GIRL

On 30 January 1903 Nora Lefurgey, a young teacher and intimate friend of L.M. Montgomery, arrived at the Macneill homestead in Cavendish, where she would stay as a boarder until the end of June 1903. During the cold winter months, Montgomery shared her downstairs bedroom with Nora. That same night, the two women began keeping a collaborative diary recording their daily adventures. The diary, reproduced in chapter 1 of this section, is full of comedy and humour, as they indulge the joys of 'man(i)curing,' teasing and titillating the local bachelors. 'Dear James,' James Alexander Stewart, a shy man in his thirties, is the focus of their suggestive talk and aggressive flirtations, along with other heroes, including Artie Macneill, Freddie Clark, Rob MacKenzie, and Joe Stewart. 'Unmentionable' undergarments, including Montgomery's infamous yellow garter, provide no end of allusive fun. A light-hearted and liberated Montgomery surfaces in this diary in high-spirited badinage and wisecracks, as she competes with Nora for ever more outrageous provocations. Although she was twenty-eight when she wrote it, the diary has an adolescent exuberance and reveals the extent to which Montgomery was able to use humour and laughter as a strategy to fend off depression.

The diary is followed by two essays analysing its text. Jennifer Litster argues that we need to consider Montgomery's performance of self as a 'harum-scarum girl' as an important part of her make-up, equal to the more serious and tragic selves performed in the journals and explored in Part 2. In the second essay, Mary Beth Cavert probes the biographical dimensions of this diary, that is, Maud's relationship with Nora and the ways in which it illuminates the mysterious relationship with Isabel Anderson many years later. Ultimately, the collaborative diary is a perfect metaphor for the close female friendship.

1.1 'Secrets' – L.M. Montgomery and Nora Lefurgey, 1903. (L.M. Montgomery Collection, Archival and Special Collections, University of Guelph Library.)

1

'... where has my yellow garter gone?' The Diary of L.M. Montgomery and Nora Lefurgey

Edited, annotated, and illustrated by Irene Gammel

Cavendish, P. E. Island, Can.
Monday, January 19ᵗʰ, 1903

Nora[1] arrived today, bag and baggage ... principally *baggage*. She gave me a glass *pen*, a glass inkbottle, *and* an empty mucilage bottle. She is a good soul. I am grateful for the mucilage bottle. One never knows when a thing like that may be of use. That is the beauty of it. There is a charm and fascination in uncertainty.

Nora unpacked ... a fearful and wonderful proceeding. I stood by and watched her. It did not embarrass her.

Then we had tea. Somehow or other *grace* was interrupted. I hope it will not impair digestion. Nora says I am not a *decent* person. I don't know whether to be mad or not. I wish I had asked the minister when he was in.

Nora's eyes are dim. She says she can't see. I would cry with sympathy but I won't after her insulting me.

I am going to bed. I must make Nora some cocoa first. She is furious because I did not introduce her to Hamilton Macneill[2] and I must do something to appease her.

---

1 Nora Lefurgey (1880–1977; see figs. 3.1, 3.2, and 3.3), twenty-three, also referred to as N.L., is the co-author of the diary and a close friend of L.M. Montgomery. For details, see chapters 2 and 3. In addition to the sources indicated, the 1901 Census (PEI Archives) and the family lineages provided by the Island Register (www.islandregister.com) were invaluable tools in identifying the characters in the diary.

2 Hamilton Macneill, son of William C. Macneill of Cavendish and brother of Montgomery's close friend Amanda.

As regards Hamilton,
'There's times you knows you mightn't
And there's times you think you might.'

L.M.M.

I bid farewell to every care and came up to cast my lot with Maude[3] for the next five months. I have long been thinking of casting my lot with this little 'freak of natur' but never dreamed I would make it out. Well, after a great deal of grunting and sighing, my trunk was at last unpacked, ditto two valises and a band-box. Then I wiped my 'dazed' eyes and went to supper.

It was not without a pang that I left the dear (ahem) old room where I have spent so many pleasant hours and it seems now so very far away.

The Rev. George brought me up and though it was sixteen below zero yet my 'lugubrious' face assumed a very April-like character. Bro. Wilson[4] called to inquire for me this eve and of course that cheered my palpitating heart ... or rather that part of my anatomy which answers to a heart. For since I met Dear James[5] ... tears ... well, words are inadequate. What is an aching void? For three weeks I have been trying to find out and now at last, oh glorious revelation! Maude's hollow tooth and my headache.

N.L.

---

3 Maude: Frequently, although not always, Nora spells Montgomery's first name as Maude, with an *e*. Intentional misspellings are part of the diary's humour and anticipate the comic spelling mistakes in *Emily of New Moon*.

4 Bro[ther] Wilson is the Reverend C.P. Wilson, the Baptist minister who was leaving Cavendish in May 1903.

5 Dear James, also known as James Alec or The Soulful One or Jim Stewart, is James Alexander Stewart (1867–1941) (see fig. 1.2), a farmer, son of Alexander and Margaret Stewart, and brother of Penzie, Elizabeth (Lizzie), William, Emma, Annie, Garfield, Fenner, and Charles (Baptism Index, PEI Archives). Montgomery was a frequent visitor in the Stewart home in Cavendish, one of the oldest homes in Cavendish still standing. In the diary, James became the main focus for Maud and Nora's matchmaking pranks until he moved to Bridgetown in May 1903. James never married. In 1941 he died at age seventy-four in Falconwood Hospital, Charlottetown (record from Cutcliffe Funeral Home, PEI Archives), and was buried with his parents in the Cavendish graveyard, his gravestone erroneously noting his birth year as 1871. In an ironic twist, Montgomery was buried in close proximity to his gravestone just one year later, in 1942.

1.2 'The Soulful One' – James Alexander Stewart, the diary's 'leading man' (front, left). Clockwise: Mrs James Robert Stewart, Lizzie Stewart (James's sister), and James Robert Stewart (James's cousin). L.M. Montgomery was a frequent visitor in the Stewart home. (Daguerreotype, copper and silver plate. Courtesy Ruth Stewart Gallant, Ontario.)

Tuesday, Jan. 20th, 1903

Last night when we went to bed I put a chair by the bed so that if Nora should kick me out during the night I would have something *soft* to fall on. She did not do so, however, and it was just as well she did not for, as the mercury was registering sixteen below zero all night, I think it probable I would have frozen stiff to the marrow before I had time to crawl in again.

Today passed uneventfully. I filled my new ink-bottle and spilled about half the precious fluid in so doing.

When evening came Nora and I 'wiped our weeping eyes' and resolved to go to prayer-meeting. We got a chance over in Rob MacKenzie's (see fig. 1.6)[6] capacious pung sleigh (see fig. 1.3)[7] with Bob and Bertha (see fig. 1.6)[8] and Mary Laird.[9] Bob and Nora sat up in front and carried on in their usual scandalous fashion. Finding my exhortations to them unheeded I decided to ask Howard Simpson[10] to pray for them. If that will not check them in their mad career I know of nothing that will.

There was a pretty fair turn-out at prayers. We sat in a row around the room. Nora got as close to Howard as possible but he never even looked at her nor offered to share his hymn-book.

When p. m. came out Nora and I started 'immejutly and to onct' up the road. We were followed by a sleigh which seemed to be possessed with the blind staggers. It stopped directly in front of us and stayed there until it got ready to move on again. Nobody knows just what it was after.

Nora and I had been hoping we would be lucky enough to get a drive but as nobody had asked us by the time we got to the middle gate we

---

6 Rob MacKenzie, also known as Robbie, Bob, or Bobs, is Robert MacKenzie (1864–1952), a farmer, thirty-eight, brother of Bertha (see below) and Milton. He would marry Jennie Alveretta Stevenson.

7 pung sleigh: A low, one- or two-horse box sleigh, it was a common method of transportation. In chapter 19 of *Anne of Green Gables*, Anne, Diana, and Diana's cousins from Newbridge 'all crowded into the big pung sleigh, among straw and furry robes' (*AAGG* 216).

8 Bertha MacKenzie (born 1867), sister of Robert. L.M. Montgomery was Bertha's bridesmaid when she married Milton Green. Bertha was a dressmaker.

9 Mary Laird (1858–1930).

10 Howard Simpson, fifty-one, farmer from Bay View.

had become a prey to despair. Just at this dismal time we observed a toboggan careering madly up Uncle John's field. As it drew near we found that the driver was the famous Russell Macneill.[11] He saluted us with,

'Lucy Maud and Miss Lefurgey, come and have a drive.'

So Lucy Maud and Miss Lefurgey hurried over and scrambled in. We drove east first until we met Artie Macneill (see fig. 2.1)[12] going westward, driving girls 'in moderation.' We at once turned and pursued him through Cavendish, up as far as William C.'s[13] lane. Here we met the unfortunate creature on his way back. Russell stopped and shouted, 'That's her all right. You had no business to do a thing like that.'

There is a sad tragedy veiled in those words but I don't know what it is.

We turned and came back also. R. kept us laughing with his ridiculous speeches, especially about the Forresters' banquet at New Glasgow.[14] He informed us that one young lady who was there had a *blue bow* on. The inference being that she had nothing else I *blushed*.

We promised R. that we would put up a prayer for him before we got into our little trundle bed. I tried to yank some fur out of his coat for our scrapbooks but it was too firmly rooted in. Russell drove away warning me not to tell Nora everything about him when we got into bed tonight.

We came in and solaced ourselves with some hot chicken broth. I will close this chapter in our strange eventful history with the following appropriate and touching quotation: –

'Jingle bells, jingle bells, jingle all the way,
Oh, what fun it is to drive with Russell in a toboggan sleigh.'

L.M.M.

---

11 Russell H. Macneill (1874–1950), also referred to as R., is the brother of Pensie and Alec Macneill of Cavendish. He would marry Margaret Warren.

12 Artie Macneill is Artemas Macneill, twenty-three, a farmer, the brother of Montgomery's friend Alma Macneill.

13 William C., also known as W.C.M., is William C. Macneill, seventy-three, father of Amanda and Hamilton and husband to Christy Ann Cameron. He committed suicide in May 1907 (see chapter 7).

14 New Glasgow: PEI village southwest of Rustico in Queen's County, named by Scottish immigrants who arrived in 1820. See chapter 7, for the 'Forresters' banquet' reference.

Wed., Jan. 21, 1903

Well, the decree has gone forth that write I must. I have tried my very best to get clear but no, that Maude will just make me do it, so here goes.

In the beginning of the day her ladyship 'cribbed' one of my beautiful new woollen stockings, but I got it back so let it rest.

Well (and I daresay you notice that it is a word of mine) Dr. S.[15] arrived in his toboggan as soon as school was out.

'And then and there was hurrying to and fro.'

Maude and I 'wiped our weeping eyes' and proceeded to business. I robed myself in my bran new night frock but let me say had I foreseen the 'melancholy catastrophe' never on this earth would I have sacrificed that sky-blue frock with 'trimmen' but there, the doctor says that the best and most 'modest' people sometimes make mistakes, but he is *so* sarcastic.

O, I am dead tired so I will not write any more. I know this will sound rather crude along with Maude's but I don't care. I wish the Stanley or Minto (fig. 1.3)[16] would hurry up and get unfroze for it is a matter of importance. 'The shades of night were falling fast' but the shade of the window stayed up, much to Maude's alarm for it occasioned her many a trip to the back door to watch the effect on the 'virgin' snow. The doctor was standing by the bed with his arms loosely folded over the broad convexity of his stomach, idly watching the 'hysterical' female in pale blue, tossing and groaning on the bed when sharp and quick rang a pleading voice from without ... 'draw the blind.' The doctor felt that something dreadful was about to happen, madly rushed to the innocent window and though it was past prayer time he indulged in a few words of Hindoo grace for the poor fellow could not find the place.

N.L.

In regard to the above I think that like *Murray R.*[17] he did not accomplish much when he did find the place.

L.M.M.

---

15 Dr. S.: Dr Stuart Simpson of Stanley.

16 The *Minto* and the *Stanley* were ice-breaker vessels that provided winter passenger and mail service runs from PEI to the mainland.

17 Murray R. is Murray Robertson (1851–1925), a farmer in Cavendish living on Kirk View Farm, with a view on the Presbyterian Church. He was married to Emily Woolner Robertson.

1.3   Winter transportation in Prince Edward Island in 1903. Top: pung sleigh. (Courtesy PEI Heritage Prints.) Bottom: the *Minto*. (Acc. 4400/1. Public Archives and Records Office of Prince Edward Island.)

Thursday, Jan. 22ⁿᵈ

Nora and the doctor probably bewitched the bedclothes in their weird incantations last night. I went to bed early, being considerably the worser of the nervous strain to which I had been subjected on account of that window blind. At the unearthly hour of four o'clock in the morning I was awakened by Nora frantically clawing me, under the impression that she was pulling in the bed-clothes. I assured her that I had not swallowed them and told her to pull away ... Could stand it as long as she could. So she pulled and finally got them on and lay down with a grunt. But evidently something was wrong yet for our bare feet were protruding uncomfortably at the foot. So we had to scramble out, light a lamp and re-make the bed. Nora attended to this and then, as she had another of her virtuous fits of 'trying again,' I crept into the next room and looted a Victoria Regina.

Finally, we got to sleep again. When I woke this morning I found that one of my garters (see fig. 7.3) was missing and hunt as I might I could not find it. Once I thought sure I had it and grabbed at it joyfully but no, it was only Nora's toe. The garter has never turned up. I suppose Nora made away with it out of some mean, small, malicious petty spirit of revenge. The loss has cast a gloom over my entire day. I had to go about feeling the stocking sliding down my leg. Finally I got two safety pins and pinned it to the edge of certain garments not mentionable in polite society. This proved effective. Nora has just been in, 'trying again.' But I can assure her that if she gobbles down people's garters it will take more than part of the Minto's cargo to recruit her shattered system.

I took about an hour to eat my tea tonight. Grandma[18] began retailing to us certain tid-bits of sixty-year old gossip. Evidently 'human natur' was human natur then just the same as now. There was a certain David Simpson who seems to have been a villain of the deepest dye. But did he ever steal a garter?

'Oh, where, tell me where has my yellow garter gone?
Oh, where, tell me where has my yellow garter gone?
I dinna ken what dreadful fate my garter has befel
But it's, oh, in her heart that Nora kens full well.'

L.M.M.

---

18 Grandma is Montgomery's grandmother, Lucy Ann Woolner Macneill (1824–1911), with whom Montgomery lived at the Macneill homestead in Cavendish. Grandma Macneill was not welcoming of the boarder Nora Lefurgey. '[Unfit] to have any stranger in the house,' Montgomery notes, she behaved 'childish' (*SJ* 1:288).

Monday, Jan. 26th, 1903

From this gap one would infer that something fearful had happened of late ... probably that Nora had murdered me out of hand to prove that she didn't absorb my garter. However, nothing of this sort has happened. We are both alive and have not yet come to blows over the garter ... although relations are getting somewhat strained ... as is also my stocking and the aforesaid garments not mentioned in polite society.

Well, on Friday evening Nora's medical friend and adviser appeared and carried her off bodily to New Glasgow. By way of being extra swagger she put on a veil. I had to tie it for her and of course got 'jawed at' for my pains. Nevertheless, being of a forgiving disposition (except in the matter of garters) I promised faithfully that I would burn her private documents if she 'never came back any more.'

That night I had to sleep alone and actually found myself lonesome. It seemed so weird and unnatural not to be compelled to be on the alert lest my other garter should vanish. I would have been willing to sit up all night to watch it if only Nora had been home. Boo-hoo.

Saturday night I had the most exquisite felicity of cutting Nora completely out. Her best young man brought me home from practice. So you see there are compensations even for lost garters.

I fondly hoped Nora would be home Saturday night but no ... the vacant chair continued vacant still. In vain I lay awake for hours, listening for a sleigh to stop at the door, all ready to leap out of bed and let the prodigal in. I began to fear that she and 'the famous Artie' had eloped.

Yesterday morning my depression over her absence ... or something else ... made me really ill and I had to make quite a sensational exit from church in the middle of the service.

Last night just as I was going to bed Nora turned up beamingly. I put on a skirt and shawl over my nightdress and in this classical costume made her some cocoa and listened to her tale of woe ... which she will now proceed to relate herself and tell 'how fair the realm *imagination* opens to the view.'

L.M.M.

Mon., Jan. 26

'There are lots of things in this old world I don't pretend to know
And Maude may think perhaps that I am a trifle slow ...'

Well ... humph ... but one thing I *do* know

I never stole her dern old yellow garter! So there!

Well, garter discussion has become a dissipation with us, a wily, seductive habit that seems to be growing upon us with marvellous rapidity. (I am sure that is classical)

I heaved a sigh of relief when Mrs. C. came to the house for I thought surely delicacy would keep that yellow article out of sight, but not a bit of it. Maude, with that delightful candor that is so characteristic of her, informed Mrs. C. that I had stolen her garter. Just think of it! Stole a garter! I am indeed an afflicted mortal but never mind, there will come a time some day!

Well (same old word) Dr. took me to Glasgow Friday night. Fought all the way over and finally got lost in a snowstorm on the river which occasioned quite a lot of fun. I shall not attempt to journalize that experience for no pen of mine or *imagination* could do it justice. However, necessity (which they tell me is the stepmother of invention) compels me to touch upon it. Fought all the eve with the medical adviser and at 12:30 took my brick and trotted off to bed with these jeering words ringing in my sensitive ears, 'Well, if I were a girl, 21 years old, and could not get anything better than an old brick to take to bed I'd stay over in Cavendish where they give a fellow raspberry jam and cheese for supper.' This was followed in rapid succession by some good advice which, as I suppose I shall have to pay for but am going to take, I will not put in here for Maude to read. No, sir. She has damaged me enough already.

M.D. told me to stay in bed till the affair was over. I consented but little did I dream that he was going to keep me there penned up till nearly Saturday night, but I hope I may never have to go through anything like that again. I close my eyes, yes, sister, weeping eyes and in *imagination* I am back on that little bed, tossing, crying, scolding, and calling the doctor all the fancy names out of the dictionary, while in the distance I hear his No. 10s pattering downstairs for ether, d...ing my poor fluttering heart and 'nervous temperament.' However, he laced up my long boots so I'll forgive him. He is the only man I know who can swear to music. He is also very complimentary for in the midst of my moaning he snapped out, 'you're an unqualified crank,' while poor me, stupified by chloroform roared at the top of my voice, 'I'm not' but through the gloom and stupor surrounding me came the replay like the voice of an angel, 'you are.' However, let me say in concluding the unfortunate affair it turned out that it was not *imagination* and everything came off *honey well*[19] and I got up, but kept the whole house or the greater part of it awake all night rolling around the bed which had considerable musical ability in it. Both Artie and Jo[20] arrived to take me home so I came with Jo, but 'hypnotized' the doctor before I left and so got even with him which was by no means easy. Jo poured out his tale of woe to me on the way home. We could sympathize with each other for he is not the only one who is persecuted by his friends. No, indeed, oh no. My friend does not ask me to buy the bottle but she ... well, there, I am too full for utterance along that line. Jo and I got home about ten and Maude, bless her sinful heart, got up out of bed and made me a cup of cocoa. I gave her the only things Stuart could find that looked like a garter. Just imagine, that dreadful article of female attire has never turned up yet and didn't that terrible girl send word to Everett Laird[21] that he'd *stole her garter*! Poor fellow, I can feel for him but never mind, I'll fix Miss Maude. I hereby swear that I will *tell* yes, sister, tell, every male creature that comes to this house that she lost her garter!!! I will! I stole her garter, indeed! I wonder what she tried to steal from me while I was away! My James, heart and hand, bag and baggage! And the new Dundas farm! All clean gone and swept out of my life like magic! So now I have only Artie left ... there, I am too full for utterance.

N.L.

'Oh, young Jamie Stuart[22] came out of the west
Through all the wide border his steed was the best,
He stayed not for brake and he stopped not for stone,

---

19 There was a Dr Honeywell, hence the joke. My thanks to Jennifer Litster for this reference.

20 Jo, also known as Joe, is Joseph Stewart, twenty-six, of Bay View. In 1917 Montgomery notes: 'Joe Stewart, a good-looking inanity, drove me around one summer and was quite madly in love and horribly cut up because he knew there was no chance for him' (*SJ* 2:206).

21 Everett Laird, thirty, son of James (Jimmy) Laird and brother of Ellice (see below). Known for his 'dry, funny remarks' (*SJ* 1:70), he was among the 'boys and girls who formed our "set" that gay winter at Park Corner' (*SJ* 2:125). '*He* could and did talk enough for four' (*SJ* 2:255).

22 Jamie Stuart is James Alexander Stewart; see footnote 5. The poem is a parody of Sir Walter Scott's 'Lochinvar.'

He drove up to the post-office where gate there was none,
But ere he alighted at the post-office door
Nora had gone to New Glasgow and his hopes were all o'er.'

L.M.M.

Wednesday, Jan. 28th, 1903

Peace and quietness reign in the household of Macneill tonight for Nora is away. I shall take advantage of the fact to chronicle a few unimportant events of yesterday and today.

Yesterday morning Everett's father came and took me down to Mr. Laird's[23] in spite of that atrocious statement made by Nora to Ellice[24] regarding Everett and my garter. Evidently Laird, Senior, put no faith in it.

When I got back after taking the Rev. George and his affectionate brothers in three different poses I was dog-tired. A short nap refreshed me, however, and when old Mrs. Wyand[25] came in I had enough energy to introduce Nora to her very gracefully. She asked Nora if she came from Vernon River.[26] Mrs. W. came from there herself and I suppose she thought Nora looked as if she did too.

After tea Joe came along to borrow a book and tell us a few more tales about beloved Freddie (fig. 1.4).[27] Poor dear Fred! Well may he pray to be delivered from his friends!

In due time we toddled out to prayers. I was full of bottled-up deviltry until about half through the service. Then, without any reason whatever I just

---

23 Mr Laird, also referred to as Laird Senior, is either John or William Laird. My thanks to Jennifer Litster for help with the Laird family.

24 Ellice Laird is Everett's sister and James Laird's daughter.

25 Mrs Wyand is Mrs John Wyand of Cavendish. The Wyands are the owners of the large cow field on which Montgomery and her cousin Lucy, in 1891, met the two unfriendly cows that scared the two girls (see *SJ* 1:68), a scene dramatized in *Anne of Green Gables*.

26 Vernon River: in Queen's County in central PEI at the Vernon River.

27 Freddie, also referred to as Fred, is Frederick Clark, twenty-one, Baptist, son of Cavendish farmer Darnley Clark and brother of Chesley, Wilber, Maggie, Ernest, and Campsie (see fig.1.7).

1.4 'Beloved Freddie' – Frederick Clark, circa 1903. (L.M. Montgomery Collection, Archival and Special Collections, University of Guelph Library.)

'Went to pieces all at once,
   All at once and nothing first,
   Just as bubbles do when they burst.'
I felt as *flat* as James' society. Oh dear, but I was in the doleful dumps. Couldn't even smile. As for laughing ... well, that was something I had *once* indulged in ages upon ages ago.

This melancholy mood lasted all night. Nora became infected also. She did try once to say something about the garter but I became so bitterly sarcastic that she didn't go for to do it again. Garter, indeed! What did a girl who felt as I felt want to hear about the pomps and vanities of the world as represented by yellow garters? Had there been a convent handy I would have gone into it on the spot ... and then Lord have mercy on the soul of the poor nuns.

I suppose when Nora saw how blue I was she became alarmed and thought the garter business had gone far enough so she put it behind my trunk and there I found the ill-fated thing this morning. Nora tried to look as if she were surprised but such a flimsy pretence did not deceive *me*.

However, even this partial repentance has worked wonders for her already. There was something in the mail for her today. Next time she exasperates me beyond endurance I shall stick pins in it.

She is away tonight, as aforesaid, and I ought to be as happy as a clam but strange to say I am not. I suppose when one has become accustomed to being harried and worried and punned to death one kind of misses it when it is lacking.

'If ye come back to me, Nora, Nora,
   In the old likeness that I knew,
   Never a word about garters shall grieve you,
   Nora, Nora, tender and true.
   Never a word about garters shall grieve you
   I'll smile on ye sweet as James could do,
   And I'll put my cold feet on your feet, Nora,
   Nora, Nora tender and true.'

                                                                L.M.M.

Sunday, February 1st, 1903

Some people are born to do things, others to have things done for them. *I* am one of the former. By the same token Nora is one of the latter. It is her turn to write up this journal but so far she has wiggled out of it. So for sheer shame's sake I will fall to. She is curled up on the sofa reading a novel and I am here with my feet in the oven, cudgelling my gray matter as to the harmless events of the past days.

Wednesday night, after writing this journal, I covered myself with eternal shame and disgrace by making a pun. I did it on the impulse of the moment but Nora says it was on the cat! *'Facile descensus Avernus.'* I had never made a pun in my life before but that night I made three or four. It's always the first wrong step that counts.

That night also, after we went to bed, Nora finished telling me a 'serial' she began to tell me one night when the famous MacDougall[28] was evangelizing the dark places in Cavendish. Freddie interrupted us on the hall hill and I never heard the rest of it until Wednesday night.

On Thursday evening Nora went up to Y.P.U.[29] in the Baptist church. I thought it was a good place to go so I let her go willingly. I even went part of the way with her. But judging from results it was a mistake. Late at night Nora arrived home in a vile state of mind and quite horrified me by swearing at Jerry.[30] Jerry is someone whom I cannot have abused, sweet soul. I got her to bed and calmed her down. The real reason she was so mad was that she found out that 'the soulful James' had been here that evening when she was absent and she had missed him.

Friday night it poured rain so we did not go to Literary but stayed home. When we went to bed I read Nora to sleep with THE LOVE LETTERS OF A WORLDLY MAN.

Yesterday morning Nora washed ... not herself but her clothes, all of 'em, even those she had on her back. I hung around and sympathized with her. Sympathy is a splendid thing! It is so cheap too.

In the evening I went to choir practice at Uncle John's (see fig. 1.5).[31]

---

28 MacDougall, a revivalist who pretended to be Presbyterian but was really Baptist, is fictionalized in one of the Pat books. My thanks to Jennifer Litster.

29 Y.P.U., the Young People's Union, also referred to as Union, is a social gathering for young people organized by the church.

30 Jerry, also referred to as J.C., is Jeremiah S. Clark, thirty, a schoolteacher born in 1872, and son of John Cavendish Clark from neighbouring Bay View. Jerry worked as a missionary to Indians, as did two of his nine siblings, Martha and Zella, which explains the jokes about 'Injuns.' Jerry married Belle Pratt.

31 Uncle John is John F. Macneill (born 1851), Montgomery's uncle and Lucy Woolner Macneill's son. His farm was close to the Macneill homestead.

Nora stayed home. She pretended that she wanted to go to the practice up at Clark's (see fig. 1.7)[32] but when that shamefully abused boy, Freddie, arrived to take her up she went off and hid. I suppose the real reason was that she thought James would be down and that she could grab him when I was out of the way. But if so she got left, for James dear was at our practice, looking as sweet and sanctified as any angel about to enter the sacred portals. Moreover he drove me home in a big mud sleigh.[33] There were a few dozen other people with us but that was not James' fault. I am sure that he would have preferred me alone. So great was his delirious joy over it that he lost his head and drove me all the way down to Lairds'[34] before he found out where he was at. I almost froze for poor James does not understand the fine art of keeping people warm. I suppose his heart has been so frozen by Nora's former coldness ... before she found out how other people appreciated him ... that it will take me some time to thaw him out.

I woke up in the night with a bilious headache. At first I thought I must have caught the 'jaunders'[35] from Nora for I felt absolutely *yellow* ... at least I felt like *yell*-ing with pain. That is *not* a pun, cross my heart solemn and true it isn't. Nora will say it is but then she is always looking for a chance to jump on me. There is some more of today but Nora has got to write about it. I feel that I have done my duty by my country.

L.M.M.

Mon., Feb. 2ⁿᵈ

Well! (I tell you I feel thankful for that interjection!) I suppose I shall have to write up tonight. I have tried my best to get clear but the effort was unsuccessful. Was up to church yesterday morning. Nearly froze to death on my way up and on the way home. I told the minister's wife a big fib but I should be excused for that when you hear that I was

---

32 Clark's: Darnley Clark's in Cavendish.

33 Mud sleighs were used when roads turned to mud; there were large mud-sleigh
    buses, which might have a stove for heat.

34 Lairds': William and John Laird's, who lived close to the Cavendish beach.

35 jaunders: jaundice.

awakened at 4 A.M. (*hour, hour*, you see) by Maude prowling about the bed. Poor little girl had a sick headache and when I 'wiped my dazzled eyes' I spied her ladyship vainly endeavoring to give up all for her country. (There now, I did not intend to put that in for it is 'not refined, you know.') However, she got mustard (I wonder why) and in the end was completely cured.

I spent the afternoon in reading OLD LOVE LETTERS and THE AUTOCRAT. I like the latter very much. I tell you the old 'doll' comes down on puns like the Assyrian. (I am full of allusions.)

Maude came near having a *scene* with Cousin Toff[36] before she got dressed for church. She can put on speed when it is necessary now. I can tell you!!

We went to P[resbyterian] church and though it was 'Sabbath eve' (as Mrs. Ewen[37] says) we had some difficulty in keeping our wayward feet in Sunday line. However, we were saved the inconvenience of vain effort on the way home by Russell's cheery voice,

'Is *them* my girls?'

Them turned out, or rather *in*, to be his and away we went over the icy fields, the wind nor'east and the horse's tail serving as a fan.

I guess we would have almost frozen, had he not kept us constantly laughing by his crude speeches which I am not qualified to journalize (and I am not sorry for I am so sleepy).

Maud and I went away through Lover's Lane[38] this eve for a walk and I for one enjoyed it very much. The scenery was perfect but the walking rather treacherous. But I had to stick to the ice while her ladyship ... there, it is no use for me to try to be smart for I have not energy enough to do anything tonight. However, I might just say in regard to Maud and her 'etherealism' ... 'it's in this poor human critter but she can't get it out.'

N.L.

---

36 Cousin Toff is Theophilus MacKenzie (1843–1915), a farm labourer and Grandma Lucy Woolner's nephew. Montgomery remembered him in her journals: 'I can't picture Cavendish without Toff. He was a central figure in our social life as long as I can remember – jovial, friendly Toff. He never seemed to grow old' (*SJ* 2:174). A lifelong bachelor, Toff took care of his ageing mother.

37 Mrs Ewen, also referred to as Mrs Ewen MacKenzie, is Margaret Bell, wife of James Ewen MacKenzie.

38 Lover's Lane: a little woodland lane in Cavendish, named by L.M. Montgomery.

Thursday, Feb. 5th, 1903

Nora tried to be poetical in that last entry and witness the result. She has got so tangled up that I shall have to come to her rescue and extricate her. I think that she was trying to say that *she*, being 'of the earth, earthy,' had to stick to the solid ice, while I, in my *more ethereal* nature floated lightly over the snow-crust without floundering through. We had a bee-*yet*-tiful walk that night, though, in Lover's Lane. The only drawback was that there were no lovers, but we contrived to enjoy life tolerably well even so.

Since then we have been doing absolutely nothing worthy of chronicling. Our only resource has been to discuss the soulful James in all his aspects. He has more than replaced the garter. When the latter was found that was an end of its usefulness. But the interest in James is perennial.

Friday, Feb. 6th, 1903

Nora and I have decided that it will take *both* of our inspired pens to do justice to tonight. So here I come with my side of the story.

First however, I must jot down a word or two concerning Thursday night. In the evening Prescott,[39] Lucy[40] and I started off, leaving Nora simply green with jealousy because I was going to spend the evening in James' exhilarating company and she was not. We started west for Will Moore's but eventually turned up at Alec Macneill's (fig. 1.5)[41] down

---

39 Prescott A. Macneill (1879–1910), twenty-three, is John Franklin Macneill's son, brother of Lucy (see below) and L.M. Montgomery's cousin. He was unmarried.

40 Lucy Macneill (1877–1974), also referred to as Lu, twenty-five, is Prescott's sister and an intimate friend of Montgomery's. Montgomery notes in her journals: 'Lucy is my cousin. She lives just across our field' (*SJ* 1:2). In November 1903, Lucy married Benjamin F. Simpson, and the couple moved to Lynn, Massachusetts.

41 Alec Macneill is Alexander C. Macneill (1870–1951), thirty-three, one of Montgomery's beaux. Son of Charles Macneill and May Buntain, brother of Russell and Pensie Macneill. Montgomery notes in her journals: 'Alec has always been an excellent friend of mine and is very fond of me in a harmless platonic fashion to this day' (5 Jan. 1917; *SJ* 2:205). Alec married May Hooper and lived on Gartmore Farm, Cavendish, where Montgomery visited them in the 1920s and 1930s.

1.5 Montgomery's social life in Cavendish: Left: 'choir practice at Uncle John's' – John F. Macneill and his wife, Annie. (Courtesy Jennie Macneill, Prince Edward Island.) Right: 'dancing at Alec's' – Alexander Macneill, circa 1900. (L.M. Montgomery Collection, Archival and Special Collections, University of Guelph Library.)

east. There were four sleighs of us and we spent the evening playing whist with 'nations' cards. James was not at my table, I regret to say, but of course he wished he was. He lost the rubber ... no doubt because his eyes and thoughts were wandering from the game in my direction.

When I got home at twelve I was almost frozen and more than glad to crawl into a warm bed beside Nora who speedily thawed me out. We laughed and talked for about two hours. It is unnecessary to say whom we were discussing. There could be only one person. I may say we have hit upon a plan for settling at once and forever our rival claims. I am to take one end of his moustache, Nora the other, and tug hard. To the victor will belong the spoils.

This afternoon, there being no school on account of the storm, Nora and I went to work and made up a saucepan of candy with peanuts in it. It was a howling success. When Russell came we treated him to it, hoping that he would thereby be induced to take us to the lecture. But R. only got so far as to ask us if we were going to walk. So our candy was wasted.

We sped to the lecture all the same in Uncle John's box sleigh. But no lecturer appeared. The indefatigable Jerry, however, who had been minding his own business all day ... so he told us ... bustled around and got up a 'hat night' ... a thing which is a relic of the dark ages. Various floods of eloquence followed. Howard Simpson and our Freddie made *the* speeches of the evening ... the former on photography, the latter on 'card-playing.' Jerry also discoursed feelingly on pork-packing and 'Pa'[42] began on prohibition and got tangled up in politics.

When we came out Joe elbowed up to us in the porch and said we'd better go along with him. Unsuspectingly we did so. When we got down to the hollow whom should we behold, off to one side, but the Soulful, sitting all by his lone in his sleigh. I thought I smelt a rat and when James followed us 'straight' on up the road instead of turning in at his own gate I felt sure of it. Presently he began throwing out hints, asking Joe if he wasn't crowded, etc. Finally he drove up on one side and said he would 'take one of the ladies.'

---

42 'Pa' is Arthur Simpson, sixty-four, farmer and Baptist. As Montgomery notes: 'The Deacon is known to irreverent young Cavendish as "Pa" and his pallid, malicious wife as "Ma" because of their habit of addressing each other thus upon all occasions. I think Arthur Simpson is the one and only man in the world I hate with an undiluted hatred' (*SJ* 1:70).

This was a hint for *me*, of course. But I resolved to be self-sacrificing for once and let Nora have him. So I was blind and deaf, while Nora joyfully skipped out of our sleigh and into James.' Joe and I were left to amuse each other and he did his part by talking horse all the time. I was bored to death and got awfully cold into the bargain. I wish Joe would stick to 'the New Glasgow route' and leave me alone. However, my tale of woe is unimportant so I will now stop and let Nora relate hers.

Oh, my heart's up at 'Alec's' my heart is not here,
My heart's up at 'Alec's' a-chasing James dear,
A-chasing James dear and a-following Joe,
Oh, my heart's up at 'Alec's' wherever I go.

L.M.M.

Friday, Feb. 6th, 1903

Had I known how my poor pen was going to suffer by comparison I would never have consented to this partnership affair!! Would that my pen were inspired also and I could walk on snow!!!

As Maude has written the events of the day I shall just state a few facts (??)[43] in reference to 'Tabby'[44] and ... no, I won't have even my pronoun connected with that feline creature. By the way that makes me think of a 'widdle.' Why is James like Maude's cat?

We arrived safely at the hall and were scarcely seated when Maude observed that the object of our affections had arrived. My heart jumped as it generally does on such occasions. It did not come into my mouth however, as it is accustomed to do in most 'hysterical females' the reason being there was no room on account of some choice 'cuss words.'

I was bored nearly to death the whole eve and the only comfort that rendered it bearable was that Maude also was bored!!! (Oh no, I am not selfish!!)

At one time however we almost became interested in the science of 'pork-packing' when the door opened with an emphatic creak and in

---

43 (??): It's difficult to identify the author of these question marks in parenthesis. Montgomery could have inserted them when she transcribed Nora's text, questioning that Nora is really reporting the 'facts.' Conversely, Nora could have inserted them herself for she had a habit of inserting question marks to signal irony, as seen repeatedly in her entries.

44 Tabby is Montgomery's cat.

stepped Artie, tall and stately, with a stove-pipe hat and 'his pale hands clasping a gilt-edged book.' So we were 'done' for the rest of the eve.

Jo Stewart (the little brat!) came up to drive us home. He turned up west and when we discovered a 'lone traveller by the wayside brook' my suspicions of Mr. Jo were at once confirmed. Of course my *dignity* (was it?) prevented me from making a scene and I went with the *dern* fool! (I don't care if it is Sunday night I will say a 'cuss word' for it is only one thousandth of what is inside me.)

How I loathe and detest the creature! Did I ever imagine I could come down to even sitting beside him in a sleigh? I think if he dared touch me the very flesh on my bones would fall off!! (yes, it would!)

I can just picture him driving up and asking for 'one of the girls.' Although it is Sabbath eve,

'A feeling of *hate* comes o'er me that my soul cannot resist.'

There, I will not waste time and paper writing about the 'Rust*icus*' but let him dare ask me to go driving again!!!

I will stop for I am sure this is Sabbath-breaking.

N.L.

Sat. 7th

I suppose I shall have to write up the fun for today.

Maude went down to Mr. Macneill's this afternoon and I to bed, being on the sick list.

I had just finished dressing for practice which was to be held here when along came Fred and took me down to the 'Parsonage.' I went for I feared that Satan might appear later.

Very few were there, as the night was cold and we soon came home. Were in time to see the others off.

N.L.

Sunday, Feb. 8th

'It's easy to talk of the patience of Job, humph, Job had nothing to try him. But if he had known James Alec Stewart folks wouldn't have dared come nigh him! Trials indeed, now I tell you what if you want to be tired of your life just come and change places with us awhile for ... well, we know the 'darn fool.'

Was in bed nearly all day. Maude went to church this morn and came home 'madder'n' a wet hen because there was to be a missionary meeting Friday night and she could not go to the party at J.C.'s. I observed that there were worse things in Cavendish than *Miss[ionary] Meetings* but she did not seem inclined to carry on the conversation so we went to dinner and after man(i)curing ourselves with orange sticks and warm water Maud got her book and I went to bed. I felt better this eve and got up. We had just settled down to a nice quiet eve when along came Fred to take us to the Baptist Missionary meeting. (They are all the go now.)

I fled and Maud had to give my excuses. I was much relieved when I heard her do it so well but it was only temporary for I heard Fred remark that he had J.S. with him!!! I must confess I flew into a regular passion and actually swore and I know Maude will think I am very rude but I can't help it and found relief in tears after she had gone and got myself 'all flusticated up' so now I am fit for nothing.

Since writing the above Maud and James arrived. She is going to W.M. Macneill's to stay till after the funeral.[45] I suppose she is going to do penance for all the 'fibs' she has told.

N.L.

Tuesday afternoon
Feb. 10th, 1903

There has been a great fall in beef lately and Nora's nerves have suffered in consequence. But that is not what I started out to say. I am going to give *my* version of Sunday.

Firstly I went to church and everything there conspired to ruin my temper. A draught from the window gave me the sniffles, the choir sang out of tune and finally Mac[46] announced the missionary meeting for *half past seven*. That was the last straw. I hope he won't get a red cent at all to pay him out!

Nora was in bed part of the day and the rest of the time was lounging in a comfortable *un*dress. At about seven o'clock we heard a sleigh and

45 funeral: Amanda Macneill's mother had died. My thanks to Jennifer Litster.
46 Mac, or Mr MacIntosh (born 1868) is Major MacIntosh, the Presbyterian minister in Cavendish. My thanks to Jennifer Litster.

Nora made a wild dash for the room door. In walked Freddie and said he had come to take us to Missionary meeting. I went in to interview Nora who was running about gathering up the sheets of this self-same volume which she had scattered in her flight. She would not go, however, even when it transpired that the Soulful was waiting outside. So I went and Nora, on her own confession, wept tears of rage because I had secured dear James that time.

James has a dandy team anyhow. We just flew up to the church. Going through a fearful pitch in John Macneill's field *I* flew too about three feet in air. If I had lit on James or Freddie when I came down they would never have been heard of more. I risked my immortal soul telling them the most fearful stretchers about Nora having neuralgia of the heart. I represented her as at death's door, with myself vainly trying to bar him out in the watches of the night.

The Missionary meeting was not too bad. Jerry expiated on the Indians of course. Jerry's idea of heaven seems to be in poring over the Indians.

After church I went down to W.C.M.'s and stayed there all night and until after the funeral today. It is not a subject to be treated flippantly else I could a tale unfold. Suffice to say that I almost froze to death Sunday night, hugging a brick for warmth and comforting my sad heart with thoughts of the Soulful.

We got some foreign mail yesterday for a change. But I don't really see why people are going on so about the lack of ma(i)l(e)s. Nora and I are overwhelmed with them and in some cases cannot get rid of them. It's always the case that what you want you can't get and what you've got you don't want.

But there are some things I *will not* endure. I am *not* going to have my dearly beloved cat compared to James Alec! The idea! I suppose Nora thought that conundrum funny. The answer is simple enough ... it's because he always comes back of course. Like James, 'Bob's' faith in humanity is unbounded and does not grow dim for any amount of ill-treatment. But there all resemblance ends. Poor Bobs![47] 'That was the most unkindest cut of all.'

I must now tog up and wade out in the snow to choir practice for that old missionary meeting ... may the pigs get it.

---

47 This, of course, refers to Bobs the cat, not Rob MacKenzie.

I nearly forgot to say that Nora and I heard a 'banshee'[48] last night. Perhaps it was the last despairing cry of James Alec.

'The passionate wail of a breaking heart
Of a heart slow in breaking alas.'

L.M.M.

Friday afternoon, Feb. 13th

Tuesday evening I went to choir practice at Uncle John's. Nora would not go because she was too deeply absorbed in *Rupert of Hentzau*[49] to tear herself away.

But she wished she had later on, for ... what do you think? The Soulful was there and he drove me home all by my lone. Nora felt so bad when I came home and told her that she had to put a mustard plaster on her heart before she went to bed.

Last night there was practice again and Nora went but James did not appear so she felt pretty blue. She pretends she does not care but that is all bluff.

Well, tonight our missionary meeting was to have been and also the party at J.C. Clark's.[50] But present indications do not point to much hilarity. It has been storming furiously all day. Nobody seemed to be abroad but James who drove past here in the worst of it. Evidently no weather can squelch *him*.

Nora has taken to nursing Bobs who is submitting under protest. His expression plainly indicates that he is making the best of a bad business.

I have often heard that the gods sometimes punish people by granting their wishes. Last Sunday in my anger I wished for a howling snowstorm tonight. The gods heard and granted and here I am madder than ever. There is no mail either ... spell it whichever way you like.

---

48 A banshee, in Gaelic folklore, is a female spirit believed to predict a death.

49 *Rupert of Hentzau*: a novel by Sir Anthony Hope Hawkins (1898), an author better known for his novel *The Prisoner of Zenda* (1894).

50 J.C. Clark, also referred to as J.C., is John Cavendish Clark (1835–1914) of Bay View, Baptist. He was married to Anne Simpson and was the father of Jerry, Annie, and eight others. J.C. Clark's was a rich place for socializing.

Nora and I are in desperate want of someone to take us to the party and have gone around all day singing this doleful ditty.

'Oh for a man ... a man ... a man ...

A man ... sion in the skies.'

L.M.M.

Tuesday, Feb. 17th 03

Suppose I shall have to get my wits about me and write up the first (and I suppose the last) party of the season ... for us. There is to be another on Friday eve but as there will probably be a practice for the missionary meeting I may not be able to go (???)

It snowed most beautifully all day and as we had no one to take us we were lamenting about our lot for you know there was to be a missionary meeting (as usual) and Maud could not go till after that so we could not go together anyhow. I may just say here in regard to missionary meetings that they are our chief entertainment this winter. It seems to me that we just get through tramping to practice for one and begin to enjoy life without the heathens when we are startled with the report there is another on the go. I sincerely hope the poor heathen are warmer than we are this cold weather.

However, it was Friday eve and I had just settled down to work when along came 'the idol of my heart' in the person of Jerry. Of course this put all my cares at rest (???) I began to worry about Maude but had I only known what was in store for me I would just simply have let Miss Maude's affairs alone. Well, there, I suppose I might just as well blurt out the whole trouble at once and get it over with! I think I said that Jerry took me. Yes, the creature did and *he left me there* too! Home time came but no Jerry turned up. I don't know what he meant ... perhaps it is just one of his 'cute ways' and if I didn't have to gooseberry⁵¹ home with Maude and Fred! Perhaps I wasn't mad! I know he did not want me but though my reception was cool he did not succeed in freezing me out though it was near it for he ran me into a snowbank and just covered me with the 'virgin snow' but still I remained seated.

The time passed very pleasantly at the party. Maude and John J. got a prize for flowers and Roger and I for books (though somehow and I

---

51 gooseberry: to chaperone.

don't know how James heard it was John and I but I declare that was not true. I know he was angry with me for he did not smack his lips when he said it was 'the last quarter of the moon,' and that is a sure sign. N.B. Those marks mean a deep sigh) but perhaps it is all for the best.

However, I got Neil Simpson[52] on the string and we went out to supper. (James was not there.)

Maude and I tried to 'swipe'[53] as much stuff as we could but alas, we lost it all!! So you see though it was a 'swell' time in a way I had a great many troubles. I really don't know what I could have done to Jerry to merit such treatment. I talked 'Injun' all the way up, discussed Baptist preachers and conference meetings, then back to the Indians again. I tried my very best to appear interested and when he asked me if I would like to be a missionary I said 'yes' and clasped my hands in an ecstasy of delight as the vision arose before me of Jerry and I away in the western lands teaching the Indians, but somehow it was no use. I need not have added more sins to the already large list but I suppose 'it will all turn out for the best' and he may yet ask me to take the 'long road' with him, same as Holmes did that other 'missus.'

I forgot to say we had our fortunes told during the eve and mine turned out to be an 'immediate marriage' so that is encouraging.

Wednesday, Feb. 18th, 1903

'The Man' arrived Friday afternoon ... that is Jerry came down and told Nora he would call for her as soon as he had sold the Baptist church. People did not seem anxious to invest in Baptist churches that day however as Jerry was soon back. I had to fly to my room and stay there in the cold while Nora dressed for I dared not try the effect of my 'frizzed' hair on Jerry's delicate nerves.

Evening came and everybody went to the party except myself. I

---

52 Neil Simpson (1876–1940), Montgomery's school friend, would marry Margaret Sarah MacLeod and reside in Vancouver. Montgomery recalls about his recitation at the Cavendish school concert: 'Neil always read as if he had a hot potato in his mouth' (*SJ* 1:22).

53 For a discussion of Montgomery and Lefurgey's game of 'swiping' mementoes, see chapters 2 and 7.

togged up and went to the missionary meeting just as mad as I could be. Of course only a few turned up and Mr. MacIntosh postponed it until Sunday night. We sung a hymn and the benediction was pronounced.

I started out boiling with rage. Here I had lost my chance to the party and was not to have even a missionary meeting to cheer me up. But when I got out to the porch there was that blessed Freddie. 'No sun upon an Easter day was ever half so fine a sight.' At that moment I forgave Freddie all his sins.

When we got up the party was in full swing and Nora was prowling around trying to 'swipe' things. The whole affair was very good. Of course it was pervaded with Jerry. Fred and I learned to play ping-pong and Jerry explained very carefully to us what 'love' meant in this game. He seemed to be afraid we might mistake its meaning. Ping-pong is a game you play with a ball. You try to hit the ball all the time you aren't chasing it around the floor or digging it out from under the sideboard.

One of the amusements was telling fortunes by shooting at a heart. My luck was to be married five times. It is enough to discourage anyone.

Here is a conundrum Jerry got off at supper. Why is a sheet of foolscap like a lame dog?

Nora kept on swiping things. I tried but to no luck. Irene Simpson[54] watched me every time. I did manage to secrete a brown paper heart but lost it later on. In the end my only spoils consisted of a piece of string, a green rose worn by Jerry, and a piece of Fred's whip. Jerry didn't bring Nora home so Freddie and I toted her along. I don't think her entry shows her to have been very grateful.

We employed Saturday and Sunday recovering from the effects. Sunday night that famous missionary meeting came off at last. We discovered that Cavendish was Jerusalem. I have often heard it compared to heaven because there is neither marrying nor giving in marriage in it, so I suppose it is the new Jerusalem. Also, the province of Quebec is Samaria.

When we came out dear James came up and asked if he might drive us home. His idea of driving us home seemed to be taking us clean down to Rob MacKenzie's corner. I am afraid James' bump of locality must be lacking. Nora wouldn't talk so I had to. If I stopped there would be a horrible silence and after vainly racking my brains I would

---

54 Irene Simpson (1884–1971), Cedric's sister from Bay View.

at last remark, 'We've been having some storms lately.' And James would respond, 'Yes, the moon is in her last quarter.'

It has been doing nothing but storm ever since and we have not even seen James. Never mind.

'Summer will come again,
Snowbanks will thaw again,
We shall see James gain,
We shall see James again
By and by!'

L.M.M.

Judging by the above Miss Maude seemed very glad that James asked her to go for a drive Sunday night. Dear me, what on earth will I do if she cuts me out? But you see I will have vengeance in some other way. Of course, she has no 'gigermandi' to stick pins into but I will do something that is worse than that, yes, I will.

As it was only fourteen below zero Sabbath eve and a nor'wester blowing with force enough to blow Artie down and the roads bad as a three days' storm could make them that 'flabbergasted' creature whom they call James asked if he could take us over home but I declare it never took me so long to get home before. I guess he thought we had rented a summer residence down at South Rustico,[55] judging by the frantic effort he made to get us there. I nearly perished and one would think to be near me that I was in that country where 'the wind from Thule freezes the word upon the lip.' However, my silence was not noticed and in time we got home.

N.L.

Sat., Feb. 21

The 'little time' as James says has come off, viz. the party at Alec Macneill's.

Two 'gents' by name Jo and Jim Stewart took us girls up to Literary[56]

---

55 Rustico: South and North Rustico in Queen's County, close to Cavendish. Known for Acadian populations.

56 Literary: Cavendish Literary Society, where Montgomery and Nora Lefurgey read essays.

where Maude read an excellent paper to a 'highly intellectual audience,' Arty Moffat[57] being there. It was a good paper and I was sorry to see so many vacant seats.

After Literary the above-mentioned took us down to the festal scene. The seat room being somewhat limited we had to economize space and I would rather sit on the stove with my hollow tooth full of water and wait till it ... well, I won't say the rest ... than sit where I sat. However we arrived in good time, well supplied with curling tongs, camphor ice, safety pins and other things too numerous to mention. I danced a set of lancers with 'Bobs' and had I been able to get clear of that without being rude!!!

Maude flirted with 'Bobs' (fig. 1.6) all the eve and I did not care very much but you'll see now when she goes to write up she will say quite prim, 'Nora was just green with envy.' Yes, she will. She always does. However, I will just say that as she professes to be my friend she acted a very mean art, so there!

James 'waxed sarcastic' about coming home. We stayed till nearly five in the morning and I bet the next time I attend a social function in Cavendish I will get home early.

N.L.

Tuesday, Feb. 24th, 1903

Lent begins tomorrow so I must write up the history of our worldly vanities before turning my thoughts to holy things ... I mean several garments which are in need of darning and patching.

Well (I've caught that word from Nora) there was a glorious dance at Alec Macneill's last Friday night and we were invited. For a wonder there was no missionary meeting to detain me but just as bad there was Literary and I had to read a paper for it. Nora and I expected James to come down for us, as he had been in the evening before and said he would 'come for *yes*.' We got ready in a peck of trouble for everybody in Cavendish ... more or less ... came in while we were dressing and we would have to bolt. But all was in readiness at last and in due time

---

57 Artie Moffat, fifty, labourer, presumably lacking education. He was an old bachelor from New Glasgow with very red hair who was always proposing to women. My thanks to Jennifer Litster.

1.6   'Maud flirted with "Bobs" all the eve' – Robert MacKenzie (second from left), with his sister Bertha on her wedding day, Christmas 1905; L.M. Montgomery as bridesmaid. (Courtesy Jennie Macneill, Prince Edward Island.)

James and Jo appeared and drove us to the hall. Nora had to sit on the farmer's knee and she nearly tilted over going up a particularly bad piece of road on David's hill.[58] 'Well,' we got the Literary over and I read my paper and we started for Alec's. Arriving there we found the party in full swing and presently we were in the swim. From that in till five o'clock we had an alama-glorious time ... at least I had. Nora fought with Bob MacK. over that everlasting 'valise,' condoled with Henry (see fig. 2.2)[59] and also discussed platonics with him, and snubbed poor James until my heart ached with pity for him and I did my best to be kind to him. That is what Nora calls 'flirting with him' mark you, when I was literally sacrificing myself on the altar of friendship. Why, I even went and played whist with James with those horrible old 'nations' cards when I might have been dancing!!! And I grinned all the time, mark you. Here behold heroism incarnate in the person of Maud M.

At supper time Joe and I sat on the back stairs and flirted amiably while James and Nora sat in the corner below and gazed lovingly at each other. When James begins to look sentimental out of those soulful orbs of his it is enough to make one turn Mohammedan or Mormon.

We kept the dance up until five o'clock and then came home in state under 'the last quarter of the moon.' Next day we felt like the dickens. Nora's fatigue got on her nerves and she began to talk about dancing being a *sin*. That night I had to trail away down to E.J. Mackenzie's for practice ... but wait until I tell you. James, dear James, came and took me. He didn't ask Nora to go either. So you see I am rewarded for my devotion to him at the party. He nearly spilled me out in a snowbank on MacKenzie's hill so I was horribly cold and tired and cross when I got home.

Sunday morning 'Prophet Edwin'[60] preached for us. And lo and behold, our minister has resigned. We can be as wicked as we like for awhile.

---

58 David's hill: folk name for the hill at David and Margaret Macneill's in Cavendish.

59 Henry, also known as Henry M. or Hen-ry is Henry McLure, a farmer of Rustico and Montgomery's beau in 1899. In her journals, she notes about him: '[His] best point is the possession of a dandy gee-gee [horse] and I neither like nor dislike him' (*SJ* 1:242).

60 'Prophet Edwin' refers to Edwin Simpson (1872–1955), the Baptist Reverend of Belmont Lot 16. Montgomery had been engaged to him for nine months in 1897 when she taught school in Belmont and Lower Bedeque (for more details, see chapters 4 and 7).

Tonight Nora and I started out for a 'logical' walk, in to the old Baptist church and along Lover's Lane. We tried to see how many different ways we could make fools of ourselves and succeeded beautifully. Nora told so many fibs that her tooth has been aching ever since. But that is her own fault for I gave her an infallible cure for it ... fill it with kerosene and set fire to it. But she would not try it.

We have seen nothing of James since Saturday night. What can have happened to the dear fellow? Can Nora's heartless conduct have chilled his young affections at last? Or is it that there being no moon at all now, not even a last quarter, he dare not trust himself abroad? Well, I have borne other troubles so I suppose I can live through this.

'Twas ever thus since childhood's hour
I've seen my fondest hopes decay,
I never loved a tree or flower
But 'twas the first to fade away.
I never tamed a Soulful one
To glad me with his bright blue eye,
But when he came to know me well
He coldly, sternly passed me by.'

L.M.M.

Tuesday, Mar. 3rd... 03

'I' feel about ten times as big tonight as I generally feel and that is the reason why I started this with the all important 'ego' and I expect Miss Maude will remark on it but I don't care. If she knew the reason of my inward exaltation she would be as mad as ... they generally are under the circumstances. I feel beautiful. I have an empty tooth and I don't even feel it so great is my joy.

Maude and I very quietly planned to go down to Darnley Clark's (fig. 1.7)[61] to spend the eve. Of course we have both been intending to go for a long time and we just were going down to see the 'old folks'

---

61 Darnley Clark, sixty, a Cavendish farmer, father of Wilber, Freddie, Chesley, and Maggie. Montgomery notes in her journal: 'I sometimes wonder what I would have done if Darnley Clark had not had a family of boys!!! They have all been so kind to me and they are nice brotherly chums, always ready to do a good turn, with no nonsense of sentiment in the matter' (SJ 1:318).

1.7 'I sometimes wonder what I would have done if Darnley Clark had not had a family of boys!!!' Back: Fred, Chesley, Wilber, Ernest. Front: Maggie, Jane (mother), Darnley (father), Campsie. (Courtesy Janet Haslam, Prince Edward Island.)

(?). I think I can safely say that neither of us had any desire to flirt but alas!

I was ready in time for a wonder and were both sitting at the fire, talking of 'the one' nearest our hearts when we heard a sleigh. Maud made a frantic dash for her coat, ditto hat, but I simply stayed still. I knew it was not Wilber,[62] why no, it was James. He is so 'instinctive' you know! It was not long before Wilber did arrive and Annie[63] (my sister-in-law by the way) bounced in looking like a frozen crab (apple) only a great deal more so. She snapped out 'Good eve' just the same as the 'aborigines' did to Columbus. James did not come in. You know he saw Wilber in the yard with a large white article round his neck and he concluded he was after us. I do believe he was vexed but I am afraid he 'jumps to conclusions.' He'll have to get over that before ... oh never mind, I'm not going to tell all I know.

We had quite a nice time at Mr. Clark's. We both elocuted for him and after a little fun came home.

We intended to go to P.M.[64] tonight but are too tired.

I forgot to say we went to church Sunday night but Mr. Mac did not come but of course James was there. He was as cool as a cucumber and dear me, what can the matter be?

'Oh Jamie, come back to us.'

N.L.

Saturday, March 7th, 1903

I am sitting down here Saturday morning writing in this immortal record when there are stacks of other work I ought to be at. Nora is in bed doing penance for her sins and consequently I'm having some peace of my life.

Well, you should just have seen Nora Thursday night. Of all the happy girls.

She took a notion to go up to Union and I went up to W.C. Macneill's

---

62 Wilber J. Clark, nineteen, is Darnley Clark's son and brother of Freddie, Chesley, and Maggie.

63 Annie, also known as the Amiable Annie or Annie Stewart, sister of Jo, Will, Lizzie, and James Alexander Stewart.

64 P.M.: prayer meeting.

gate with her, determined to keep her out of mischief as long as I could. Then I came home and, and as Jerry says, minded my own business.

Nine o'clock came ... no Nora. Nine-thirty ... no Nora still. I began to feel anxious. Had she cut me out with our beloved James again? Heart-rending thought! Finally at a quarter to ten Nora arrived and so radiant was her physiog. when she entered that I knew at once my worst fears were confirmed. James had driven her home. I will draw a veil over my feelings!

But never mind! I paid her out when I got her into bed. I kicked all the bed-clothes up at the foot and she had to crawl out in the cold and tuck them in.

Wednesday morning I received a letter from Jerry Clark (B.A.) which he very appropriately sent down by his mother. When I saw the old lady toddling in with the missive I nearly had seventeen different kinds. The letter proved to contain the information that Jerry could not come down before Friday evening to confer about our 'newspaper' but would be along bright and early that eve and take us to the Literary. Right here I may record a very Jerry-like incident which took place two Sundays ago. Coming out of church Jerry elbowed his way up to where I stood among a crowd of people and told me in a very confidential tone that he was very much afraid he couldn't get down 'to see me' the next night as he was called away and wouldn't be back for a week. You should have seen the people rubber. I suppose they immediately scented a romantic romance whereas it only referred to a harmless business arrangement that Jerry and I had made to meet and talk over our plans for our Literary 'newspaper.'

Well, 'to resume and to continue,' as *Samantha*[65] says.

Last evening Jerry arrived with a cartload of sermons, editorials and poems. Nora had been having fits before his coming but the sight of his beaming countenance so worked on her for good that she got well immediately and to onct. I produced some MSS. I had prepared and we hoed in to work and cudgelled our gray matter getting up a lot of 'personals' and local jokes. In due time we had accumulated enough mental fodder and then we started for the hall behind 'Olive.' On the way up Jerry politely offered to drive us back after Literary and 'talk it over.' After a harrowing pause Nora uttered a faint 'Thank you' ... you

---

65 Samantha refers to the popular American humorist-writer Marietta Holley (1836–1926), whose pseudonym was Samantha Allen.

see, she hated to give up her chance of a drive with the Soulful ... and I piped out a cheerful assent too. When a few minutes later we saw James and Jo entering the hall we felt that there might be squalls.

Our 'paper' went off in pretty good style and after it was over we departed in state with Jerry, neither James or Joe daring to venture near us in his august presence.

So that is another worry over. And now I am in a peck of scrapes over the choir practice. No sooner do I get out of one pickle than I go plump into another. It is bringing down my gray hairs with sorrow to the grave.[66] Never mind! There is a land where the Jameses cease from troubling and the weary are at rest.

L.M.M.

Sat., Mar. 21 ... 03

The whole weeks of 'skulking' and here, old diary, I start in again fresh and (as Maud will stick in I suppose) *green* from my long rest. So much has transpired during this period that I fear I shall have to omit most of it. Two instances however must be cited. Viz: – James has gone and left us ... yes, honest.

'He has gone from the haunt where his dark-eyed Nora sighs'

... and I hope he will never return.

Then, to add more trouble to the already heavy burden Mrs. Murray came down on me like a 'western snow-slide' with 'By Creon'[67] and Murray[68] plus Charlie Simpson.[69] The result was a resignation.

---

66 'my gray hairs ... to the grave': Montgomery parodies the Bible: 'And if ye take this also from me, and mischief befall him, ye shall bring down my gray hairs with sorrow to the grave' (Genesis 44:29). She may also allude to the discovery of her first grey hairs in 1903; the experience was upsetting, as she confessed in her journal a full decade later in 1913: 'It was ten years ago ... I cried myself to sleep and for days the thought of those gray hairs haunted me' (*SJ* 2:130).

67 'By Creon' refers to Pierce Macneill, forty-nine, a farmer in Cavendish, whose favourite expression was 'by Creon.' In 1892, he and his wife, Rachel, had adopted 'Ellen,' the orphan girl who inspired the idea for *Anne of Green Gables* (Willoughby 44).

68 Murray Robertson: see footnote 17.

69 Charlie Simpson, a farmer, father of Emma and Mamie, Montgomery's classmates. He moved to New Glasgow in 1914, then to British Columbia in 1920. My thanks to Jennifer Litster.

I was up to J. Laird's[70] the other eve. Maude had the audacity to infer that I was trying to get Everett on the now almost *knotless* string but there is not one atom of truth in it for he was over to Tennis' playing cards.

Last Sunday eve Mr. MacLeod[71] preached us a very instructive and soul-stirring sermon. The result was that Maude has been more 'logical' than ever all the week much to my annoyance.

Last eve we walked up to Literary and Maude behaved herself most dreadfully. I did not have the peace of a 'dorg.' And then if I would do anything in self-defence she would fly to the refuge, 'I'll stick pins ...' then a dead silence which old dame Experience has taught me too well the meaning of.

However we landed at the hall somehow, me with my mouth crammed (if there is only one M in that leave the other out) Jammed (ditto) ... bet she will say that is swearing. She said 'dern' was ... full of peppermints and ... a collar, but I was full of Lord Byron so the other deficiencies were excusable.

Miss Lefurgey, the mistress of Cavendish public school, read a paper on Lord Byron.

Wilber put out the lights before we all got out so we had to hunt around in the dark for half an hour. Bob MacKenzie took us home in his chariot with a bag and no back. Of course the immortal valise was the chief topic of conversation.

We both feel relieved tonight for our connection with Cavendish literary is at an end.

I guess spring is very far away yet for even the three blue *'jays'* have deserted the place. (More air please.)

N.L.

Sunday, Mar. 22nd, 1903

It is pouring rain and we have no preaching anywhere within come-at-able distance the whole day. Under such dismal circumstances I have nothing better to do than 'slamwhang' a bit in this journal although I

---

70 J. Laird's: John Laird's, where Nora had boarded before lodging with Montgomery, and where Ewan Macdonald boarded. For more details, see chapter 2.

71 Mr MacLeod, or the Rev. J.M. MacLeod, is a minister; he had preached at Grandfather Montgomery's funeral in August 1893 (*SJ* 1:92).

have nothing to record. Please notice the new and pictureaskew[72] addition to our vocabulary in the preceding sentence.

All things considered this last fortnight has not been an exhilarating one. 'The rains descended and the floods came' most of the time and as cold as charity into the bargain. One cannot stir abroad without sinking in mud up to her ears.

But oh, think of it. Dear James has, I fear, deserted us both at last. We have seen nothing of him for over a fortnight. Nora took it so hard that she had to stay a whole day in bed and I taught school for her until she recovered from the blow. 'Men are deceivers ever.'

Friday night was Literary and Nora read a very excellent paper on Byron.[73] She had been going about for a week with her eyes staring into vacancy while she mentally rehearsed the selections she was going to recite. I wanted her to give one from DON JUAN but she was afraid it might bring a blush to Jerry's cheek and would not. We walked up and Nora, with her usual veracity, says I misbehaved myself. I didn't. I was just as logical as possible.

'Geordie' and 'Little George'[74] discussed the paper in their usual eloquent style. Father Pierce presided and I think he must have been praying in a very muddy spot, judging from the knees of the garments that clothed his nether limbs. (Nobody would think of *legs* in connection with Pierce.)

Bob MacK. brought us home and, thank the Lord, he and Nora finally and forever buried that defunct joke about the *valise.* I am grateful, beyond words. I had begun to believe that valise affair was like Tennyson's brook destined to go on forever and never get there.

It is of no use for Nora to pretend that she didn't go up the hill to see Everett. It would be much more becoming if she frankly owned up to the motive. Go she did and I went to the gate with her. On the way up we met Murray and Pierce. If they had come along about ten seconds earlier they would have seen a sight worth seeing now. Later on we met D. Clark, got in and drove back to the school with him.

---

72 pictureaskew: picturesque.

73 Byron: Lord Byron (1788–1824), author of *Don Juan,* a work considered a manual for vice by genteel readers.

74 'Little George,' also referred to as George R., is George Raglan Macneill, son of Jimmie and Jane Macneill, brother of Evie and Grace. Geordie is unidentified but could refer to George Simpson, Howard's brother. My thanks to Jennifer Litster.

It's all very well for Nora to say that Everett was away at Tennis' playing cards. In the first place, how does she know he was really away at all? He may have been upstairs hiding from her. In the second place, granting he was away, how does she know he was at Tennis'? He may have been up to see Lizzie. In the third place, if he *were* away and if he *were* at Tennis', how does she know he was playing cards? He may have been minding Mrs. Tennis' baby. The foregoing is logical I am sure.

But anyway I know Nora stayed up at Lairds' half the night waiting for him to appear. I was just going to start out and rouse the settlement to search for her when she came home.

There's something queer about Nora anyway. I've come to that conclusion. One day I took a photograph of four respectable elderly gentlemen sitting in a parlour. And when I developed the plate there was a picture of Nora on snowshoes standing out in the woods!!! (see fig. 7.3).

Upon reading over the last two entries calmly I think we have been foolish in getting so wrought up over the disappearance of three *jays*. If we did not have a *jay* Friday night we had a Rob-in the sleigh and everyone knows that a *robin* is a much more reliable sign of spring than a *jay*.

L.M.M.

Sunday, Mar. 29, 1903

Nora says it is my turn to write in our diary. It looks a lot like it! But of course I must try to fulfil her behest. Not that I have a single thing to write about. There has been nothing at all happening this week and the weather has been past praying for. I have been groaning with a sore back and Nora has been a prey to 'rinology.' The weather has been enough to give an angel the kinks. It is of a very peculiar kind. And last night it turned as cold as James' recent manner and snowed a few feet more or less, thereby saving James' reputation as a reliable weather prophet. My faith in him is justified.

Nora and I ploughed up through the drifts to the Baptist church this morning, all agog to hear the Rev. 'Craw's'[75] wonderful sermon on a given text. But there was nothing particularly biting about it except that His Reverence seemed to think that people used to be able to kill a great

---

75 Rev. Craw: Rev. C.P. Wilson; see footnote 4.

many more of their foes in the old times and rather regretted he hadn't been round then.

Nora and I both went visiting yesterday and came home with all the gossip in C.[76] with which we regaled each other in bed. The main items are that Everett has got out again after his three days' 'retreat' in bed, that Wilber 'sat out' Garfield[77] last Saturday night at 'Hughie's'[78] that Mrs. Will Sandy is hooking mats for Townsend, that Pierce and Albert[79] have had a fight, that Neil S[impson] has made an excellent choice, and that Nora's influence over Gordon is considered adverse to his spiritual life.

James dear favoured us with a call Friday afternoon. The weather has been 'way down in zero ever since. How my heart went pitty-patter when I heard his well-known footfall. You should have seen Nora hustling her feet down.

Bob MacK. spent Wednesday evening here and I had all I could do to keep the peace between him and Nora. In spite of my efforts I really thought once that they would go at each other poker and tongs. To my disgust they dug up that unsavoury old valise joke and threshed it over as of yore. Bob told Nora that she was like Mag Laird.[80] It was at this point that Nora seized hold of the poker.

We had a call from Mag Laird this week among other spring birds. When she came on I did not recognize her at first and was just going to say to Nora, 'Why, here is your aunt?' when I saw who she really was. The old lady was looking for a 'chaw' of tobacco but we did not have any left. We find it hard to keep a stock of the weed on hand since Nora arrived here. So poor old Mag had to trudge further on in her search for the staff of life.

L.M.M.

---

76 C.: Cavendish.

77 Garfield is Garfield Stewart, the younger brother of James Alexander Stewart. He married Ellen Macneill.

78 'Hughie's' could refer to Hugh MacLure's in Cavendish.

79 Albert Macneill (1860–1928), of Cavendish, Pensie's brother and, according to Montgomery, 'an old family friend, of whom I was always fond' (SJ 3:386).

80 Mag Laird is the model for Peg Bowen in the The Story Girl. Jennie Macneill recalls her mother's recollections of Mag Laird as being 'harmless' and 'wandering all over.' According to Jennie Macneill, it was 'not unusual to find Mag Laird sleeping on your couch in the winter. People would give her meals' (phone interview, July 2003).

Sunday, Mar. 29 ... 03

My task this time is a difficult one. I see plainly that I will have to give Miss L.M. a calling down. She has just done enough slam-whanging.[81] I am mad right through. In the beginning she deals me a whack about it being my turn to write. Then she goes on to state that there is nothing to write about. Humph! Nothing to write about indeed, when this is the week James came back to us!

We were talking the affair over and were 'sorter confidin' in each other about it. Maude was at the stove caressing her RAM'S HORN magazine[82] (which I may say she has taken a marvellous fancy to of late. I hope it will do her some good!) and your humble servant was ensconced on the sofa with her extremities (suppose Miss L.M. would say legs!) elevated on a chair .00716084 degrees higher than her head when a step sounded at the door and in walked the long-lost James. Yes, honest, he came in like a lamb! (Just like March.) Maude grinned and clasped the RAM'S HORN to her fluttering breast. My feet descended to the floor by magic. Otherwise I retained my calmness.

Then she errs again in her 'Birdology.' Last tome she had something very *ill*-ogical about 'Blue j's.' Now she launches forth on the 'crows' and says there was nothing biting about it. I fear she had her mind on the *Hen*-ry whilst it (not the crows but the sermon) was being delivered. She is spiritually bankrupt. Gordon ditto *and I am not to blame*. She told a downright fib in the last part for she said she thought it was my aunt coming in the morning Mag L. got out. How did she know I wonder when she never saw an aunt of mine in her life.

N.L.

Sunday, April 5th, 1903

The weather this week has been a disgrace to civilization. It has snowed and blowed and rained and hailed and 'friz' without cessation and sometimes it has done them all at once ... as for instance today. I am at my last gasp of endurance and my nerves, like those of Laura

---

81 slam-whanging (a neologism): mud-slinging.

82 The *Ram's Horn*, a popular social gospel magazine, was published in the United States during the 1890s and the early twentieth century.

MacKenzie's horse, have got 'all unstrung.' If it keeps on as it has kept on for the past month I am going to go to bed, like Everett Laird, and stay there.

There is no preaching anywhere near today and though one of those perennial missionary meetings is to be held in the B[aptist] church tonight it does not look as if we would get there too abundantly. I feel wickeder than any old heathen anyhow.

When I began this page it was pouring rain. When I got half way down it was hailing and now it is a blinding snow-squall.

Talking of preaching reminds me that last Sunday night the Rev. Wilson preached on temperance. I would not turn out but Nora marched off, hoping that James would bring her home. But she got beautifully left for he didn't. But there is worse to follow in its due order.

Tuesday evening Nora went over to help Lucy hook and dragged me along too, not even giving me time to comb my hair.

By Thursday we were both feeling red-hot mad because our samples hadn't come. They have never arrived yet. I believe old Crewe[83] has swallowed them. He did not show up at all yesterday so perhaps they have given him housemaid's knee or locomotor ataxia and good enough for him.

Thursday evening at sunset ... there *was* a little sun that day for a wonder ... Nora and I started for a ramble through Lover's Lane. We expected it would be mud to our ears. Instead we found excellent sleighing and banks of snow over the fences. We came home by Tennis' thoroughfare and had to climb across the brook hanging on by our eyelids to a fallen spruce tree. Nora was as illogical as usual. Coming over the hill we saw a 'mackerel sky' and I prophesied that it meant wind.

We had not been home long 'when footsteps were heard at the door' and in marched our two long-lost, lamented *'jays.'* Then Nora and I had to straighten up and begin to talk small talk. They sat and sat until my resources were exhausted. At last, just when several of those 'awful silences' were beginning to happen they got up and took their departure. Joe bade us all good-night but James turned around at the door and looking at me very tenderly said, 'Good-night, *Maud.'* Nora turned absolutely green. She need not aspire to James' affection any longer. She must know it is hopeless after that.

---

83 Crewe is the mailman. My thanks to Jennifer Litster.

Well, next day it blew a hurricane so I am as good a weather-prophet as James. He bobbed up serenely again on Friday evening. I suppose he came back to say good-night to us all that time. When he departed he left his mittens behind him. Whether this was a gentle hint that he was giving us each a mitten or not, I cannot say. Scarcely had we got rid of James when Russell arrived and spent the evening. We have certainly had several callers this week but I fear they are a rather poor assortment.

George R.[84] came in last night and was decidedly the best of the bunch. Thanks to his entertaining conversation Nora and I got through the evening without wishing to commit suicide. Nora was drying her nut-brown locks on the floor when George came in and you should have seen her scamper.

'I hear thee speak of a better land
Where people do not get froze as they stand.
Nora, oh, where is that happy shore,
Shall we not go and get thawed once more?
Is it where the north-east zephyr blows
And Lovers' Lanes are all full of snows,
And strange bright "jays" have mittens to wear
And samples vanish the Lord knows where,
And ma(i)l(e)men fail to come to hand,
Is it there, dear chummy, that better land?
    Not there, not there, my child.'

L.M.M.

April 19 ... 03

Last Sunday night we went up to church. It was snowing and blowing something terrible but as this is the usual state of the weather we should not complain!

I strolled up into the choir where 'old dame Circumstance' gave me a seat beside Jerry Clark. The subject of the discourse was 'Excuses' and I just wondered as I sat there so very near to Jerry what excuse he was able to give for not taking me home from the party though he was extremely obliging to take me there!

---

84 George R: George Raglan Macneill; see footnote 74.

I know now his conscience must have given him a twinge as he thought of that night so on the way down the choir steps he sidled up to me and asked me if he could take me home with him! The strange way the question was put startled me for a moment but I soon recovered. How glad I was he did ask me for when I got to the door I saw Fred looking very intently at Maud and I at once perceived his intention so Mr. Clark saved me the embarrassing position of chaperon.

We talked Indian all the way home as usual but as the roads were very bad Olive[85] commanded most of his attention.

I just got home and my coat off when in walked Maud and her escort. He stayed till nearly twelve so I guess Miss Maud can't tease me very much.

Ha! Ha! Ha!

Tuesday night we were all seated around the fire when in walked James S. as usual meek as a lamb. I was very much interested in THE TALE OF TWO CITIES at the time so I left Maude to talk to him.

Thursday we went down to Mrs. Laird's to see Hetty.[86] We had quite a little gossip chat going down for Maude having gone a piece with Amanda[87] got a drive back with Joe and consequently had some interesting news.

Hetty was very gracious and just as we came out we met Fred. He stopped to say good-evening but evidently he was 'rushed.' He cast one long look at Maud and for the first time in his life he made the first move!

I know I should have been up at union tonight but I went visiting so could not go.

Friday eve James S. came in again and the first thing he did was to talk about Jerry. I got a little cranky for it goes against me to hear him made fun of! But when he told the story about the oil it was more than I could stand so I laughed.

The story goes that Jerry missed me at union and wasted three gallons of oil trying to calm his troubled breast! But of course you know that is only report.

---

85 Olive, the horse.

86 Hetty is Hetty Laird, the daughter of William and Mary Laird. She dated Fred Clark but died young in 1905. My thanks to Jennifer Litster.

87 Amanda Macneill (1874–1949), Montgomery's school chum ('Mollie'), whom 'I loved in childhood and in young girlhood' (*SJ* 2:2). Amanda married George Henry Robertson in July 1909.

Sat. I was down to Mrs. L's again. Hetty was in a beautiful humour and the first thing she hailed me with was Jerry! Of course Fred told her all about me but I bet he did not tell about Maude.

So all the 'knights' have been fair ones this last week. I suppose the moon's (smack) in her last quarter.

N.L.

Sunday, April 19th, 1903

For a wonder today is fine ... overhead. Underfoot it is nothing but snow and slush. Ever since my last entry there has been nothing but rain and snow. Fortunately my samples arrived the next day so I was therefore enabled to get through the week alive. On Sunday of course it snowed all day. But in the evening Nora and I, driven by desperation, started up to the Baptist preaching. It was awful, snowing, blowing and slush to our knees. I tell you I wished many a time on the road up that I had stayed home and read my 'expurgated edition' of Adam Bede.[88]

Right here I may remark that Nora has been poking fun at me because of this. She thinks it is quite a good joke apparently. But I do not care. I think when one is pure-minded one should endeavour to remain so and not risk their soul reading such dreadful books as ADAM BEDE in the original!!!

Finally we arrived at church and got a seat. But in a few minutes Nora saw a vacant place beside Jerry in the choir and nothing would do but up she must go although she has not troubled herself about the choir for months! I was left alone till Amanda dropped in and then she and Annie and I amused ourselves for a time by picking the straws off John Macneill's coat.

Rev. 'Craw'[89] preached eloquently about 'excuses' and in due time 'meetin' came out. Then, bless you, didn't Nora and Jerry depart in state, without so much as a glance at me. I just stared after them with my mouth hanging open. Goodness knows how I would ever have got home ... for it was snowing thick and as dark as a black cat ... if that blessed Freddy had not come to my rescue gallantly and convoyed me

---

88 *Adam Bede*, an 1859 novel by George Eliot.
89 Rev. Craw: Rev. C.P. Wilson; see footnote 4.

home. On our way we met Jerry returning over Pierce's bridge and by the way 'Olive' was getting over the ground I thought Nora must have 'snubbed' him. She has a reputation for that sort of thing.

Sunday over we relapsed into apathy again until Thursday evening. Nora ought to have gone up to Y.P.U. but she did not, sad to say, for Jerry's disappointment was so great that he dropped a demijohn he was carrying into church and spilled three gallons of kerosene oil over the floor. He must have been trying to make a funeral pyre of the church.

Amanda came in and I went part of the way home with her and was unfortunate enough to put my foot in it with an innocent remark about Jerry which she seemed to take as a slur at George Henry, though I do most solemnly protest that such a thing never entered my thoughts. Meeting Joe on a sulky I mounted thereon too and risked my neck driving back with him. But I was rewarded by a bit of gossip and all's well that ends well. Soon as I got back Nora and I started for Laird's to interview Hetty who was most gracious. We would not stay long for fear of encountering Fred and we only just got away in time for we met him in the yard. But Freddy was not inclined to hang around doorsteps *that* night so we were not detained. I may also remark that I borrowed a *novel* at J. Laird's but it did not come up to my expectations, being in fact *no worse* than one I had of my own.

James dear called Friday night and was his usual loquacious and brilliant self. He seemed very exultant over the fact that Jerry had tried to drown himself in kerosene oil but Nora, being as usual absorbed in THE TALE OF TWO CITIES paid but little attentions to James' tales and left me to do the agreeable. That is always the way; and yet when James testifies his appreciation of my efforts by some delicate attention Nora gets fairly frantic at me and says I am a traitress.

'There was a little man and he had a little sleigh
And he drove Nora home to her door,
And he went to church and spilled a lot of oil
Right on the floor, floor, floor.'

L.M.M.

Tuesday, April 28 ... 03

It will be rather hard to write up this time and give everything justice. We have been having quite a sporty time this last week and this is so unusual I fear it has left a bad effect on us.

136
"There was a little man and he had a little sleigh
And he drove Nora home to her door,
And he xxxxxxxx went to church and spilled a lot of oil
Right on the fixxx floor, floor, floor."
                                    L.M. M.

                          . . . .
                                    Tuesday, April 28...03
It will be rather hard to write up this time and give everything
justice. We have been having quite a sporty time this last week and
that is so unusual I fear it has left a bad effect on us.
                                                        Thursday Maude
went up to Dan Simpson's to cut rags! (Ahem) I have heard of girls going
out to hook but to cut rags .... however, she can't hook so she said
she would cut rags. The simple truth is she thought she would "hook"
into Howard and cut the "widow" out! But she got nicely left and she
was so disappointed that she took xixkxxxx sick as soon as she got
home and had time to think it all over.
                                    Sat. we all started down to
Toff's and she behaved quite respectable till we took a walk on Cape
Turner and then the beauty of the scene seemed to turn her head   for
she said something terrible to Toff but as usual blamed it on me!
         We were tired out when we arrived home and I was starting for
bed when in walked little George. We chatted away for a few minutes
and bless your heart in walked Wilber! Maude produced "the pack" and
there we sat till nearly eleven, opposite two young men one of which
looked vicious enough to kill them the other without a prayer but despite the fact that they did not speak to each other we had a great
game.
         Sunday morning we trotted up to church and derived much benefit
from the sermon, "Parents' Influence in the Home."???
         Went up to church in the eve and that Stewart fool came
home with me. Henry came with Maud as the noble Fred had his Hetty
there.
                    K. L.
                          . . . .
                                    Tuesday, April 28th, 1903
If Nora were writing this journal alone what a fearful mass of mis-
statements it would be! Fortunately I am in the biz. too, and so can
correct her terrible fibs about my character. The idea of her saying I
said that to Toff ... and connecting it with such a vile pun, too,
which is adding insult to injury, why, she said it herself. And I can
call upon "Charlie Martin" to prove it. If he has ever stopped running
that is. If he is still going at the rate he passed here yesterday
morning he will soon be too far away to be an available witness.
         Last week, as Nora says, was quite a sporty one for us. In fact we
were hugely dissipated. Everything seemed to come on with a rush.
         Firstly, last Sunday evening, Nora and I in sheer desperation,
started out for a walk up to "Mac's" barn. We encountered some bogs and
had to snag one of Hamilton's longers to ferry us over. We left it
lying there also and I expect we will be getting a bill of damages some
of these long-come-shorts. We had some vague idea of hunting up Freddy's
stone quarry but concluded it would be too much exercise for one while
so we came home instead via the Cavendish Road.
Tuesday Thxxxdxx afternoon we spent quilting at Uncle John's.   Thursday
morning Lu and I went to Dan Simpson's. Nora could not go, hence her
jealous slur about me and Howard! I did go to cut rags and I cut them!
As for "hooking" Howard, all I've got to do is to raise my finger and
everybody knows it. But I don't want him. His "widder" is quite welcome
to him and no sour grapes about it.
                    On Friday evening Nora and I started

1.8   Montgomery's diary entry of 28 April 1903. (Typescript page. L.M. Montgomery Collection, Archival and Special Collections, University of Guelph Library.)

Thursday Maud went up to Dan Simpson's to cut rags! (Ahem.) I have heard of girls going out to hook but to cut rags ... however, she can't hook so she said she would cut rags. The simple truth is she thought she would 'hook' into Howard and cut the 'widow' out! But she got nicely left and she was so disappointed that she took sick as soon as she got home and had time to think it all over.

Sat. we all started down to Toff's and she behaved quite respectable till we took a walk on Cape *Turner* and then the beauty of the scene seemed to *turn her* head for she said something terrible to Toff but as usual blamed it on me!

We were tired out when we arrived home and I was starting for bed when in walked little George. We chatted away for a few minutes and bless your heart in walked Wilber! Maude produced 'the pack' and there we sat till nearly eleven, opposite two young men one of which looked vicious enough to kill the other without a prayer but despite the fact that they did not speak to each other we had a great game.

Sunday morning we trotted up to church and derived much benefit from the sermon, 'Parents' Influence in the Home.'???

We went up to church in the eve and that Stewart fool came home with me. Henry came with Maud as the noble Fred had his Hetty there.

N.L.

Tuesday, April 28th, 1903

If Nora were writing this journal alone what a fearful mass of mis-statements it would be! Fortunately I am in the biz. too, and so can correct her terrible fibs about my character. The idea of her saying I said that to Toff ... and connecting it with such a vile pun, too, which is adding insult to injury. Why, she said it herself. And I can call upon 'Charlie Martin' to prove it. If he has ever stopped running that is. If he is still going at the rate he passed here yesterday morning he will soon be too far away to be an available witness.

Last week, as Nora says, was quite a sporty one for us. In fact we were hugely dissipated. Everything seemed to come on with a rush.

Firstly, last Sunday evening, Nora and I in sheer desperation, started out for a walk up to 'Mac's' barn. We encountered some bogs and had to snag one of Hamilton's longers to ferry us over. We left it lying there also and I expect we will be getting a bill of damages some of these long-come shorts. We had some vague idea of hunting up Freddy's stone quarry but concluded it would be too much exercise for one while so we came home instead via the Cavendish Road.

Tuesday afternoon we spent quilting at Uncle John's. Thursday morning Lu[90] and I went to Dan Simpson's. Nora could not go, hence her *jealous* slur about me and Howard! I *did* go to cut rags and I cut them! As for 'hooking' Howard, all I've got to do is to raise my finger and everybody knows it. But I don't want him. His 'widder' is quite welcome to him and no sour grapes about it.

On Friday evening Nora and I started back to the woods to look for 'the devil's punch-bowl' about which Freddy had been yarning when he called Wednesday night. We did not find it however and presently we were brought to a standstill by the sound of footsteps pattering over the leaves not far from us. But 'whether "twas the deil himsel" or the "wild man"' who has been roaming at large of late or merely Tennis out for a constitutional we did not stop to investigate but beat a hasty retreat homeward.

Saturday afternoon we spent at Hammond's and Nora actually *proposed* to Toff. I felt so mortified about her. We had just got home when in walked George R. Later on Satan appeared also ... at least I guess George R. thought it was he. In plain English Wilber Clark arrived and by the sign of the white collar he meant to stay. George R. grabbed his hat but before he could flee I roped them all in for a game of whist. It was too good fun, too, in spite of the fact that our young men were at daggers drawn and never spoke to each other the whole evening. Nora and I kept the conversation ball rolling, however.

Sunday morning we went up to B.[91] preaching and heard Father Wilson expound the duties of a parent. It all went in at one of my ears and out of the other but I saw Nora storing it up in her mind. I suppose she thought it would come handy some future day when the little Jerrys begin to arrive and she has to hit on some scheme to distinguish them from the pappooses. I may remark that the church reeked so of kerosene that we could hardly stay in it.

In the evening we went again. Coming out we started off instanter but presently we heard airy footfalls behind us and up came Henry and James. The latter and Nora stepped off together and disappeared down

---

90 Lu: Lucy Macneill; see footnote 40.

91 B.: Baptist.

the road at a headlong rate. That girl must surely be more frigid than an Arctic glacier or James' persistent devotion would have thawed her ere now.

Henry and I amused ourselves tolerably. The principal side-show of the walk was Pierce throwing a fit or two on the road. We met poor James in our lane going disconsolately back. Nora opened the window when we reached the house and we had a friendly chat. We have found out what it means when Henry shaves his moustache.

'Here's to the girl who's strictly in it,
Who never loses her head for a minute,
Plays well the game but knows the limit
And yet gets all the fun there's in it.'

L.M.M.

Wed., May 6 ... 03

This pen is crazy tonight, the writer ditto. So this will be short and to the point. (No I won't.) The mad impulse took hold of me there to make a pun but I won't. Maude made one today so I will stop.

I am dead tired tonight but I must write in some way for I guess Maud thinks I am a regular shirker (never mind what it means).

Last Friday I took half a day off to attend the only social function that Cavendish knows ... a funeral. I came home in a very 'lugubrious' frame of mind and was preparing tea when my eyes caught sight of a stalwart form steering for the door. I rushed to the foot of the stairs and in a helpless voice howled out,

'Maude, Artie is here!!!!'

'For heaven's sake,' came the muffled response from the bottom of an Eaton's dry-goods box.[92]

Seconds passed, minutes ditto, and no Maude appeared but Artie was patient and at length she arrived.

Sat. I was down to Mrs. Ewen's[93] and Mr. James A. Stewart of

---

92 Eaton's dry-goods box: Timothy Eaton's department store began as a dry goods store on Yonge Street in Toronto in 1869. In 1885 he introduced out-of-town customers to the mail-order catalogue.

93 Mrs Ewen, or Mrs Ewen MacKenzie, is Margaret Bell, wife of James Ewen MacKenzie.

Cavendish, P.E.I. but now of Dundas[94] met me and kindly gave me a 'lift,' which proceeding seemed to have a disastrous effect on his sister Annie's temper. She was unable to appear out to church.

Sabbath morning, as Mrs. Ewen says, we had a fern frolic in the woods and a mayflower show in church.

Sunday eve the above-mentioned cavalier called and took us to church in Rustico. Artie arrived while he was tying the horse and took us to a top seat. In he came and there was Artie with his two girls. During the service the mad idea took possession of me to elope but I did not. Henry came home with Maude.

                                                                      N.L.

'I'll hang my harp on a willow tree
And I'm off to the farm again,
My peaceful home has no charms for me
And my sister's scowls no pain.
The lady I love sat by Artie's side
In a beautiful velvet hat,
Oh, why did she flatter my boyish pride
If she meant to leave me like that?'
        Extract from 'James' Lament.'

                                                                      L.M.

Wednesday, May 6th, 1903

I wonder if Nora thinks that that weird picture resembles my beautiful James. No, it cannot be. She must have been trying to depict Artie though I don't see why she should represent him as deserted at the altar. But there is no accounting for the queer things she does. Artie

---

94 Dundas: village in King's County, PEI, about fifty kilometres from Cavendish. On 8 May 1903 James A. Stewart purchased two parcels of land in the Bridgetown area, near Dundas of township 54, one parcel of 107 acres and another parcel of 115 acres, from Calvin M. Clay and his wife, Alice Clay (Land Conveyance # 221, King's Co., 8 May 1903, Prince Edward Island Provincial Archives). James Stewart moved to Bridgetown, where he was a farmer; later he was joined by his siblings Garfield and Annie.

called here on Friday afternoon and wanted to take Nora home with him but she would not go ... I suppose because James' sojourn in C. was drawing to a close and she did not want to lose any of the precious time.

Saturday afternoon Lu and I went Mayflowering and Nora went to Mrs. Ewen MacKenzie's. Judging from her account she had an interesting time of it. Mrs Ewen has seven different diseases and Ewen is minus half a lung!

I arrived home from the barrens and went to practice. Thereto also came Annie Stewart looking as black as a thundercloud and as amiable as she usually is. Among other eccentricities she was determined to have ABIDE WITH FAST FALLS THE EVENTIDE sung at three o'clock in the afternoon. As we would not agree to this she suggested satirically that we'd better have a chant! Later on I discovered that her disgruntled condition was caused by the fact that James was driving Nora. Coming home Nora informed me that she had been nice to James for the purpose of getting him to take us to Rustico the next evening and that he had fallen into the trap and we were to get.

That night I slept upstairs alone ... or rather I *stayed* upstairs for sleep I did not but nearly froze to death. At last about two o'clock I rose with a grim expression, hunted out all the spare quilts in the house and piled them on the bed. Then I got to sleep but have not tried upstairs again.

Sunday morning Nora and Lu and I remembered the Sabbath day to keep it holy by going back to 'The Devil's Punchbowl' ... or 'washbasin' as Tot[95] calls it ... to gather ferns. With these and our mayflowers we decorated the church very spluxiously[96] for we were going to have preaching for the first time in seven Sundays. We did it all with an eye single to Annie Stewart's criticism but we need not for the Amiable Annie did not show up at all and the choir had to worry on without her 'chanting.'

Early Sunday evening James appeared with a dandy turn-out and leather boots on his gee-gee.[97] We started off and were feeling pretty good when down in MacKenzie's hollow we came upon a sight that struck us dumb. A Frenchman and his lady love were strolling along blissfully hand in hand. They were certainly the two ugliest ducks I

---

95 Tot is Annie, John F. Macneill's daughter, and Montgomery's cousin. My thanks to Jennifer Litster.

96 spluxiously: combination of spurious and luxurious.

97 gee-gee (child's word): horse.

ever put my two optics on but *so* happy. I just thought, 'Oh, if James and I might walk like that!' But alas, it can never be, and the bitter thought made me mute for the rest of the drive.

Arriving at church as we whizzed past I saw something very dazzling away up in the air off to one side. I did not know what it was then but later on I knew it must have been the setting sun shining on Artie Moffat's red hair.

We were late and when we went into the porch the folks were standing up to sing. We couldn't see a vacant place at all. Just then Artie loomed up above us and promised to find us a place. He marched up to the top, turned and beckoned to us, and we sidled up the aisle to the pew he had for us. Everybody thought he took us there, of course. Goodness knows what James thought of it ... if he ever thinks at all.

When we came out something loomed up by the name of Henry MacLure, and, as I did not want to be gooseberry any more, I went with him. I knew James wanted to have a farewell chat with Nora, poor fellow, for he was going east to his new farm the next day. We wished him good-bye at the door so that chapter in our 'romance' is closed. Heaven only knows what we will do for a joke now unless Providence raises us up some new victim.

'I go to find a pew for you that where I sit there ye may sit also.'
'Beautiful beckoning hands.'

L.M.M.

Sunday, May 17th

One of the early lessons of my youth was 'Brevity is the soul of wit.' How poor Mac used to try to drive that into us. We had a spell of it every day and if he could see this journal he would feel proud that at least one of his pupils had not forgotten it.

Last Sunday afternoon I went to the beach (that sounds more romantic than shore). In the eve Maude and I walked up to the Baptist church to hear Mr. Wilson's farewell. It was blowing a regular hurricane but as that is all the style Sunday eves it should be unmentionable by this time. Bob acted the flirt for which he will be sorry, for from that night our valise bargain is broken. I was sitting in the choir trying to keep my mind on things spiritual when I caught her casting glances over in his direction. Oh, no, of course, I would not dare to be so bold as to insinuate that she had an object in view in directing her 'bonny blues' in that direction. However, the result was that he went home with her and left me. Yes, honest, she left poor black-eyed Henry in the lurch but he very kindly came to my assistance and I knew she was mad as a wet hen but she can just get over it. However I bet a quarter the next time we go visiting she will up and tell the whole thing in her own inimitable style. It is generally the way she treats my good luck. She imagined, I suppose, that I was going to pass the graveyard alone with naught to console me but she and Bob in the distance. I guess she got left. However, to return to Bob, she completely hoodooed (don't curl up your nose, miss, that spelling will do) him on the way home for he forgot all about our bargain. This is what happened.

(In the original there are some 'illustrations.')[98]

Nothing has happened during the week to write about. Thursday evening I did not go to P.M. on account of a previous engagement viz. to go to bed. Fred came home with M. and I suspect he wants to trap her also like the rabbits.

Yesterday afternoon we decided to go to McLures'. A few minutes before we started I took Maud in the room, quietly shut the door and kindly told her how to behave. But alas, advice and castor oil are two things she does not take. The consequence is easily conjectured. She acted something terrible. She said everything to me she could think of and told all she knew. She even dared to mention poor J.S. and

'I heard them speak of his eastern land
But I calmly sewed at the work in my hand,'
while Toff loomed up in the distance.

Oh, I wish I could make some sensible poetry. I know she will laugh at this.

BOB.

I

'The hue of his hair was whitish brown,
His body was lean and his neck was slim,
One eye was turned up, the other turned down
But he loved the girls and was strong of limb.
With a Roman nose and a love-like wail
And ribs like the hoops of a home-made pail.

---

98 'In the original there are some "illustrations"': This is L.M. Montgomery's typescript notation. Unfortunately, the illustrations are lost, as the original diary is no longer extant.

HENRY.

II

His human passions were quick to rise
And many a mark did his forehead wear,
For he said many a passionate parting shot
Had left upon him a lasting spot.'

N.L.

Sunday, May 17th, 1903

Nora did herself proud in the foregoing entry. Really, it is quite credit-
able to her. Of course, as we say in a newspaper office, 'errors will creep
in' and several have crept into her statements of current events. However, I will correct them so no harm will be done.

Well, last Saturday evening Lu and I decorated the church and we
had practice here afterwards. Annie came and seemed to have recovered from her queer spell for she was all smiles. After practice I discovered that Nora was in the seventh heaven of delight because she had
heard that James was expected home that night. James has not turned
up yet, however, so her joy was short-lived.

Sunday evening we faced a south-wester up to the B. church to hear
Mr. Wilson preach his farewell sermon. As usual Nora deserted me for a
post beside Jerry and I had to sit bunched up against Cedric Simpson[99]
who was looking too saintly for any use. The folding doors were open
and Henry sat beyond but never, alas, did he once glance in my direction. All his burning and 'passionate' glances were concentrated on the
choir. I did not think Nora would do such a mean and ungenerous
thing. But worse is yet to come.

Rev. Wilson preached very entrancingly about heaven and 'Pa' had
his own troubles with his door but we all got out and Nora and I started
down the road. Presently up steps Henry but alas, it was by Nora's side
that his stately form halted and I heard him asking if he might see her
home 'or words to that effect.' Was it not dreadful? But of course I was
too proud to show how deeply I cared. I pretended to laugh and jest

---

99 Cedric Simpson (1882–1951), Irene's brother. He resided in Bay View, PEI, and
    married Marjorie I. Enman in 1923.

and hid my breaking heart under smiles until Bob, bless his heart, came up and rescued me. Poor fellow, he was feeling blue enough, too, over the way Nora had treated him but we consoled each other and I promised to go and take a whole trunk.

Along by our gate Everett Laird wandered dismally by, lamenting in his own poetical fashion that there would be no nights in heaven. At our door Henry and Nora sauntered up ... but Bob and I had to wait nearly an hour for them ... on very confidential terms. It seems that they had agreed to jog along in double harness too. They seemed very hilarious over it but Henry has never been up to see her since and *I* don't think he is a very devoted lover. It's different with Bob of course. *He* had to go and help Charlie[100] put in his crop. Besides, Henry told us all right there that he didn't believe there was any such thing as love. It was just passion. Oh, I don't envy Nora. I wouldn't like to marry a man like that!

Nora came up to sleep with me that night but she annexed so many MacLure fleas that she could not sleep herself and wouldn't let me. Finally she pattered down to her own cubiculum and I fell into a sound and refreshing slumber.

All this past week I have simply had a fiendish cold. Nora has pretended to have one, too, and made it an excuse not to go to prayer-meeting Thursday night. But I went for I wanted to get a good look at our new 'supply.' Who knows but that he is the 'coming man.'

On my way home I heard a dulcet voice breathing in balmy tones over my shoulder, 'let me see your books.' I don't know what Nora means by her allusion to 'trappers' hanging about doorsteps. I'm sure Fred did not hang around that night. He got himself away with marvellous celerity. Nora, tired of waiting for Henry to appear, dragged me down there yesterday, hoping that Henry would drive her home but he did nothing of the sort, so she got beautifully left, in spite of the most bare-faced hints to Toff. I do love to see plotting, designing girls get hoaxed like that.

L.M.M.

Monday, June 1st, 1903

What a characteristic index this old diary is of my capricious make-up. Oh, yes, miss, I intended to write in it yesterday only I didn't. Truly the way to H ... is paved with good intentions.

---

100 Charlie is Charles Simpson.

Her ladyship went off to town today in company with Mr. Crewe. Goodness knows what mischief she will get into while she is away.

The 'Sabbath' eve after we were at Henry's Fred arrived along to carry Maude's books. He paid me a very dashing compliment which if not courteous was characteristic.

Thursday evening I was down to Mrs. L's. The young and sporty Mr. Murray arrived and drove Mary and me to P.M. It poured down rain and he wanted to drive us home but no! Bob had my apron in his pocket so I had to rush off to get that and when I arrived back Maude was nearly through the hole and we walked home. I know the young minister was worried about us.

Sunday Maude went to Park Corner[101] to her uncle's funeral. In the eve I went up to one of the everlasting missionary meetings and as Maud was unable to come I had Bob to myself. We made it up and now she is mad at me.

Hetty arrived on Tuesday and despite the fact that she and Maude are rivals they got on splendidly except that Maude swore! Yes, honestly, she *swore*! Hetty left her skirt about half done and when Maude got to work to finish it she swore! Was I shocked? Well you just bet your sweet life I was. Had poor Mr. Murray heard it he would have felt anxious about the future welfare of the 'handmaiden' but he didn't hear and I won't tell on her for she gave me a nice piece of soap and I wish the dear little creature were home for I am too lonesome to live.

Saturday night we went to choir practice. Henry was there and asked us to take a drive. We climbed in and began to giggle and smirk for we were anticipating a nice long drive but lo, the turn and in we went. Now whatever happened to Henry at that fatal moment I cannot say for apparently he was himself.

Sunday night Henry and Bob walked home with us but that was all. We stood on the wet grass long enough to freeze our feet, then we came in.

N.L.

Sunday, June 7th, 1903

Bob took me for a drive Tuesday night and Maude arrived home yesterday. I was glad to see her I can assure you. Bob took us for a drive last night and when I think of it a cold shudder runs down my spine.

---

101   Park Corner: L.M. Montgomery's Campbell cousins lived in Park Corner.

Maude has succeeded in shocking me at last. She told him that dreadful story about the same process. It was simply awful.

'I saw Murray's pale light
Gleam through the rain and the mist,
And a feeling of sadness comes o'er me
That my soul cannot resist.'

We had a nice drive, though, and laughed a great deal as usual.

N.L.

June 7, 1903

Here I am at home again after my week's visit to the metropolis. I had a pretty decent time and would have stayed longer had I not feared Nora would alienate Bob's affections forever. As the sequel will show my fears were only too well grounded.

Whether or no Henry was mad at us for decamping so early from his ancestral halls I cannot say but at least he did not attempt to see us 'round the square' the next evening. That duty fell to Freddy who did *not* carry my books, Nora to the contrary notwithstanding. I had to lug 'em all myself. As for Fred's 'compliment' she richly deserved all she got. She called me a 'heartless flirt' right before him and of course he told her without any frills that it was a lie. (I have just rescued a lady-bug from drowning by fishing it out of the ink bottle. May it be imputed to me for righteousness!)

Nora and I have been given a subscription a piece to YOUNG'S MAGA-ZINE. Despite its name it is not a magazine intended for the young person!

When Thursday came around the minister called here and had prayers and supplications. Mrs. Dr. Macneill[102] says he is a young man who is very sound in doctrine. He prayed in moving terms for "thy young handmaiden" but I fear it hasn't improved me much.

A thunderstorm came up during prayer-meeting and Mr. Murray seemed quite disturbed lest we get wet going home. He offered to drive us, poor mannie, but we declined and started off through 'the straight and narrow way.' I thought we'd never find our way home. Not only had I to pilot myself but I had to drag Nora along, too, who hung on to me in mortal terror.

I could not go to the Baptist church Sunday night and of course Nora

---

102 Mrs Dr Macneill is the wife of Alexander Macneill, fifty, the local physician.

went and cut me out with Bob. He came home with her and they added insult to injury by billing and cooing under my window for half the night. Oh well, never mind. 'Men are deceivers ever' and well have I learned the sad fact. Next day nothing would do but we must go down to Bob's. In the evening he drove us home and we were very hilarious, especially when passing Murray R's,[103] when we gave vent to our high spirits unrestrainedly. We went into Mayfield and it was so cold we nearly froze to death. Between 'buttons' and 'branches' my life was a burden to me so that I did not lament when Fred came along and rescued me once again from the position of gooseberry. Bless the boy!

Last Saturday night when practice was over it was a perfectly lovely evening and Nora and I were hoping we would get a drive. We started off and presently were delighted to hear Henry's dulcet accents asking us to take a drive. We scrambled in delightedly and were just getting ready to enjoy ourselves when Henry whisked us into our lane and that was our drive. If it be true that brevity is the soul of wit then that 'drive' was quite the wittiest I have enjoyed for some time. Then Sunday evening Bob and Henry walked home with us and we caught a fresh dose of cold hanging around making love by moonlight. That does well in 'theory' but fails in being 'practical.' Dash Bob and Henry!

I went to town with many misgivings. And sure 'nuff that Bob came up and took Nora driving one night so I guess I'm out of it for good. I don't care I'm sure. James has bought a lovely place down at Bridgetown![104]

I got home yesterday and Nora had the 'brass' to pretend she was glad to see me back. We went to practice although I was so sleepy I would have tumbled off the stool if Annie had not shrieked so loudly in my ears that I had to keep awake in spite of myself. Bob took us both driving later on and as his notions of a drive are not quite so abbreviated as Henry's we had a very nice time. Nora went and snagged the verse of poetry I meant to end up with so I shall just stop right here and now.

P.S. I did *not* swear at Hetty. And I did *not* tell Bob a terrible story either. He said there was nothing dreadful about it. It's just Nora's evil mind. She reads YOUNG'S MAGAZINE and unexpurgated editions of ADAM

---

103 Murray R's: Murray and Emily Robertson's place in Cavendish.
104 Bridgetown: see footnote 94 concerning James Alexander Stewart's property purchase.

BEDE and things like that so it's no wonder she is corrupted. P.S. No. 2. Nora has come up and is sitting on the bed devouring candies. She has just swallowed a great big raspberry tablet whole and if she survives that it will be perfectly safe for her to take up nursing for nothing can kill her.

L.M.M.

Wednesday, June 17th, 1903

Tonight after milking (?) Nora and I started up to visit Darnley's (see fig. 1.7).[105] 'Twas a beautiful spring evening and we were both feeling fairly good-humored ... for us. Going up by David's[106] Roger whirled by us in such haste to get home to dear Janie that he could hardly say good-evening to us, much less give us a lift as we had been fondly hoping he would do. Along by John Macneill's 'odoriferous belt' I asked an innocent question of Nora, concerning cause and effect and got so sat upon that I vowed I would not say another word until we got to Darnley's. By what some Paddy has called 'Herculaneum effort' I kept this rash vow but it was the hardest thing I ever did in my life. I thought of a hundred funny things I wanted to say and could not.

Maggie (see fig. 1.7)[107] was at home for a visit and between her baby and her ingrowing toe-nail we did not lack for amusement. Later on Lizzie (see fig. 1.2), Annie and Hetty appeared. Annie did not seem inclined to talk about James although Maggie introduced the subject and poor Nora pricked up her ears wistfully, hoping she was going to hear something about that Bridgetown farm. But no, Annie, dear girl, was not in a communicative mood.

When they went of course Freddy followed and in his absence we also made our adieux. Wilber felt called upon to escort us home and just as we were sailing down the lane we met Fred returning. He very kindly ordered Wilber to get a 'hoss' hitched up and drive us home. Wilber started off to do so and we three sat down on the roadside and told funny stories to pass the time. Nora tried hard to get me to tell Fred the 'same process' one but I drew the line at that.

---

105 Darnley's: Darnley Clark's in Cavendish.

106 David's: David and Margaret Macneill's place in Cavendish.

107 Maggie Clark is Darnley Clark's daughter, sister of Freddie, Chesley, and Wilber.

Wilber drove us home. Poor fellow, it was too bad to take him out in the night air when he coughs an hour and a half every night after he goes to bed. Coming in the lane we put our foot in it terribly about our 'abbreviated drive' with Henry M. and had to tell half a dozen fibs to cover up our tracks.

'Speak the truth and speak it ever,
Cost it what it will,
But when the truth will hardly serve
A fib will fill the bill.'

L.M.M.

Sunday, June 21ˢᵗ, 1903

Nora's last Sunday in Cavendish has arrived. (#) This character represents a big big sigh. She and I are up here in my den with Daffy[108]... whom Providence has kindly sent to amuse us now that James has gone. Daffy is purring and acting as bad as he can and we are writing this, the last entry but one in these famous old journals.

Well, last Saturday we started off in the morning and toddled down to spend the day at Wm. Houston's,[109] Rustico. We covered the three and a half miles in schedule time and arrived there in time for dinner. In the afternoon Nora determined to learn how to do drawn work. Learn it she did but I shall not go into the harrowing details. Suffice it to say that she nearly died of a nervous headache as a result.

I came home in the evening but Nora went and stayed all night at Toombs',[110] ostensibly to visit Miss Brown[111] but in reality to strike a mash on old man Toombs who has 'one foot in the grave and the other pointing heavenward.' She did not succeed in her nefarious designs, however, as old T. merely recommended her to read the RAM'S HORN and Nora does not care for that style of fiction.

Wednesday evening we sailed down to George R.'s and spent a

---

108 Daffy is Montgomery's cat.

109 William Houston, forty-eight, a Rustico farmer and beau, although Montgomery denies he was *her* beau: 'As for Will Houston – well, *that* was not one of *my* "love-affairs" certainly' (*SJ* 2:206). He married Montgomery's friend Tillie.

110 Toombs': Mr and Mrs Wallace Toomb's, Rustico.

111 Miss Brown is Ella Brown, twenty-two, who would marry Ben Woolner.

couple of hours. They did not ask us to take off our hats but gave us a lunch of a cookie and a glass of jam drink. Aunt Jane, 'poor thing,' was very doleful indeed and assured us we would never get the one we loved best. How true that is! For example, I shall never get James and Nora ... for all she thinks she will ... will *never* get Bob.

Thursday evening Nora inveigled me down to Lairds' under the pretence of going sailing but nary a sail did we have only walk around the shore. Soon after we got home Bob arrived to take us for a drive and of course we started joyfully although it was cold enough to freeze you and we were both dead tired. We went all the way to Stanley[112] and the way Nora and Bob carried on was something scandalous even for them. I was simply shocked to death. They terrified all the inhabitants of the city with their unseemly conduct, 'mauling square,' etc.

Yesterday afternoon we went down to Lairds' and finally prevailed on two cranky Frenchmen to take us out sailing. They didn't want to go at first for it was pretty rough and I suppose they thought Nora was a queer bird to tempt the briny deep with. But in the end we went and had a glorious sail. Nora behaved pretty well, considering. She didn't try to knock me overboard more that two or three times and she didn't use *many* words more than eight syllables long. Coming in we all but got upset in the dory but the old proverb about those who are born to be hanged or to be trained nurses never getting drowned held good and we all safely reached dry land again.

Practice last night of course with the same old faithful few in attendance. Bob walked home with us and there was no especial fun. This morning we had a Highlander[113] to preach for us and he was 'chust lofely' and all the girls got struck on him. My heart pitty-patted so that I could hardly play the hymns. It's weak yet so I shall stop short with this beautiful quotation from Omar Khayam.[114]

'Nora stood on the fishy deck
And hit me on the head,

---

112 Stanley: Stanley Bridge, a village close to Cavendish.

113 The 'Highlander' refers to the new reverend, Ewan Macdonald (1870–1943; see fig. I.2), L.M. Montgomery's husband-to-be. Born in Valleyfield, he was inducted in the Cavendish Church in 1903, but commuted until he moved to Cavendish in 1905. Montgomery often misspells his name.

114 Omar Khayyam (1050? – 1123): Persian poet and mathematician. His collection of quatrains, *The Rubaiyat of Omar Khayyam*, is well known.

The sun that shone on Robbie's house
Shone round us o'er the dead (crabs)
Yet beautiful and bright she stood
Bound to brew up a storm,
For Nora will be drowned to death
Before she will reform.'

L.M.M.

*Sunday, June 21*st

Wed., June 17th we were up to D. Clark's to spend the eve. It was a perfect evening and all was smooth sailing or rather walking till Maude [came] up with one of her illogical remarks. 'Say, what is that squeaking noise? It comes from the field.'

Now how on earth she expected I was going to account for the strange noise is more than I can tell. There were some men, a horse, and a roller over in the above-mentioned field so the noise 'might mean almost anything.' I reminded her of the fact that she was prone to indulge in illogical reflections, whereupon she became suddenly angry and declared she would not speak till we reached our destination and though we were only half way there she kept her vow. (There! Maude has just said a terrible *swear*. Daffy has been trying to crawl up one of her 'branches.')

I had to call into the parsonage on the way up and Maude quietly and silently waited on the church steps. Somehow silence does not become Maude. She looks so 'can't help it' like.

They entertained us all the ev'ning with Maggie's baby and the afflictions of her big toe. Later on the Stewart contingent, piloted by Hester, arrived and much to our amusement the programme was repeated though with some variations, viz: – the baby wet Maggie's apron. Oh dear me, I do not know how ... I suppose it spilled water on it. The act did not damp her maternal enthusiasm however and she still kept talking baby till at last she changed the subject to the soulful James. Of course Maude's heart came into her mouth and I blushed ... but Annie did not care to talk so our hostess stopped.

Wilber drove us home and we told fibs to no end. It was a lovely night and Wilber, his 'lugubrious' tone belying his words, said he had never been disappointed in love. Unromantic youth!

Sat., June 13, we were down to William Houston's all day. We fought considerably on the way but Maude did not resort to silence.

I stayed at Mrs. Toombs' all night and 'Sabbath' Ben Woolner[115] drove us all around the shore.

Wed. eve we called on little George (p-o-o-r thing). His mother told us it was no use we would never marry the man we loved so it was no use to try. Poor thing, what a comforting thought.

Thursday eve I wanted to go for a sail and of course Maude did not. I trotted her off, however, but we got left for the men would not take us out. We walked home around the shore and had a merry time.

We just got nicely settled down when along came Bob and took us up to Stanley. It was simply disgraceful the way they acted. My face burns now even with the thought of it. They made terrible speeches and told terrible stories. They made all sorts of queer noises. He tried the game on me but I just told him to stop mauling me round. He obeyed me by grasping at my waist and saying he would maul me square!!

Sat. afternoon were down to Lairds' and the surly creatures took us for a sail. It was perfectly lovely and as we had an audience we fought all the time. We were over to choir practice in the eve and Bob came home with us. He came in for his mail and I was terrified he was going to stay but Maude *yawned* and *yawned* and he had to go.

'They have said in notes of sadness
I must leave my Bobbie soon,
And go off to other districts
For to try a new love-tune.
All on *branches* and in laughing
Is the way we spent the time,
But we'll find on Friday morning
It has not done any harm.'

N.L.

Thursday night, June 25th, 1903

The long-looked for rain has come at last, I knew Nora was the Jonah of this drought ... she is going away tomorrow, hence this welcome downpour.

---

115 Ben Woolner (1876–1962), of Cavendish, would marry Ella Brown in August 1903.

Last Sunday evening Nora and I had our last walk through Lover's Lane together. 'Twas a lovely evening and we got along with less slam-whanging than mostly distinguishes our walks and jaunts. We had a bit of fun stalking a rabbit but it didn't get near enough to put salt on his tail!

Monday night I had to go down to the country on church business and Nora and Bob took the opportunity of my absence to sneak off together to Stanley. A pretty mean trick. But never mind. I had the best of it after all. When I got home at 9:30 the beloved Arty Moffat was here and I had him all to myself till an hour later when Nora and Bob returned. I ran out to give Bob a bit of wedding cake[116] and he drove off with the remark that he hoped he'd dream about *me* ... so I don't think Miss Nora gained much by her trick after all.

Thursday evening Nora went into Mayfield for the night and I accompanied her along the road until we saw a certain beautiful aspect which so overcame me I turned tail and fled.

Last night I went to a practice at Alec Macneill's. Nora would not go but remained home in hopes I suppose that Bob would come in and take her to New Glasgow. He didn't, however, and so she got left again.

This evening we went to the shore and took each other's pictures on the rocks (fig. 1.9).[117] We didn't forget to pull the slide this time but I guess I moved my eyes when I hadn't orter so heaven knows what the result will be like. We left YOUNG'S MAGAZINE floating peacefully on the waves, it being too heavy to carry but too *light* to sink.

There was a prayer-meeting tonight and perhaps that brought the rain and not Nora after all for we haven't had any since the last night when little Murray prayed down a thunderstorm. Those Highlanders must have great influence at the throne of grace.

---

116 wedding cake: According to folklore, sleeping with wedding cake under the pillow meant the woman would dream of the man she would marry. My thanks to Jennifer Litster.

117 'we ... took each other's pictures on the rocks': Montgomery photographed Nora Lefurgey posing with her camera against a rock; this photo has been reproduced on the cover of Gammel, ed., *Making Avonlea*. Nora, in turn, photographed Montgomery posing against the rocks scantily dressed in an improvised bathing suit. In 1931 Montgomery inserted this photo as 'Sea Nymph' in her journal and noted: 'We hid the pictures away in terror lest anyone should see them. We would have been disgraced forever!' (*SJ* 4:145). For a detailed discussion of the sea-nymph photo, see Gammel, 'Mirror Looks,' 293–8.

1.9   'We ... took each other's pictures on the rocks' – L.M. Montgomery photographed by Nora Lefurgey. (L.M. Montgomery Collection, Archival and
Special Collections, University of Guelph Library.)

Bob toddled home with us in the rain: owing to the latter he and Nora had to cut their adieux short for which I was thankful as no doubt had the weather been fine the scene would have been too harrowing for words.

So here we are in my 'den' writing the last entry in this journal. The thought makes me feel very blue indeed but we have determined to finish up this journal with a smile as we began it and allow no tears to blister its pages. So I will just end up with a grin and the 'toast' I quoted once before, slightly improved.

'Here's to two girls who were always in it,
Who never lost their heads for a minute,
Played well the game but know the limit
And yet got all the fun there was in it.'
Farewell, James, Artie, Bob, Joe, Freddie and all the other heroes whose exploits are set forth in these pages. May your shadows never grow less!

L.M.M.

June 25^{*th*}*, 1903*

Our last entry!

Last 'Sabbath' eve we strolled through Lover's Lane. All was peace and quiet. The only thing out of the common being a rabbit. Even a man himself could scarcely have been a more ra(re)bit of scenery. (Dear me, I hope Maude won't faint!)

Monday night Maude had to make an 'ice-cream' call (you know she has taken up church work since the young ministers have struck the place). I did not go ... for private reasons!! During her absence Bob came and took me to Stanley. We arrived home about 10:30 and lo, we discerned a chariot hitched to the front orchard fence. 'Dear me,' thinks I, 'what a mischief has Maude got into since we left?'

A peep into the kitchen soon told me all! There sat Artie, glorious, nay, brilliant and on his left sat Maude! I took in the situation at a glance. I bade a hasty good-night to Bob and strolled in trying to look innocent and surprised. A look of keen disappointment flitted for a second across Maude's peaceful face, then I was no sooner inside the door than grabbing up something from the table, she bounded forth into the darkness shouting 'Bob' till the very hills sounded. Of course I know *now* what she went for. Bob was going to take me over to New

Glasgow and she just stopped it. Yes, honestly. Whatever she told him I do not know but Wed. eve, though I stayed home and primped all the eve 'No Bob' appeared! She also took him out a piece of wedding cake so he would dream of her, but she need not have bothered for he 'dreamed not at all.'

Thursday night I went to Mabel's. Maude came as far as 'the French colony' with me but the 'beautiful aspect' guarding the ascent to the hill was more than her poetical soul could stand. She looked up into my face with that longing look which only poets have and then she turned and fled like a 'motherless cat.' I took courage and strolled past.

We were in P.M. tonight. It began to pour and we waltzed off home through the hole as quickly as we could. Bob followed and I was glad when he did not come in for we wanted to end up (oh, not like the aspect) the diary. Maude won't tell me how so I will just say 'tra-la-la.' ... 'meet me there.'

'So this is the end of it all.

It rounds out the year's completeness.'

N.L.

Finis.

2

The 'Secret' Diary of Maud Montgomery, Aged 28¼

Jennifer H. Litster

> If a stranger were to read that record he would be sure to think it was
> written by a couple of harum-scarum girls in their frivolous teens ... Yet it
> was written – at least half of it – by *me*!
>
> L.M. Montgomery, 12 April 1903, *SJ*, 1:287

Maud Montgomery made a new friend when she returned to Cavendish
from Nova Scotia in the summer of 1902. Nora Lefurgey, an Island girl
(born in Summerside in 1880) and Prince of Wales College graduate like
herself, had become the Cavendish schoolteacher during the year that
Montgomery worked for the Halifax *Daily Echo*. The two young women
took to each other instantly; indeed, Montgomery wrote in her personal
journal that the friendship of the twenty-two-year-old teacher was 'a
positive God-send' since her intimacy with Amanda Macneill was now
only 'a hollow show' (*SJ* 1:283). After boarding with the John Laird
family for a time,[1] Lefurgey flitted to the old Macneill homestead on
19 January 1903, where she remained until leaving her teaching post
that summer on 26 June. At the beginning of February, Montgomery
recorded with some excitement that she and Lefurgey 'have had, are
having, and expect to have a lot of fun – just undiluted fun' (UJ, 2 Feb.
1903). 'Nora,' Montgomery wrote at the start of what was to prove a
forty-year friendship, 'fills a "long-felt want"' (*SJ* 1:283).[2]

L.M. Montgomery's want of fun in the years following her grandfather Macneill's death in 1898 will be familiar to readers of her Cavendish
journal. This melancholy record is not, however, the only surviving
account of these times. During the five months that Lefurgey roomed
with her – months that, among other events, witnessed the arrival of a

dashing new Presbyterian minister, Ewan Macdonald – Montgomery was more than usually busy in fashioning mementoes, often with Lefurgey, for her memorabilia scrapbooks. As Montgomery confided in her journal, she and Lefurgey also decided 'for sport's sake' to start 'a sort of co-operative diary, she writing it one day and I the next.' This diary 'was to be of the burlesque order, giving humorous sketches of all our larks, jokes, etc. and illustrated with cartoons of our own drawing' (*SJ* 1:287). Sadly, the original collaborative diary has been either destroyed or lost. Fortunately, Montgomery typed its contents, minus the illustrations, into the edited (and unpublished) version of her journal she made in the 1930s.[3]

Despite their good intentions, the sketches were not written on a daily basis. There are entries for only thirty-one days within this five-month period and, as the two women each provide an account for some days, there are forty-five entries in total. Montgomery wrote twenty-four of these. As longer gaps are usually acknowledged or explained in the text, it seems probable that she transcribed the collaborative diary in its entirety. This claim to authenticity is further supported by the fact that Maud Montgomery replicated Nora Lefurgey's consistent misspelling of her name as 'Maude.' If the authors failed to keep the diary each day, they were at least faithful to their initial aim, and their collaborative work is a very amusing creation. In this respect, the diary is a lampoon of actual events, which Montgomery conceded by using inverted commas – 'those two absurd "diaries" of ours' (UJ, 30 June 1903), 'those old comic "diaries"' (*SJ* 3:390) – whenever she referred to the two notebooks in which it was written.

Boy Talk and Love Games

An example from each diarist serves both to illustrate the 'burlesque' style and to introduce the complexities of interpreting such a document. There are a few provisos. Firstly, the diary is in effect a long-running private joke, and it is difficult to extract passages that will make some sense to outsiders and make sense standing alone. Secondly, unlike Montgomery's private journal, the collaborative diary provides no explanations as to who its characters are or where they are from, and many people are referred to by nicknames (often pejorative) or first names only. Some knowledge of turn-of-the-century Cavendish is therefore necessary for an informed reading. Lastly, the 'larks' in the diary principally revolve around men and matchmaking and the problem of finding a match in a man, and its humour springs from the mock intensity, irony, and sarcasm with which this pursuit of romance, and indeed husbands, is invested. When this story arc dominates, the women's diary 'tells the truth slant' (Bunkers and Huff 20).

On Tuesday, 17 February 1903, both women give an account of the preceding Friday's party at J.C. Clark's home in neighbouring Bay View, a St Valentine's party, in fact, although no dancing was allowed in this Baptist household (UJ, 21 Feb. 1903). Lefurgey goes first:

> ... I suppose I might just as well blurt out the whole trouble at once and get it over with! I think I said that Jerry took me [to the party]. Yes, the creature did and *he left me there*, too! Home time came but no Jerry turned up. I don't know what he meant ... perhaps it is just one of his 'cute ways' and if I didn't have to gooseberry home with Maude and Fred [Fred Clark of Cavendish]! Perhaps I wasn't mad! [...]
>
> The time passed very pleasantly at the party. Maude and John J. got a prize for flowers and Roger and I for books (though somehow and I don't know how James heard it was John and I but I declare that was not true. I know he was angry with me for he did not smack his lips when he said it was 'the last quarter of the moon,' and that is a sure sign [...]) but perhaps it is all for the best. [...]
>
> Maude and I tried to 'swipe' as much stuff as we could but alas, we lost it all!! So you see though it was a 'swell' time in a way I had a great many troubles. I really don't know what I could have done to Jerry to merit such treatment. I talked 'Injun' all the way up, discussed Baptist preachers and conference meetings, then back to the Indians again. I tried my very best to appear interested and when he asked me if I would like to be a missionary I said 'yes' and clasped my hands in an ecstacy of delight as the vision arose before me of Jerry and I away in the western lands teaching the Indians, but somehow it was no use. [...] I forgot to say we had our fortunes told during the eve and mine turned out to be an 'immediate marriage' so that is encouraging.

Next Montgomery takes up the pen:

> Evening came and everybody went to the party except myself. I togged up and went to the missionary meeting just as mad as I could be. Of course only a few turned up and Mr. MacIntosh postponed it until Sunday night. [...] I started out boiling with rage. Here I had lost my chance to the party

and was not to have even a missionary meeting to cheer me up. But when I got to the porch there was that blessed Freddie. [...]

When we got up the party was in full swing and Nora was prowling around trying to 'swipe' things. The whole affair was very good. Of course it was pervaded with Jerry. Fred and I learned to play ping-pong and Jerry explained very carefully to us what 'love' meant in this game. He seemed to be afraid we might mistake its meaning. Ping-pong is a game you play with a ball. You try to hit the ball all the time you aren't chasing it around the floor or digging it out from under the sideboard.

One of the amusements was telling fortunes by shooting at a heart. My luck was to be married five times. It is enough to discourage anyone. [...]

Nora kept on swiping things. I tried but to no luck. Irene Simpson watched me every time. I did manage to secrete a brown paper heart but lost it later on. In the end my only spoils consisted of a piece of string, a green rose worn by Jerry, and a piece of Fred's whip. Jerry didn't bring Nora home so Freddie and I toted her along. I don't think her entry shows her to have been very grateful.

Little boots it that in reality many of these beaux had other girls, and that a few were married before the year was out. Nora and Maud were rarely serious when playing 'the game' of love. As Montgomery writes on 10 February: 'Nora and I are overwhelmed with [males] and in some cases cannot get rid of them. It's always the case that what you want you can't get and what you've got you don't want.' There were many young men knotted on the twosome's strings: Jeremiah S. Clark (Jerry), who talked 'Injun' and would leave PEI later that year – a married man – to work with Native Canadians in Winnipeg; Jo Stewart (from Bay View); Rob MacKenzie (see fig. 1.6); Fred Clark (Chesley's brother; see fig.1.4); Artie Macneill (Alma's brother; see fig. 2.1); Hamilton Macneill (Amanda's brother); Henry McLure (fig. 2.2); and the much maligned Russell Macneill (brother of Pensie and of Alec), whose 'ridiculous' and 'crude' speeches are faithfully (and perhaps callously) replicated throughout the diary.[4] The chief object of both girls' affections was 'the Soulful James,' James Alexander Stewart (see fig. 1.2), whose nickname was inspired, as Montgomery notes, 'by his beseeching eyes,' sentimental 'enough to make one turn Mohammedan or Mormon' (24 Feb. 1903). Eventually, Montgomery writes, they 'hit upon a plan for settling at once and forever our rival claims. I am to take one end of his moustache, Nora the other, and tug hard. To the victor will

2.1   Artie Macneill with his bride on his wedding day, showing off his wedding ring. (Fall Collection, Robertson Library, University of Prince Edward Island. Courtesy of the L.M. Montgomery Institute, Prince Edward Island.)

2.2 'The Game of Love' – Henry McLure (back, left) with Jack Whitfield, George Campbell, and Stella Campbell, circa 1900. (Courtesy Jennie Macneill, Prince Edward Island.)

belong the spoils' (6 Feb. 1903). Collectively, James, Jerry, and Jo are known as 'the three jays,' and this 'birdology,' as Lefurgey styles it on 5 April, is one of the diarists' favourite jokes. When Rob MacKenzie attended social events, they had a 'rob-in,' and with Henry MacLure, 'a hen.' The Baptist minister, the Rev. C.P. Wilson, inexplicably goes by the soubriquet the 'Rev. Craw.'

Such flippant boy talk was hardly salacious. Nevertheless, the collaborative diary was kept a secret, as well it might be in a conservative Presbyterian community where giddiness was frowned upon, and the notebooks were hastily hidden when others dropped by at the busy post office Montgomery and her grandmother operated from their kitchen. The co-authored diary stayed a 'secret diary' in other respects. Montgomery alludes to it in her handwritten journals just three times (12 April 1903, 30 June 1903, and 24 February 1929), and its contents have been accessible to only a handful of researchers. On the other hand, the very coded language and jokes that enhance the sense that this is a private record can today be used to unlock the secrets of several cryptic notes Montgomery pasted into her memorabilia scrapbooks. The diary's ornithological nicknames, for instance, are also a feature of the mock 'programmes' Lefurgey and Montgomery composed after Cavendish Literary Society meetings. Their jotting for 20 March 1903 laments 'The absence of all three [blue]-jays. / Never mind we have a *Rob-in*' (USB 12/3). Montgomery's memorabilia scrapbooks house news items, jokes, and poems clipped from newspapers and magazines; portraits, pictures, and postcards; notes commemorating special events or days; and an assortment of bits and bobs (and bits of 'Bobs,' Maud's cat), including the 'stuff' she 'swiped.' Maud's fad for collecting 'screwveneers' began in the early 1890s in cahoots with Selena Robinson, another Cavendish teacher (*SJ* 1:308). Whereas the significance of many early souvenirs from Prince Albert, Charlottetown, or Park Corner is lost – as indeed their meanings were to Montgomery when she flicked through these early scrapbooks in 1926 (*SJ* 3:314–17) – the co-authored diary illuminates several album pages from 1902 and 1903. The spoils pilfered from the J.C. Clark household finish up here, inside a greeting card bearing the motto 'Inquire Within,' with the party's date and some comic quotations. The party invitation the women received is also preserved by Montgomery – or half of it at least, the remainder presumably taken by Lefurgey for a book of her own. The collaborative diary is a lexicon of sorts that allows us to decode several puzzling scrapbook items gathered in youthful high spirits by Montgomery and Lefurgey –

including the infamous yellow garter (see fig. 7.3) that is the running joke in the co-authored diary (see chapter 7 for details of the scrapbook reference).

In the diary, the mysterious disappearance of this yellow garter – down Nora's gullet, as Maud supposes – provides almost as much amusement to the diarists as the Soulful James. Forced to pin her stocking 'to the edge of certain garments not mentionable in polite society' (22 Jan. 1903), Montgomery resorts to a parody:

> Oh, where, tell me where has my yellow garter gone?
> Oh, where, tell me where, has my yellow garter gone?
> I dinna ken what dreadful fate my garter has befel
> But it's, oh, in her heart that Nora kens full well.[5]

Yellow garters were thought good luck symbols in North America, and it was a traditional belief that a yellow garter worn constantly from Easter Monday would ensure marriage within the year. The garter lark is characteristic of the riotous way in which events unfold in the 1903 diary. Maud loses her garter and blames Nora: 'I suppose Nora made away with it out of some mean, small, malicious petty spirit of revenge' (22 Jan. 1903). Maud taunts Nora by mentioning the unmentionable to all callers: '... and didn't that terrible girl send word to Everett Laird that he'd *stole her garter*' (26 Jan. 1903). The garter becomes an obsession, as Nora admits in her entry on the same day: '... garter discussion has become a dissipation with us, a wily, seductive habit that seems to be growing upon us with marvelous rapidity.' Two days later, the garter turns up behind a trunk, as Maud notes on 28 January: 'Nora tried to look as if she were surprised but such a flimsy pretence did not deceive *me*.'

Such badinage is also typical of the diary's comic style. Montgomery later recalled with some affection how she and Nora 'ragged' each other, that is, insulted and reproached one another, and bandied jests (*SJ* 4:192). The collaborative diary replicates these oral spats. The young women tease each other mercilessly about men, of course – about which young man is most attracted to which woman, about how flirtatious or immodest the other has been, about how one has audaciously cut the other out of some poor soul's affections. They chart their adventures with a series of particular beaux and particular *bêtes noires*. They laugh at each other's clothes and hair. They poke fun at the ministers and their sermons and the elders and their wives. As Nora admits, they have 'some difficulty in keeping their wayward feet in Sunday line' (2 Feb. 1903). They quote and misquote, attempt to outdo each other with puns, and write parodies and verses to accompany their little dramas. They delight in dropping each other in embarrassing situations and generally carry on, as Maud writes, in a silly and 'scandalous fashion' (20 Jan. 1903). And when Nora visits friends, family, or town for a few days, Maud misses 'being harried and worried and punned to death' (28 Jan. 1903).

When left to their own resources, by preference or by bad weather, the two friends cook, sew, wash clothes, turn over gossip with grandmother Macneill, and read to each other: *A Tale of Two Cities*, Oliver Wendell Holmes's *The Autocrat of the Breakfast Table* (which, in its condemnation of puns, answers perfectly their condemnation of this dreadful habit in each other), and Lucy Lane Clifford's *Love Letters of a Worldly Woman*. Montgomery also reads an expurgated edition of *Adam Bede*, protesting on 19 April that she didn't want to risk her 'soul reading such dreadful books as ADAM BEDE in the original!!!!' Her tongue-in-cheek comment is also fiendish, for in 1890, the Cavendish minister, the Rev. Mr Archibald, had told the Literary Society that George Eliot led 'a life of immorality and her works were not safe to read especially to the young' (Cavendish Literary Society minutes, 27). In the winter months, the Literary Society was the main social function outside of church activities and provided ample opportunity for flirtations when the censorious eyes of the local guard, Arthur 'Pa' Simpson and Pierce 'By Creon' Macneill, allowed. The 1903 program included a paper delivered by Lefurgey on Lord Byron, a debate on Prohibition, a hat night, and the production of a magazine that included L.M. Montgomery's story 'The Strike at Putney Church.'

Montgomery and Lefurgey enjoyed a friendship based on intelligence, irreverence, love of literature, and, to some extent, the knowledge that these traits set them apart. In this vein there is evidence in the cooperative diary of friction and animosity between the Cavendish neighbours, and even a lack of respect at times. Despite the jokes and jests, Maud Montgomery seems a little put upon in the community, especially by church duties. This problem increased when she became organist in January 1903, although she was to find that the position brought some benefits. The previous incumbent, Mabel Simpson, would marry the minister, Major MacIntosh, and Montgomery greeted news of MacIntosh's resignation with a joyous cry of 'We can be as wicked as we like for a while' (24 Feb. 1903), a wickedness perhaps intensified by the arrival of Prophet Edwin, that is, her ex-fiancé Edwin Simpson, in Cavendish the same day.

Here in this 'absurd' diary we are treated to Montgomery's first impressions of her future husband, Ewan Macdonald (see fig. I.2), a secret she did not include in the handwritten copy of her personal, intimate journal until their engagement was a *fait accompli* in 1906. Having exhausted, possibly, the gamut of local farmers, Montgomery developed a healthy interest in the prospective ministerial candidates, moving Nora to comment cattily that Maud 'has taken up church work since the young ministers have struck the place' (25 June 1903). The candidate on 21 June in particular caught Maud Montgomery's eye: 'This morning,' she swooned, 'we had a Highlander to preach for us and he was "chust lofely" and all the girls got struck on him. My heart pitty-patted so that I could hardly play the hymns.' The tone is strikingly different from that of the journals. Thus the collaborative diary's observational humour can reveal important aspects of Montgomery's Cavendish life that are missing from other sources.

The diary is a snapshot of ordinary life: of the extent to which the young people attended the Baptist and Presbyterian churches regardless of their own denomination, but, nevertheless, of the antagonistic undercurrent that ran between the congregations. We discover the everyday disruptions the winter weather could bring; we understand the problems the lack of mails cause in an isolated community; we encounter Mag Laird (the model for Peg Bowen in the 'Story Girl' books) calling at the homestead for a 'chaw' of tobacco; we sample the delights of home-made candy and hooking parties and heating cold feet in the warm oven; we feel the thrill of winter walks in Lover's Lane and after-meeting drives; and dance at Alec Macneill's until five in the morning. In short, this diary portrays a less staid and more leisured community than we might think existed from a reading of either Montgomery's fiction or journals.

A Bad Girl's Diry

Both of L.M. Montgomery's personal diaries – her childhood diary (c.1883–9) and her adult journal – have a literary antecedent. As a nine-year-old, she 'first got the idea of keeping a "diry"' (*SJ* 1:281) from Metta Victor's best-seller *A Bad Boy's Diry* (1880), a comic catalogue of mischief purportedly written by 'little Gorgie.' Montgomery replaced the 'silly' diary suggested by this book with 'a new kind of diary' in

1889 (*SJ* 1:1), two years after the posthumous *Journal of Marie Bashkirtseff* was published. It was 1924 before Montgomery read this Ukranian artist's diary, but as a 'young girl' she was alive to the 'tremendous sensation' it made and 'longed to read it' (*SJ* 3:187). Although she does not claim it as an inspiration, the teenaged Montgomery shared Bashkirtseff's 'passionate longings for fame and success' (*SJ* 3:187) and must have been thrilled that a portrait of a young artist (Bashkirtseff died of tuberculosis when she was twenty-three) could appeal to readers. Such was its success in translation that many a young girl, like Oscar Wilde's Cecily Cardew in *The Importance of Being Earnest*, was motivated to keep a 'record of her own thoughts and impressions [...] consequently meant for publication' (Wilde 377).

Despite being 'bookish and dreamy' by nature, in aping Metta Victor's book, young Maudie 'schemed and planned many naughty tricks' (*SJ* 1:281) that she could write about. For this juvenile diary, then, Montgomery constructed, from a literary model, an alternative identity for her diary-self. In much the same way, her adult journal plays with literary conventions to engage with, and even create, different versions of herself, as a romantic or tragic heroine, for instance, within a private text (Buss, 'Decoding' 80–100).[6] The collaborative diary presents another self: a playful, self-confident young woman and proverbial social animal. Although a few of the entries she made in her private journal in the five months of Lefurgey's stay look optimistically at this flourishing social life and her burgeoning literary career, others are emotionally taut, and the general tone is one of dissatisfaction and dislocation coupled with dismay at the effect of her limiting circumstance on her personality. 'So many things bore me now,' she wrote, 'I stand rather appalled at the changes I see in my inner self' (UJ, 30 June 1903). This anguished journalist was both surprised and discomforted by the 'harum-scarum' Maud.

If Montgomery's journal exposes her private life and self, she would have its readers believe that the parallel self in the collaborative diary – the girl whom she had such difficulty recognizing – is a false one. By implication, this merry socialite is as much a literary affectation as the bad girl persona she adopted in childhood. There is, however, a crucial difference. Montgomery's juvenile diary was an entirely private document and one that she burned when she outgrew it. The collaborative diary was not only preserved, it was written with, and read by, Nora Lefurgey. Either the two young women embarked on the project with a common literary purpose – to write a skit, possibly, of rural life for girls of marriageable age – and the collaborative diary is essentially fiction, or the diary, at the very least, shows a different and unfamiliar but nonetheless true side of L.M. Montgomery. After all, for all that the diary is of the burlesque order, its events and larks are genuine enough – indeed, it contains more of Montgomery's public life than her journal does – as is the friendship that sustains its comedy.

The collaborative diary was initiated by Lefurgey and Montgomery for 'sport's sake' and was a logical creative development from their scribbled notes or faked Literary programs, which date back to November 1902, when Nora still lived in 'Lefurgey's Roost' at the Lairds'.[7] Like collecting scraps or souvenirs, keeping such diaries may have been a fad among girls or young women, and other examples do survive of co-authored journals, more often those kept by relatives or families than friends (Bunkers, *Diaries* passim). There does not appear, however, to be a specific literary precedent, although there are some superficial resemblances between the Lefurgey-Montgomery diary and Kate Douglas Wiggin's mock travel book *Penelope's Experiences in Scotland* (1898).[8] Like an account of a journey or a vacation, the collaborative diary has a finite span from its inception and therefore a predetermined plot: it will commemorate the time the women board together.

The resulting fictional overtones are enhanced by the fact that both women were writers. Lefurgey kept a journal and wrote an unpublished novel. Lynn Bloom has noted that 'once a writer, like an actor, is audience-oriented, such considerations as telling a good story [...] can never be excluded' (24–5). Margo Culley emphasizes in introducing her study of American diary literature that the importance of audience cannot be overstated (218). Throughout the writing process, Maud Montgomery's audience was Nora Lefurgey, and Nora's, Maud. Moreover, the co-authored diary is more than the work of two pens; it is a dialogue between two pens, with each author dependent on her audience for her inspiration. The women begin their project as a cooperative endeavour, but their two distinct personalities and the sparring nature of their friendship ensure that they compete as diarists just as much as they compete in love.

To some extent this competition has a serious side. Although Nora is light-hearted enough when teasing Maud about her fondness for *Ram's Horn* magazine, which had published Montgomery's story 'After Many Days' in March, Montgomery's status as a professional writer seems to give Lefurgey feelings of literary inadequacy: 'Had I known how my poor pen was going to suffer by comparison I would never have consented to this partnership affair!!' (6 Feb. 1903). This said, their rivalry is primarily jocular and evidences itself in their competing desire to relay the 'truthful' version of events. In the diary entries of 28 April, Nora and Maud jest about two old bachelors, Theophilus 'Toff' MacKenzie (Grandma Macneill's nephew) and Howard Simpson of Bay View, each woman providing a very different assessment of the same proceedings. According to Lefurgey:

> Thursday Maude went up to Dan Simpson's to cut rags! (Ahem). I have heard of girls going out to hook but to cut rags ... however, she can't hook so she said she would cut rags. The simple truth is she thought she would 'hook' into Howard and cut the 'widow' out! But she got nicely left and she was so disappointed that she took sick as soon as she got home and had time to think it over.
>
> Sat. we all started down to Toff's and she behaved quite respectable till we took a walk on Cape *Turner* and then the beauty of the scene seemed to *turn her* head for she said something terrible to Toff but as usual blamed it on me!

Montgomery is 'outraged':

> If Nora were writing this journal alone what a fearful mass of mis-statements it would be! Fortunately I am in the biz. too, and so can correct her terrible fibs about my character. The idea of her saying I said that to Toff ... and connecting it with such a vile pun, too, which is adding insult to injury. Why, she said it herself. And I can call upon 'Charlie Martin' to prove it. [...] Thursday morning Lu and I went to Dan Simpson's. Nora could not go, hence her *jealous* slur about me and Howard! I *did* go to cut rags and I cut them! As for 'hooking' Howard, all I've got to do is raise my finger and everybody knows it. But I don't want him. His 'widder' is quite welcome to him and no sour grapes about it.

This rivalry is an act in which each woman has defined a role to play: 'Maude' in the co-authored diary is a dutiful, if reluctant, church-worker who is blessed with an 'ethereal nature' that enables her to float 'lightly over the snow-crust'; Nora, by contrast, is plagued by a tooth-ache that incites her to profanity, and being, as Maud sneers on 5 February, 'of the earth, earthy,' has 'to stick to the solid ice.' Their rivalry is also a performance to an unnamed external audience, to whom they plead veracity of their case. In the resultant bickering, the exchanges between Montgomery and Lefurgey are rather reminiscent of those of Beatrice and Benedict in *Much Ado about Nothing*: Nora waspishly refers to Maud as 'her ladyship'; and Maud urges Nora to fill her tooth with kerosene and set fire to it (24 Feb. 1903). 'Men were deceivers ever' (II.iii.63) is a recurring refrain. If the diary is thereby part Shakespearian comedy with marriage as the desired outcome, it is also part pantomime, part farce, and part musical play, with many songs abused in parody, from the popular ('Jingle Bells,' "Twill Be Summer By and By') to the pious ('Oh for a man ... a man ... a man ... A man ... sion in the skies').

The development of plot within the collaborative diary is not a truly linear prose narrative, but rather a series of scenes. As the heroines of these scenes also write them, they can manipulate and engineer events to serve their dramatic purpose, and the diarists adopt a variety of roles (and even don costumes) to serve their plot. To this end, Culley's finding that 'evidence exists that the persona in the pages of the diary shapes the life lived as well as the reverse' (219) is especially pertinent. It seems probable (and the diary entries suggest as much) that as it becomes clear that the supporting cast of suitors are going to dominate their diary entries, Maud Montgomery and Nora Lefurgey goad each other into increasingly 'scandalous' behaviour. This brings more enlivening sport to their humdrum daily existence, but also provides better literary fodder. Unlike the influence naughty little Gorgie exacted on young Montgomery, however, the literary models of mischief come from within the diary itself.

The collaborative diary is life writing that dramatizes rather than narrates events; it is autobiography as theatre, as Evelyn J. Hinz has theorized it ('Mimesis' 195). The diary obeys Aristotelian dramatic rules: plot takes priority over character delineation, especially where the plethora of young men are concerned; this plot unfolds through action not introspection, for the entries stop on dull weeks and gather pace in livelier times; and the protagonists are raised above the common level. The diarists also sit with the gods as critical spectators: of the petty community dramas; of their neighbours' coarseness and prejudices; of the hapless efforts of the local farmers at courtship. The comedic script has firm grounding in oral culture and local sayings (see Alexander in this volume). Linguistically, the diary is Montgomery's most colloquial writing, and her most hyperbolic. She and Lefurgey are hamming it up centre-stage in the roles of popular flirts.

Whatever the harsh realities of PEI women's lives in 1903, especially for those who were, like Valancy Stirling, 'twenty-nine on the morrow, and unmarried, in a community where the unmarried are simply those who have failed to get a man' (*BC* 1), Montgomery and Lefurgey write themselves into a position of power, including sexual power, on the collaborative diary's pages. When Nora presents her paper on Byron to the Literary, and has to choose a recitation, Maud 'wanted her to give one from DON JUAN but [Nora] was afraid it might bring a blush to Jerry's cheek and would not' (22 March 1903). When two sworn enemies call in at the Macneill homestead, Maud and Nora force the swains to keep company all evening and play cards with them. Although all the local men are designated their 'heroes,' more telling is Montgomery's comment when 'the Soulful James' relocates to a new farm outside Cavendish: 'Heaven only knows what we will do for a joke now unless Providence raises us up some new victim' (6 May 1903). In turning the tables on men, the diarists invent a new reality for themselves, and, despite their dire offence and mighty contests, confirm their united front.

'... this immortal record ...'

On 25 June 1903, the day before Nora Lefurgey left the Macneill homestead and Cavendish, the two room-mates added their final entries to the diary that Maud had earlier called 'this immortal record' (7 March 1903). Montgomery delivered a closing toast:

> Here's to two girls who were always in it,
> Who never lost their heads for a minute,
> Played well the game but knew the limit
> And yet got all the fun there was in it.

Then, as Montgomery recalled in her journal, they 'bound them in covers of fancy paper, with adornments of gold paint and ribbon, and [...] illustrated them with "home-made" pen-and-ink sketches which are so ridiculous that I howl every time I glance over them' (UJ, 30 June 1903). In this final performance act, the diaries were wrapped up – in both senses of the phrase – costumed, and presented as a visual treat, yet despite their showy fronts 'those two absurd "diaries"' remained a private joke. Interestingly, Montgomery divulges in the same journal entry that her grandmother's intolerance had made the five months of Nora's stay bitterly unpleasant, so much so that she had been 'worried to distraction nearly all the time' (*SJ* 1:288). With her vocabulary emphasizing the diary's function as a diversion and a fancy, Montgomery repeats the assertion that the diary was escapism from what she called her inner self.

Lefurgey and Montgomery probably met again in 1903: Nora was the bridesmaid when Ewan Macdonald married Major MacIntosh and Mabel Simpson on 23 September (USB 12/6). In the summer of 1904, Montgomery and Lefurgey enjoyed some perfect days together when Nora paid Cavendish another return visit (*SJ* 1:296). Montgomery made no entries in her personal journal during the fortnight of Nora's stay, but the two friends may have laughed over their old collaborative diary one evening. Around 1919 Montgomery lost touch with Lefurgey (see chapter 3). Montgomery may have uncovered the diary again on one of her attic rummages, perhaps in November 1926 when she dusted off her memorabilia scrapbooks and found in them the mock programs for the Literary (*SJ* 3:315). She certainly kept the covered volumes, preserving them 'as one of the curiosities of literature' (*SJ* 1:281). The voices of the collaborative diary also had potential as a source of fiction: in Nora's and Maud's friendship and banter, we can see the roots of Anne's and Phil's jests at Patty's Place in *Anne of the Island*; and the two cousins in the 1913 short story 'How We Went to the Wedding' pun and parody in the diary's witty style (reprinted in *Against the Odds*).

Nora Lefurgey reappeared in Maud Montgomery's life in September 1928, when her husband, Ned Campbell, started a business in Toronto. The beneficial effect to Montgomery was instantaneous, for she considered that 'nine years of unbroken repression' with no close friend nearby were now over (*SJ* 3:378). Some four months later, at the end of February 1929, Montgomery took the two collaborative volumes to Nora Lefurgey's house, and the old friends 'sat before the open fire and read them over – and laughed until we nearly cracked our ribs and the people in the flat below must have thought us drunk or mad' (*SJ* 3:390). As was Nora herself, the diaries became for Montgomery a reminder of her youth, and a reminder of the fun to be had from mixed-up love lives and muddled romance. Her next novel was to be *A Tangled Web* (see chapter 12).

When typing a copy of her journal for whomever of her sons did not inherit the handwritten volumes, L.M. Montgomery transcribed the two collaborative notebooks into their chronological place. Why did she do this? She may have copied out the diaries as a therapeutic distraction from her daily worries, as she did with Charles Macneill's farming diary in 1925; or, she was perhaps trying to safeguard the diary's survival after her death. By so doing, however, she was also opening the diary's contents to an audience other than Lefurgey, should this edited journal be published posthumously. Had Nora Lefurgey not reappeared in Maud Montgomery's life, it is by no means certain that the collaborative diary would have been preserved. However, throughout the 1930s Montgomery drew strength from the fact that the two diarists could successfully rekindle their old friendship, laugh over their old jokes, and fashion new ones, despite the turns their lives had taken since young womanhood. The collaborative diary thus not only functioned as a reminder of happier times, but it also offered a glimpse of a happier Montgomery. By transcribing its pages into her journal, L.M. Montgomery was, at some level, incorporating this diary and the diary's playful self into her life story.

This collaborative diary is a portrait of two clever, witty, popular young women. It also portrays two friends who got all the fun they could out of the imperfect surroundings and companions that fell short of their romantic or intellectual expectations. The diarists, in other words, were optimists. They were also, as Montgomery's closing toast shows, social pragmatists who 'knew the limit' of their play. This curtain of respectability, the fabric of the world onto which the absurdities are sewn, adds to the collaborative diary's value as a document of life writing. In the believability of its domestic scenes and its focus on community life, the 'comic' diary, for all its nonsense, is in fact the clearest view we have of Maud Montgomery's public face. More than this, the collaborative diary's charm is such that readers will find in it the effervescent and irrepressible L.M. Montgomery they might expect existed from a reading of her fiction but of which they receive only rare glimpses in her personal journal, a friend she turned to more often in darker times.

The Maud Montgomery of the collaborative diary seems very 'real.' This is in large measure a result of the shared authorship – reading the diary, we see Montgomery with someone else, reacting to someone else, and through the eyes of someone else. We see her as others see her. And this public self – whether a performance, a disguise, or a true picture – is Montgomery at what some might find her most appealing. To assume that this harum-scarum girl was a front, the personal journal must be classed as truth, and the collaborative diary as, in its own vocabulary, a stretcher. Rather than the journal being 'real,' and the collaborative diary pretense, both are self-portraits that demonstrate that Maud Montgomery shared Nora Lefurgey's 'capricious make-up' ('Diary,' 1 June 1903). In the final analysis, it is unproductive to polarize these selves, a conclusion Montgomery herself possibly acknowledged by belatedly merging the parallel lives in her journal typescript.

NOTES

I am grateful to the British Academy for a travel grant that allowed me to attend the L.M. Montgomery and Life Writing Conference, University of Prince Edward Island, 2002. I also thank all those who provided feedback on this chapter and the diary.

1 Ewan Macdonald also boarded at John Laird's when he moved to Cavendish in 1905.
2 Here Montgomery quoted from the libretto of *The Nautch Girl* (1891), by George Dance and Frank Desprey, a Savoy Opera production.
3 The diary is on pages 113 to 147 of volume two of Montgomery's typed journal, inserted after the entry of 30 June 1903, which records Lefurgey's departure from Cavendish.
4 Rob (Bob) MacKenzie and his wife, Jenny, were close friends of Montgomery, whom she visited on her vacations to Cavendish; Henry McLure (of Rustico) was her former (and rejected) beau (*SJ* 1:242). Russell Macneill's phrases are also repeated in Montgomery's fiction, by Peter Craig (*The Golden Road*) and Tillytuck (*Mistress Pat*).
5 Montgomery parodies the first verse of a traditional Scots song, 'The Bluebells of Scotland': 'Oh where, tell me where is your Highland laddie gone? / Oh where, tell me where is your highland laddie gone? / He's gone with the streaming banners where the noble deeds are done / And it's oh! in my heart I wish him safe at home.'
6 As Margaret Turner observes, in her journal Montgomery is 'experimenting [...] with who and what L.M. Montgomery is, particularly in relationship to Maud Montgomery and Maud Macdonald' (97).
7 Folded paper dated '4 Nov. 1902, Lefurgey's Roost, Cavendish P.E.I.' (USB 12/10). A note for 29 Nov. 1902 (USB 12/2) outlines that evening's Entertainment Committee meeting.
8 Montgomery read this book in 1904, although it is possible that she was rereading it (unpublished letter to G.B. MacMillan, 7 April 1904).

3

Nora, Maud, and Isabel: Summoning Voices in Diaries and Memories

Mary Beth Cavert

It's only very foolish people who talk sense all the time.
Montgomery's inscription in Nora Lefurgey's copy of
The Blue Castle, 29 March 1929[1]

In '"A Dusting Off": An Anecdotal Account of Editing the L.M. Montgomery Journals,' Mary Rubio explains that L.M. Montgomery acknowledged her journals served the specific function of 'expressing the unhappiness that she was conditioned as a woman to suppress' (58). However, Montgomery's 'grumbling' often overshadows the evidence sprinkled throughout the published journals of powerful, enjoyable, and supportive relationships with other women. Not only are her journals a record of her life, but they also provide snapshots of her friends' lives and their impact upon her. Montgomery profiled them in her own journals, knowing the journals would be read and remembered. She thus assured these women a lasting place in history. This essay is about one of Montgomery's close and intimate friends, Nora Lefurgey, whose story is also intertwined with Montgomery's far more conflicted relationship with a fan named Isabel Anderson, whom Montgomery befriended in her fifties. In writing of these women, Montgomery records vivid and powerfully sustaining friendships, but she also brings to our notice the lives of her contemporaries, women who lived equally interesting and creative, albeit less famous, lives.

Since the journal biographies provide only one person's – Montgomery's – perspective, I have conducted interviews with relatives and family descendants of Montgomery's friends to present a fuller picture that complements and at times even contradicts Montgomery's journal portraits. To summon the voices of Nora, Maud, and Isabel, I will be drawing on memories, unpublished diaries, and on unpublished creative work and photographs. Covering a span from before 1900 up to Montgomery's death in 1942, this is an intimate portrait of Montgomery from the rare vantage point of one of her female friends.

Nora: '... but always there was Maud'

Nora Lefurgey Campbell was born on 15 August 1880 in Summerside, PEI. Her father, Thomas Lefurgey, was of French Huguenot descent, and her mother, Janet McMurdo, Scottish. She was one of seven siblings: Alden (the oldest son, who moved to Boston), Montague, Will, Walter, Archibald (who was killed in the First World War), and one sister, Jessie. Nora attended Prince of Wales College and received her teacher certificate on 28 July 1902. She also received a teaching certificate in Ontario on 18 August 1905. She passed the Civil Service exams in Ottawa in 1907 but did not work for the Civil Service, as far as her family knows, although her sister, Jessie, did. Nora's son, Edmund Jr, writes the following about his mother in a letter to his fiancée, Bette, in 1939: 'My mother even looks French and her face and those deep wide brown eyes, which I myself have, give evidence of a depth of soul and a definite literary and cultural tendency.'

Nora Lefurgey, whom Montgomery names 'a brilliant woman of the world' (*SJ* 4:192), has no separate biography in the journals, and her story is incomplete, as she outlived Montgomery by over three decades. A highly trusted confidante, she entered Montgomery's journals early, and then reappeared many years later. Like Frederica Campbell, one of Montgomery's Campbell cousins in Park Corner and Montgomery's close friend, Nora was an intellectual and a keenly witty equal. And like Montgomery, Nora placed a high value on close friendship with women. She always had at least one 'bosom friend,' as her son Edmund remembers, 'but always there was Maud' (E. Campbell, letter, 1995). Nora, who had written a novel but was unable to get it published,[2] matched Maud in every aspect of her life except for literary success. Like Montgomery, she created her own lifelong collection of diaries, photographs, and letters, and her written record provides a rare glimpse into Montgomery's private life and personality.

Twenty-two-year-old Nora Lefurgey first appears in Montgomery's journals in September 1902, when she came to Cavendish to teach. Shortly after their meeting, Montgomery wrote, 'Nora suits me exactly.

3.1   Nora Lefurgey. Studio photo taken in Charlottetown, 1901. (Courtesy Bette Campbell, Ontario.)

We never bore each other and we have no end of fun together' (*SJ* 1:283). As she did with Frede, Montgomery often sat up talking with Nora until the small hours of the night (*SJ* 1:284). Years later, she remembered their year together: 'we made every day an adventure for ourselves – our wild exultant dips in stormy waves – our walks together over shadowy hills – all the fool things we did for the fun of doing them' (*SJ* 3:378). The two friends went to Literary Society meetings and walked together in Lover's Lane. It would seem that Montgomery would have already mined the romantic possibilities in Cavendish, but with the arrival of Nora, newly creative flirtations were conceived. Montgomery later wrote in Nora's copy of *Anne of Green Gables*: 'To dear Nora, with the author's love, in memory of many happy hours spent together in "Lover's Lane" and elsewhere with a "kindred spirit."'[3]

Nora left Cavendish in June 1903. She taught in North St Eleanor's from 1904 to 1906 (the same community that was home to Amy Andrew, whose diary is discussed in chapter 5), and in August 1904 she visited Montgomery in Cavendish for two weeks:

I've had a *good* fortnight. Nora has been down ... we spent most of our spare time together and I just lived with all my might. Several afternoons we spent at the shore, going down with our cameras and lunch baskets, donning bathing suits as soon as we got down and living a sort of amphibious life, wading and diving and snap-shotting. One day we had a never-to-be-forgotten surf dip. It was glorious.

Nora went home today and I shall miss her terribly. But I'll live on the memory of those two weeks for many moons. (*SJ* 1:296)

Already a year earlier, Nora had taken photographs of Maud on the rocks looking out to sea. One of these photos, which Montgomery called 'Sea Nymph,' retained its magic for her even twenty-seven years after the 'perfect day,' as she noted in the journal (*SJ* 4:145). Two months later, they again visited in St Eleanor's. Then follows a long silence.

For the next twenty-five years, from 1903 to 1928, Nora all but disappears from Montgomery's journals. In many ways, their lives were parallel during those years of separation: both married, had children, struggled with tragedy, wrote, and pursued a passion for photography. On 12 October 1910 Nora Lefurgey married Ned (Edmund) Campbell in Nelson, British Columbia.[4] The oldest son of Daniel Campbell and Eva Compton, Ned was born in Belmont, PEI. His father was a school

3.2   Nora Lefurgey Campbell in androgynous garb (centre) with a guide (left),
British Columbia, circa 1915. (Courtesy Bette Campbell, Ontario.)

trustee in Belmont, where Montgomery had taught in 1897, and she
once went sailing with Ned, his sister May, and his cousins from the
Compton family (SJ 1:188). Curiously, Ned Campbell is not mentioned
in Montgomery's journal during the year that Nora lived with her, but
she must have known that Nora was 'engaged' to him, at least infor-
mally, because Nora's daughter-in-law, Bette Campbell, reports: 'Ned
was a childhood sweetheart – wasn't he the patient man?' (letter, 1995).

Their engagement was unusually long (longer than Montgomery's five-year engagement); Nora did not marry until she was thirty years old. She insisted on 'proving herself before she tied herself down to any man' (B. Campbell, letter, 1995).

Nora's life with Ned is entirely missing from Montgomery's journals, although her biography is a truly picturesque story of adventure with dramatic ups and downs. Ned Campbell left the family farm against his father's wishes and studied at McGill University. After graduating in 1908 as a mining engineer, he worked in South Dakota for a mining company. Meanwhile, Nora lived with her sister, Jessie, and taught in Ottawa. After her marriage, the couple spent some time in Valdez, Alaska, where Nora climbed mountains and ran a dog-sled team with her beloved dog, Sam. Three of their four children were born in British Columbia. However, tuberculosis forced Ned Campbell to relocate his family to the warmer and drier climate of Jerome, Arizona, where he began his own mining research corporation. He was frequently away from home, but Nora loved and found comfort in the mountains and the austere beauty of the desert. She air-conditioned their house using wet towels and lived a full life, caring for her young family and reading and writing. They lived in San Diego, California, from 1921 to 1924, and Nora, her daughter-in-law reports, 'belonged to a writer's club. She wore pants and smoked cigarettes (most elegantly!) And thought herself to be very avant-garde' (B. Campbell, letter 1995).

In California, Nora's world began to change irrevocably. She rode a train all night holding in her arms her sick infant son, Donald, in a desperate and futile attempt to reach a hospital. Bette Campbell reports that the baby died of what was probably pyloric stenosis (letter, 1995), a common abnormality that today is corrected by a simple operation. But that was not the end. Her oldest children became ill with polio: Jessie died of the disease at age twelve, and David was crippled and wore a brace on one leg. They moved to Kingman, Arizona, where they stayed for four years in the Mohave Desert near the Hualapai Mountains, as her son recalls: 'Nora so loved to pick cactus blossoms. In spite of the recent death of her daughter Jessie, and the partial crippling of her son David, it was the time of her life that I remember her to have been most vibrantly and happily alive' (E. Campbell, letter, 1977). They did not stay long, however. In 1928, at age forty-eight, Nora Lefurgey drove her car across North America with her two boys to join Ned, who had started a consulting firm in Toronto. She enrolled the boys in Upper Canada College and made yet another home for her family. In her memoir, Mary E. Campbell remembers her grandmother's characteristic style, marked by the years in the Southwest: 'Gran's apartment was filled with heavy Spanish oak furniture, oriental carpets, book cases with shelves full of leatherbound books and artifacts such as a brass incense burner and a Spanish Mission wrought-iron candle holder' ('Gran's Scarf'). When they were settled, she finally wrote a letter to Montgomery, who in 1924 had moved with Ewan and their two sons to Norval, just a few miles away.

In September 1928, Montgomery came to Toronto to see Nora. Montgomery's journals record her delight, but also her dread that the long-neglected friendship would not hold up. 'It was twenty-four years since I had last seen Nora. A life-time lay between us. Could we clasp hands over it?' (SJ 3:377). Once they met, it seemed as if they had never spent twenty-four years apart. 'We "clicked" as well as ever we did,' Montgomery notes and continues: 'Nora looks older of course – some grey in her hair – some lines on her face. But otherwise unchanged – her bright black eyes as bright and black as ever – her smile as elfin' (SJ 3:378). Nora's son Edmund was present at the reunion, and he writes:

> I remember vividly when I first met Maud, in 1928 when we first arrived in Toronto. She was seated in the sofa, Mother diagonally in front of her in a big armchair. I, 10 years old, on the floor, small, skinny, fascinated to at last meet this woman of whom I had heard so much. To me she was a massive woman, formidable, with a strong voice which expressed her feeling of self-importance and superiority. My Mother [was] ecstatic at seeing her old friend again but slightly hostile at Maud's air of superiority. I cannot remember what they talked about; all I remember is a feeling of relief when Maud at last left, – I had my Mother back. (Letter, 1995)

Montgomery was aware of her social status, which derived from her success and fame, and she was not above using it to her advantage.[5] Among her friends and acquaintances, she may have enjoyed the mystique that comes with creative and financial success. Nora and her son may have sensed this at their first meeting, but it was most probably dispelled soon enough by the strength of Nora's own personality. Ed never thought that his mother was awed by her friend's success as a best-selling author. The women's shared history, intellectual abilities, common interests such as photography and poetry, and sharp wit would have been quite enough to put them on an equal footing. Nora had also

3.3   Nora Lefurgey Campbell – glamour photo, circa 1920. (Courtesy Bette Campbell, Ontario.)

achieved social status through her husband's business success, which Montgomery admired. With these factors to balance their lives, their friendship was egalitarian, and Montgomery was happy to once again have a confidante nearby to share very private troubles, as she would have with Frede. Seeing Nora again was like 'drinking in great gulps of clear gay mountain air' (*SJ* 3:378). When she finished *Magic for Marigold* in October, she dedicated it to Nora: 'In memory of a world that has passed away.'

The words were prophetic: a year later, more of Nora Lefurgey's world passed away when her oldest son, David, still partially paralysed with polio and encumbered with a heavy brace, drowned when his canoe turned over. The sad details of Nora's life receive no mention in Montgomery's published journals, although she must have been aware of those that took place after Nora's return to Toronto. There is no obvious explanation for these omissions – she often noted the sorrows of friends, even those with whom she had lost touch.[6] Normally, she used grief as a way to bond with old friends. She felt disconnected from her peers if their lives were too happy in contrast to her own. When she learned that her friends had experienced hardship, she welcomed them as fellow sufferers.

It is possible that Montgomery did not want her life compared with Nora's. For every tragedy and hardship in Montgomery's life, her friend had experienced similar, if not more devastating, losses. It may be that Nora's way of dealing with tragedy would not have fit comfortably within Montgomery's '"grumble" book.' Unlike Montgomery, Nora rarely dwelled on sorrow in her diary. Bette Campbell writes, '... in all the years I knew her I never once heard her complain of the heart-break and loneliness of losing 3 children and of enduring long separations from her husband' (letter, 1995). Stoic and pragmatic, Nora never sought sympathy or used others for a sounding board. She most often assumed the position of adviser and was a tower of strength in times of trouble.

For Montgomery, those visits in the early 1930s were as memorable as the days they had spent on the beach at Cavendish nearly three decades earlier. She could let down her guard. Nora knew a private side of Montgomery that few others saw, especially during 1932, a watershed year for revealing elements of their friendship. Nora Lefurgey's diary entry of 19 August 1932, a profile of a week she spent at the Macdonald home in Norval, begins, 'Maud is a dear – with reservations!' She does not explain this statement except to hint that Maud was upset when the milk was not delivered: 'I cannot just understand that milk episode. One day the milk didn't come – oh well. Shall not waste my time on that. But I do hate duplicity.' Nora does not elaborate, and readers are left with the tantalizing and judicious silence – who was duplicitous? And why? It is a small thing, but it testifies to the personality differences between women of strong character.

Their child-rearing practices also differed. While Nora implies that Montgomery was too lenient, Nora herself clearly was not. She wrote in her diary entry: 'Her method of bringing up her boys is at complete variance with my methods. We shall see how they turn out. My own cherub is not so hot! There is an innate refinement in him though – which he inherits from Ned, I'm quite sure – that saves him from too obvious a selfishness' (19 Aug. 1932). Edmund remembers his mother's disciplinary methods vividly: 'She was an astute disciplinarian, a good example of an iron fist in a very soft velvet glove.' Their children would inevitably have been topics for discussion as the two old friends forged a new relationship as mothers. Chester's failure in school had been a source of acute pain to Montgomery in 1931. It is tempting to connect Nora's quotation from Sir Joshua Reynolds in her diary at this time – 'The Only Possible Substitute: "If you have genius, industry will improve it; if you have none, industry will supply its place."'[7] – to Chester Macdonald's lack of academic success – or 'Just pure laziness, that is all' (*SJ* 4:119), as his mother wrote.

Edmund Campbell's memories, Nora's diary, and Montgomery's journals give us a glimpse of a woman of strength and powerful character, whose energy and vivacity would have been a welcome presence in Montgomery's life. By 1932 Montgomery had long been a famous author, but her marriage was an unhappy one, and the comfort of Nora's friendship was sorely needed. Both women had also suffered the loss of children. Montgomery's journal entry for Nora's visit does not mention the death of her own infant son, Hugh, but it does refer to the death of Nora's daughter (*SJ* 4:190), which they must have discussed. In her own diary, Nora writes, not about her daughter, but about her first son (born in 1911), who had died only three years earlier:

Away down in the subconscious stratum of my mind was a now twenty-one year old scene – a meagre hospital room in old Phoenix [British Columbia] in which was born to my husband a son! – the whole thing was lived again and always hammering on my heart with excruciating thuds the 'why, why' of everything. (19 Aug. 1932)

Clearly, it was not only Montgomery who found in the visit a time to resurrect old pain and, perhaps, to heal it. Nora brought back a combination of traits and interests to Montgomery's life that had been missing: the shared history of a youthful friendship, humour, poetry, and trusted companionship. Montgomery wrote on 20 August 1932, 'I have never met anyone in my life, not even Frede, to whom nature means as much as it does to me, except Nora' (*SJ* 4:190). They shared long walks under a bright moon that week, as Montgomery once had with Frede Campbell. The two quoted poetry from their remarkable memories: 'our minds seemed to strike sparks from each other' (*SJ* 4:190). Montgomery used several paragraphs to describe the experience in detail on 20 August 1932 (*SJ* 4:189–91; see also *My Dear Mr. M.* 164–6). In contrast, Nora Lefurgey wrote only one sentence about the walk: 'Maud and I walked in the moonlight so bright that we could see the expressions on each other's faces, and quoted reams of poetry' (19 Aug. 1932). She added a verse of the 'reams of poetry,' which slightly misquotes Bernard F. Trotter:

> And when I come to die I will not look for jasper walls
> But cast about my eye
> For a row of wind-blown poplars
> Against the moonlight sky.[8]

The verse actually extols a slightly different landscape:

> And so I sing the poplars: and when I come to die
> I will not look for jasper walls, but cast about my eye
> For a row of windblown poplars against an English sky.
> > (Quoted in Wilmshurst, 'Montgomery's Other Novels' 79)

Trotter was killed in 1917, during the First World War at the western front, at age twenty-six, and the poem, 'The Poplars,' appears in *A Canadian Twilight and Other Poems of War and Peace* (1917). The change from 'English' to 'moonlight' appears to be deliberate, as Nora and Montgomery were accustomed to personalizing verse. It is difficult, given the sorrow that filled their lives, not to make connections between Trotter's yearning for the quiet English countryside in a world of war, and these two women's desire to remember this moment of friendship and beauty, in lives that had become so complex. After the Trotter lines,

Nora quotes Montgomery: '"The laughter of the river underneath the moon" – Maud, while strolling along the Credit in the moonlight. Aug. 1932.'

Nora's visits to Norval sustained Maud with what she called 'the bread of friendship' (*SJ* 4:199).[9] The more they saw each other, the more Nora observed first-hand the troubling aspects of Montgomery's married life. Edmund Campbell recalls a truly bizarre event from about 1932 (he is unsure of the exact date), when he would have been about fourteen years old. The occasion was a dinner with the Macdonalds in Norval. That night at the dinner table, Ewan Macdonald shocked the company. With no apparent provocation or forewarning, as Edmund recalls, 'he threatened my Mother with a shot gun' (letter, 1995). Edmund continues:

My Mother and Ewan were at the other end of the table and I felt I ought to do something but I – and everyone else – froze. Eventually Ewan put the gun away, apparently joking. He was peculiar. He looked unbalanced. Afterwards, my Mother did not talk about the incident except to say that we ought to have sympathy for Maud's marriage. (Telephone interview, 1995)

As it turned out, Ewan's gun was unloaded and the entire episode was a cruel joke, but for Edmund, who was a teenager at the time, the event left an indelible impression: 'Mr Macdonald terrified me,' he recalled. 'I instinctively felt he was crazy.' This episode was not recorded in the diary of either Maud or Nora, and it invites speculation about possible tensions between Ewan and Nora. Although Nora was a fellow Islander and a friend of his wife, she did not have the same history with him or his family as, for instance, Frede Campbell had had. Ewan's married life and career had been complicated by a series of mental breakdowns since 1919, shortly after Frede's death. By 1932, he may have resented Nora's access to Montgomery and felt threatened by her role as a confidante and supporter; he may have been trying to assert his own position in the family with the gun incident. To Nora's family, Edmund Campbell reports, Montgomery was always known as 'my poor Maud' (telephone interview, 1995). Especially after Ewan's demonstration, Montgomery could not hide the stresses of her life. Now she had a friend, aside from her journal, with whom she could share her greatest troubles – her husband's illness, her son's scandals, and, by the late

1920s, the troublesome attentions of a persistent, infatuated fan named Isabel, whose role in Montgomery's life has remained unexplored.

Isabel: '... but your own dear self I love'

Montgomery was an intensely guarded person in public, keenly attuned to social status, propriety, and codes of behaviour. Her intimate circle of friends, including Laura Pritchard, Frede Campbell, and Nora, was established early, before she was famous, and few new people were admitted to it as she grew older. In the late 1920s, a fan, simply called 'Isobel' in the edited journals, tried to enter this private realm, seeking from Montgomery an exclusive friendship that she was not prepared to share, but was also not strong enough to refuse.

Isabel Anderson (fig. 3.4), named Isabella at birth on 13 March 1896, was born in Crewson's Corner, a small Ontario village settled by Gaelic-speaking Scots just a few decades earlier. Her father, William, was fifty-eight years old when she was born to his second wife, Matilda Cripps. A blacksmith, he worked on the construction of the Grand Trunk Railway around 1856. He became the town's first postmaster three years before Isabel was born; he also played in the first band in the area in about 1864. He was a highly respected farmer and member of the community when he died in 1924, two years before L.M. Montgomery Macdonald moved to Norval. He left three daughters from his second marriage, eight children from his first, twenty-six grandchildren, and nine great-grandchildren ('History').

Isabel was an elementary schoolteacher who wrote poetry[10] and short stories, and who had loved Montgomery's books since she was young. She was thrilled when, in 1926, Montgomery moved to nearby Norval. She soon wrote passionate fan letters to the author. Montgomery first mentions Isabel in her journal with amusement as a self-appointed protector of her privacy. In an effusive letter from the summer of 1926, thirty-year-old Isabel vowed she would guard Mrs Macdonald like a 'saint in a shrine' from all 'annoyances' (*SJ* 3:299). On the surface, it would seem that the two would have had much in common despite the difference in their ages. Both were raised in a Scottish community by an older couple who were postmasters, farmers, and active Presbyterians. Both women were teachers, and they shared a love of poetry. Their correspondence started out well; Montgomery enjoyed Isabel's 'very witty and brilliant and entirely delightful' letters (*SJ* 4:33). She might

3.4   'Your own dear self I love' – Isabel Anderson, the passionate fan of Maud Montgomery. (Courtesy the Family of Isabel Anderson, Ontario.)

have welcomed a new acquaintance at this point, as she was new to the area and had no intimate friends: by 1926, Frede Campbell had been dead for seven years, and Montgomery had yet to renew her correspondence and friendships with Laura Pritchard and Nora Lefurgey. However, Isabel was self-conscious and awkward in person and very quiet. She lacked the essential characteristics of all Montgomery's closest friends – the ability to be at ease, generate laughter, and, most of all, to talk (*SJ* 4:33).

In the years (nine, at least) to follow, Montgomery came to view Isabel as far more than a complex friend and annoyance. Their relationship began to deteriorate in 1928, which coincided with the death of Isabel's seventy-five-year-old mother and the return of Nora Lefurgey to Montgomery's life. After three years of unwanted attention, Montgomery's patience had ended. By 1930 she began to keep a written journal record of Isabel's 'obsession' and her own series of tempered and direct rebuffs, possibly to protect her own reputation. As she notes on 10 June 1932:

> But I am completely out of patience with her and have written her as follows: – My dear Isobel: – You must forgive me if I say candidly that I think it is wiser that this unsatisfactory correspondence of ours should cease for a time. All winter and spring I have been nearly distracted by several pressing worries [...] and your letters of reproaches because I cannot be some person whom you have created out of your imagination and called by my name – a person utterly unlike the practical elderly woman I am – have been the proverbial last straw.
>
> If the time ever comes when you can feel contented with what contents my other friends – a sane friendship with an occasional friendly visit or letter I shall be very glad to respond. Until then I think it better for both of us that this unhappy condition of affairs should cease. (*SJ* 4:184)[11]

Isabel replied:

> My beloved darling: –
> Yes, indeed it must stop for I, neither, can stand any more. I have been so bitterly heartsick. Let us forget it all and be real friends; I love you so. Please believe me that it is not an imagined creature, but your own dear self I love. (*SJ* 4:185)

In a tone that reveals more about Maud's panic than about the young woman, she calls Isabel's adoration 'the horrible longing of the Lesbian' (*SJ* 4:185). Montgomery repeatedly acquiesced to a limited friendship until Isabel reverted to the language of love and intimacy. Then Montgomery would admonish her and begin the cycle over again, unable to fulfil Isabel's need for attention, yet incapable of ending the relationship entirely.

When Montgomery shared this dilemma with Nora Campbell in July 1932, the relationship assumed an intriguing triangulation. Nora advised her to end the potentially scandalous association – 'cut her off completely' (*SJ* 4:186). Together, they contrived to ostracize Isabel when Montgomery invited them both for a visit in August 1932. They planned to make her uncomfortable by their sarcastic banter to exemplify how Montgomery's true friends could interact. Nora was skilled at this in earnest as well as in jest, as Bette Campbell attests: '[Nora] was elegant, refined ... But she was cursed with the "Lefurgey tongue" meaning she could issue the cruelest barbs if one did not measure up' (letter, 1995). Montgomery recorded Isabel's reactions in her journal: 'Isobel sat and listened to the insults ... as if she couldn't believe her ears' (*SJ* 4:192). In the presence of the intimidating Nora, Isabel retreated into her usual protective silence. Nora wrote in her diary: 'Isabelle Anderson ... visited Maud a whole day while I was there. Her ability for complete abeyance of all speech is phenomenal ... How can Maud stand her? Is not even pretty' (19 Aug. 1932). However, Isabel sent Montgomery a gracious thank-you letter after the visit (*SJ* 4:195). Her life story in Montgomery's journals is abridged and ungenerous, and the incident reveals neither Montgomery nor Lefurgey in a compassionate light. Yet it does demonstrate the strength of their friendship, united against Isabel, whom they were unable, given their own strengths and experience, to accept.

Montgomery wrote in her journal that she had only been trying to help Isabel by 'filling a life [according to Montgomery] otherwise piteously empty of everything that makes life worth living' (*SJ* 4:35). Isabel might well have been lonely, still grieving for her mother and missing her sisters. Yet much of her poetry is written about or dedicated to family members, suggesting close relationships. About her mother, Isabel wrote this poem entitled 'Mother Image':

I'm glad my mother never wore
Hotpants or slacks or jeans,
But covered up her aft and fore
And all her in-betweens.

I'm glad she always wore her hem
At least beyond her knee;
She was no liberated fem,
But lavished love on me.

She never was a suffragette,
Nor held such tactics dear.
She never smoked a cigarette,
Or knew the taste of beer.

To funeral services and church
She always wore a hat;
She knew traditional research
Demanded this and that.

Well – now that she is laid to rest
Beneath the sacred sod,
I treasure most her best bequest,
A sterling faith in God.[12]

On at least one occasion, Isabel invited a niece to have lunch with her and Montgomery (M. Coles, telephone interview, 2000). Her younger sister, Mary Ellen (Nellie), became a missionary to Koreans living in Japan, and Isabel wrote a biography of her. Isabel clearly missed her, as evidenced by the title of one of her poems, 'To My Sister (Following Her Departure for Yet Another Term on the Mission Field).'

Montgomery had characterized both Frede Campbell and herself as 'lonely and misunderstood' (*SJ* 2:303), so that she may have initially found Isabel's neediness familiar during a period when she had few other intimate friends. However, as the tenuous friendship quickly turned to unease, she eventually vented her frustrations with Isabel by creating the fickle Hazel Marr in *Anne of Windy Poplars* (1936). The character has a notorious crush on Anne Shirley: 'I want to possess you *exclusively*' (205). Montgomery wrote Hazel's character sympathetically, even affectionately, in contrast to the feelings she expressed in her journals. In the book, Anne Shirley's friend Rebecca Dew, like Nora, cannot understand how Anne endures Hazel. However, Anne sees Hazel in a reflection of herself, who recalls her own youth with all its 'raptures and ideals and romantic visions' (205); and Anne confesses that she likes being worshipped. Isabel might have written as Hazel did: 'I'm so different ... Nobody understands me ... But when I saw you, some inner voice whispered to me, "She will understand ... with her you can be your real self"' (204).

It was not with newcomers and latecomers like Isabel that Montgomery felt truly comfortable. In spite of her failure to become more than a fan to L.M. Montgomery, Isabel's so-called empty life lasted for almost ninety-nine years and was filled with teaching, summer travel, writing, and church work. She was a member of the Presbyterian congregation for eighty-one years. She wrote a history of her 'Kirk' for its 100th anniversary, and the booklet was reissued for the 150th anniversary. Isabel was active in the Young People's Society, taught Sunday school, and sang in the choir. Although Montgomery claimed that Isabel did not like teaching (*SJ* 4:34), she had a forty-year career which colleagues and students characterized as exemplary: 'Her interest in her pupils, her dedication to having each achieve his/her personal best and her keen sense of humour ... made her room a superior place of learning. Discipline was firm but fair, and respect for good morals was taught by example as well as by words' (Obituary, 1994).

Montgomery's lack of success in defining the borders of her relationship with Isabel became less important after 1935, when Montgomery's family relocated to Toronto (*SJ* 4:430). Her son, Chester, married and, with a family of his own, was no longer available to drive his mother to visit Isabel. In addition, Montgomery's family problems and financial stress in the last few years of her life (Rubio and Waterston 127) left little room for worry about Isabel. However, Montgomery's deep-rooted friendship with Nora Lefurgey continued. After the death of her husband in 1937, Nora lived alone in Toronto. Perhaps Montgomery's last correspondence with her was a postcard from Prince Edward Island in September 1939: 'Dearest – I am having a good time in one way. But the cloud is over all. Hope you are keeping well.' Montgomery's health declined quickly after the beginning of the Second World War, and she died in 1942. Nora Lefurgey lived exactly thirty-five years longer than Montgomery. She died in 1977, shortly before her ninety-seventh birthday. She had written, in 1958,

Sometimes I do not want the world to know
That I exist
I want to see
but not be seen
Like the gulls in the mist. (Diary, 30 March 1958)

She did not get her wish. Montgomery's fame and faithfulness to her own life writing, a lifetime record of journals, correspondence, photographs, fiction, poetry, and scrapbooks, ensure that the world knows that Nora and Isabel did exist. Perhaps Isabel's poem wraps it up best:

> To live in many a heart
> As years fleet by
> Is merely to depart
> And not to die.

NOTES

1 On 24 February 1929, Montgomery remembers the comic diary discussed by Litster (*SJ* 3:390), and the recollection probably accounts for the personal inscription in *The Blue Castle*. The novel is in the personal collection of her granddaughter, Mary E. Campbell.

2 Her granddaughter's (loving) assessment of her unpublished manuscript was that it was a 'dreadful novel' (M.E. Campbell, telephone interview, 1995), although Edmund Campbell has a different view: 'My mother was also a writer and wrote a novel but couldn't get it published. She probably wrote in a more serious vein than Maud and even possibly sniffed at Maud's success with a simple story' (telephone interview, 1995).

3 Nora's copy of the book remains in the personal collection of Mary E. Campbell.

4 The following information about the lives of Nora and Ned Campbell comes from letters and telephone interviews with Edmund Campbell Jr (son), Bette Campbell (daughter-in-law), and Mary E. Campbell (granddaughter).

5 On another occasion, she wrote in her journal: 'I wonder if those men had known I was "L.M. Montgomery" if they would not have been a little more considerate. I have often seen it work out so' (*SJ* 4:105).

6 For example, she noted that her childhood friend Nate Lockhart lost his son in a 'tragic shooting,' even though she had not heard from him since 1896 (*SJ* 4:171).

7 This quotation is from Sir Joshua Reynolds (1723–92), *Seven Discourses on Art*: 'You must have no dependence on your own genius. If you have great talents, industry will improve them: if you have but moderate abilities, industry will supply their deficiency' (http://www.gutenburg.net /etext00/artds10.txt).

8 Montgomery cites the same passage in *Jane of Lantern Hill*, where Jane's father remembers knowing Trotter in the First World War (153).

9 The phrase 'bread of friendship' was also used by Montgomery in *Mistress Pat: A Novel of Silver Bush* (143), where it is attributed to Bliss Carman.

10 Information about Isabel has come from public documents, M. Coles (grand-niece), and P. Hansen (grand-nephew). Although Isabel's verse expresses a highly Romantic angst-filled writer's passion, this excerpt from 'Erato,' supplied by Isabel Anderson's family, also documents the particular struggle Montgomery would have recognized, of a poet torn between the duties of writer and woman, Erato being the muse which inspires the lyric poet:

O muse, why must you come at night
And torture me to rise and write?
Must my poor bones tomorrow ache
Because tonight a poem I make?
Yet, if I stay upon my bed
It is my heart will ache instead!

11 Montgomery's response here echoes Phillipa Gordon's words to Anne Shirley in *Anne of the Island*, published more than ten years earlier. After Anne refuses Gilbert Blythe's proposal, Phil tells her, 'You don't know love when you see it. You've tricked something out with your imagination that you think love, and you expect the real thing to look like that' (190).

12 Isabel's poems are in a collection compiled by her family. I am grateful to Isabel Anderson's family for making these available for publication in this essay.

PART 2

CONFESSIONS AND BODY WRITING

The diary writer who playfully chased boys in Part 1 seemed carefree and slightly immature. The journal writer in Part 2 is more conflicted and compulsive. The journals – and their artistic control of intimately personal subject matter – are the focus of Part 2. Inspired by Little Georgie's popular 'Bad Boy's Diry,' Maud Montgomery had begun keeping a diary at age nine in 1883 (*SJ* 1:281). At the age of almost fifteen, she burnt these diaries, in which she had written 'religiously every day and told what kind of weather it was,' and she began 'a new kind of diary': her journals (*SJ* 1:1). In 1919 she illustrated her journals with photographs, thus further emphasizing her aesthetic control of the embodied self in carefully staged visual self-portraits. Part 2 opens with my own essay on Montgomery's account of her intimate affair with Herman Leard and my probing of some of the biographical gaps in her account. The writer, I argue, oscillates between expressions of melodramatic hyperbole and frustrated desire, ultimately revealing her discomfort with sexuality and her need to manage the experience through artful masquerade. In the second essay, Mary McDonald-Rissanen addresses the selective silences of Montgomery's journals – and of Amy Andrew's diary – to argue that the writer's self-censorship, her controlled web of gaps and silences, ironically also creates its own speech which can be deciphered and read as a story. Depression is the focus of the third essay in Part 2. While documenting the journal writer's terrifying unravelling of self, Janice Fiamengo argues that the rhetoric of depression allowed Montgomery not only to disclose a painful secret but also to define herself as a writer. Ultimately, all three essays reveal the consummate writer expertly controlling the imaging of her intimately personal life.

4

'I loved Herman Leard madly': L.M. Montgomery's Confession of Desire

Irene Gammel

On a late Saturday afternoon in October 2001, I walked down a tree-lined lane toward the former Leard farmhouse in Lower Bedeque, Prince Edward Island. The house had not changed much since 1897, when Montgomery was meeting her lover for secret late-night trysts. Herman Leard (fig. 4.1) might have emerged from the door, smiling and affable. According to her journals, he was the love of her life, yet in her journals he was rarely accorded the right to speak. He died in 1899 at age twenty-nine, surrounded by an intriguing silence. Today the memory of their romance looms large in the published journals, presenting the single most important account of physical pleasure in the author's intensely guarded life. With pent-up passion, the romance writer exalted the farmer as the most erotic lover of her life, setting him an epitaph in a long fervent journal entry of 8 April 1898, totalling eighteen pages in the published text (*SJ* 1:204–21).

Discussing the Lower Bedeque year, scholars have highlighted the fictionality of Montgomery's journal account, a story 'infused with a narrative dynamic of its own' (Rubio and Waterston 36). Helen Buss has traced Montgomery's 'sophisticated use of that most dominant of nineteenth-century literary conventions: the two-suitors convention' ('Decoding' 90); in simplified terms, the story recounts the popular courtship plot of dropping Mr Wrong for Mr Right. At the same time, scholars have also tacitly accepted that the affair was central in the author's life, even though biographical information has remained scant and sketchy. Montgomery's journal is the only source documenting the events, and, as we shall see, she was careful not to reveal the full story.

To shed light onto the affair, I visited Lower Bedeque and interviewed, among others, Nancy MacFarlane, a retired history teacher

4.1 'His face was elusive, magnetic, haunting' – Herman Leard of Lower Bedeque, circa 1898. (Courtesy of Jim and Anne Nichols, Prince Edward Island.)

who had recorded the memories of her friend Jean MacFarlane, the daughter of Herman's sister Mae; and Waldron Leard, a PEI genealogist, who shared his father, Raymond's, first-hand observations of the Leard family. As we delved into this most intimate story of Montgomery's life, it was the play of gaps and disclosure, of speech and silence, that helped unravel the most hidden parts of her life and personality. Ultimately, the story of Herman Leard laid bare important aspects of the author's sexual self, an identity which has remained submerged behind an armour of repression. Behind the hyperbolic tale of passion there was a story of frustrated desire, perhaps a microcosm of the story of her life. At the same time, this tale of love and sex helped me capture Montgomery as a 'performative subject,' a subject who knows, as Amelia Jones wrote in 'Performing the Other as Self,' 'the strategic value, of playing the game too well' (74). Ultimately, my research indicates that Montgomery covered her discomfort with sexuality by excessively masquerading the flirtatious role, a role she would perfect in the parody courtship games with Nora Lefurgey in the 1903 diary. But before unveiling Montgomery's feminine masquerade – her artful posing as the woman in love – we shall reconstruct the events at the interface of rhetoric and truth telling, life writing and fiction, biography and autobiography.

Herman Leard: 'I pushed his clinging arms from me'

The tale began in late October 1897, a month before her twenty-fourth birthday, and was recorded six months later, on 8 April. Dressing herself in the rhetoric of high romance, Montgomery described herself watching 'the great burnished disk of the sun sink below the violet rim of water' (*SJ* 1:208), as she crossed Bedeque Bay after an all-day journey by train and ferry from Cavendish to Summerside into Lower Bedeque. Nancy MacFarlane, who knows the geography intimately, identified the exact location and time: 'The ferry made three trips a day from Summerside at 8:00 A.M., noon, and 5:00 P.M. Maud caught the last crossing, landing at the end of the wharf road which ran along the east end of Thomas Wright's farm, now John Wright's farm, connecting to the Lower Bedeque road' ('Summary' 1). The Leard family, where Montgomery was boarding, was 'well off' and 'highly respected in the community' (Leard, telephone interview, 2003); they lived on the Lower Bedeque road, just two houses from the school. The local teacher, Herman's brother Alf (fig. 4.2), was attending college to become a

4.2 Alphus Leard with his school class, Central Bedeque, 1894. Back: Ettie Schurman (second from left), Priscilla Schurman (third from left). (Acc. 3466/HF 75.9.5. Public Archives and Records Office of Prince Edward Island.)

dentist and had hired Montgomery as the replacement teacher. She was chosen because her fiancé, Ed Simpson, was Alf's friend (MacFarlane, interview, 2002; *SJ* 1:212), an intervention that anticipates Gilbert Blythe's helping Anne secure a school in the Anne novels. With only fourteen students to teach, Montgomery enjoyed a nice reprieve from the large class in Belmont, which had left her exhausted and burnt out.

But who was Herman Leard? Born in 1870, he was the third in a family of eight children and was 'slated to take over the Leard farm' (MacFarlane, interview, 2002). He was a 'better than average-looking fellow' (MacFarlane, interview, 2002), yet Montgomery, who had a discerning eye for handsome beaux, was not immediately taken with him. She thought his brother more attractive:

> [Herman] was under medium height, slight, and – I thought then – rather insignificant. Calvin impressed me far more favorably. I thought him much better looking than Herman – nevertheless, all through supper I found myself looking again and again at the latter. He was dark-haired and blue-eyed, with lashes as long and silken as a girl's. He was about 27 but looked younger and more boyish. (*SJ* 1:208)

In the portrait photo (see fig. 4.1), the rounded cheekbones give his face a gentle expression; the lips are sensual; his eyes, piercing and intense, speak of a confident personality and appear to look into the future. Indeed, Montgomery was drawn to his 'elusive, magnetic, haunting [face]' (*SJ* 1:209). Also, Herman loved to jest and tease (*SJ* 1:209), and soon they enjoyed a close bond that anticipated her bantering friendship with Nora Lefurgey.

According to the journal, the affair began on the moonlit night of Thursday, 11 November 1897, 'the *first step* on a pathway of passion and pain' (*SJ* 1:209). A highly charged buggy ride of '3-miles or 25 minutes' (Leard, telephone interview, 2003) took the couple from the Central Bedeque Baptist Church, opposite the cemetery where Leard lies buried today, to Lower Bedeque:

> I remember every turn of that road – we drove down to Colin Wright's corner at Central Bedeque, thence down the long shadowy Bradshaw hill over the creek ... up another long hill to Centreville and 'Howatt's turn.' I was tired and sleepy that night and did not feel like talking so I was very silent. Suddenly Herman leaned over and drew my head down on his shoulder.

I was about to straighten up indignantly and say something rather tart
but before I could do so there came over me like a *spell* the mysterious,
irresistible *influence* which Herman Leard exercised over me from that
date – an attraction I could neither escape nor overcome and against
which all the resolution and will power in the world didn't weigh a
feather's weight. It was indescribable and overwhelming. (*SJ* 2:209)

'Up to the time of my going to Bedeque I had never *loved*,' she recalls
(*SJ* 1:208). Or, as she would note twenty years later, in January 1917:
'For the first time I experienced the overwhelming power of senses – of
sheer physical passion. It had never touched me before' (*SJ* 2:205). In
the book of her life, at the age of almost twenty-three, she heralded a
sexual rite of passage, her initiation, claiming Herman Leard as her
erotic soulmate.

As seen in the description above, most remarkable in Montgomery's
'confession,' as she calls it, of 8 April 1898 is her specificity, as her
internal references to days and events allow us to reconstruct the exact
dates, places, and times of their tête-à-têtes, underscoring the veracity
of her record. The first secret date, for instance, took place in the Leard
parlour on Sunday, 28 November, two days before her twenty-third
birthday. 'Will you stay down a little while with me tonight?' (*SJ* 1:211),
Herman had whispered earlier in the evening. This sentence, one of the
rare quotations by Leard recorded in the journal, is important in that it
corroborates his interest in her.[1] There are at least three such invitations
for late-night dates: on Saturday, 11 December, they meet in the kitchen,
after others had gone to bed; and on Saturday, 25 December 1897,
Christmas Day, even though Montgomery's 'clear brain and unrelent-
ing conscience both told [her] it would have been far better not to [go],'
as her fiancé, Ed, had just been visiting (*SJ* 1:213). For each of their
secret dates, the same sentence is repeated in the journal, using identical wording, like a code in this carefully guarded affair. Apparently, the
family was oblivious of Montgomery's 'double life' (*SJ* 1:212), although
the ever-vigilant Mae later reported that she saw 'Maud chase Herman';
Montgomery would 'run to the window' when she heard Herman's
buggy (MacFarlane, interview, 2002). Herman fetched the mail from the
post office, delivering her letters, magazines, and presumably correspondence with editors.

If there is a scandalous note in this Victorian record of secret passion,
it is the spatial metaphor, for beginning with Sunday, 26 December,
their trysts moved to the bedroom which Montgomery was sharing

with Helen. Later she recalled Helen disparagingly as 'a surface friend,' remarking on her 'bitter tongue,' but in 1897 she entrusted Helen with the secret of her engagement with Ed Simpson. Engaged to Howard MacFarlane, Helen in turn was busy with her own dating. She was absent on several evenings, overnighting with friends, so that Montgomery's dating schedule with Herman neatly mirrors Helen's social schedule, further strengthening the plausibility of her record. With his sister gone, Herman quietly appeared late at night, sitting on the sofa and listening to Montgomery read her letters. On one occasion, she reports, he played with her jewels on the dresser, trying on her rings, as if he were one of the girls. Between 11:00 and 12:00 A.M., on the night of Friday, 4 February, one of the snow-blockaded weekends, her room became the setting for a steamy scene and turning point. That night Herman's whispered sentence, 'a request whose veiled meaning it was impossible to misunderstand' (*SJ* 1:215), sent her spinning with panic, as she confessed to her journal: '... only a faintly uttered, hysterical "no" had stood between me and dishonor' (*SJ* 1:216). The spectre of premarital pregnancy, which she would describe with such tragic poignancy in *The Blue Castle* (1926), was a risk she would never take – not for all the ecstasy in the world. The Victorian armour is back in place. According to the journal record, Herman repeated his efforts to cajole Maud into intercourse on Thursday, 17 February, three days after Valentine's Day, again in vain. It is interesting that his sentence, though central to the events, is never quoted or paraphrased in the journal, underscoring its taboo content, yet also leaving an intriguing gap. What exactly did Herman say? we are left wondering. After 17 February, their affair was effectively over, although the couple did reunite for a brief epilogue of parlour trysts and sleigh rides from 21 March to 1 April 1898, after her grandfather's death on 5 March had enforced her decision to return to Cavendish for good.

Since this is Montgomery's most explicit claiming of pleasure in a liaison with a man, it is important to ask: Just how sexual was her fling? And what does this affair tell us about her sexuality? In her journal's rhetoric, oral and haptic pleasures – kissing, caressing, touching, pressing, tapping, nestling, snuggling – predominate by far over other sensory perceptions, including smell, sight, and hearing; sexual desire and fantasy predominate over sexual activity. Following Victorian fiction codes, hair – a silken and dusky surface to be stroked, kissed, and arranged – is the most eroticized body zone along with flushed and burning facial skin. Although the sex act remains unconsummated, there is a great deal of kissing of lips and faces; on at least one occasion, Herman kisses her fingers, wrist, and bare arm – but that is the full extent of nudity revealed in Montgomery's journal. Her sexuality is maternal, seeking the comfort zones of childhood. The lovers 'nestle' in each others arms, one of her favourite words to describe their bodily connection; she is in the 'shelter' of Herman's arm; Herman's head is 'pillowed' on her shoulder. In the only reference to her breasts being touched, she notes, 'I can feel ... the warm pressure of his dear curly head on my breast' (*SJ* 1:217), as if he were a baby. She instructs her boyish lover like a mother who keeps a vigilant eye toward the clock – 'You must go' or 'Go to your room at once' or 'Lad, it's time for you to go' – and who praises: 'He obeyed me at once' (*SJ* 1:216). 'I pushed his clinging arms from me,' she writes when he pleas to stay in her room past twelve o'clock (*SJ* 1:217). Although four years older, Herman plays the complementary role of petulant child, routinely withdrawing when she scolds him, thus reinforcing the off-on pattern of their relationship. It is Montgomery's role to police the borders and decorum of their sexual activity. For sex to her is a dangerous precipice, an abyss, a vortex, and herein lies its difference from the modern non-consequential and unemotional flapper sexuality of the 1910s and 1920s. Her journal's rhetoric is consequently obsessed with frames and boundaries – the clock striking twelve or Herman lying rather than sitting when his head touches hers. These are the traffic signs that regulate their physical contact. If they are not obeyed, panic and chaos will follow. Her sexuality is activated within the classical Victorian gender codes: he takes the initiative, she reacts; he desires, she yields. Yet what is daring and modern is that she proclaims herself as a woman who is capable of quasi-orgasmic arousal in a relationship she has no intention of legitimizing through marriage. Even while she protests her shame, she is in fact quite shameless in claiming her sexual desire in her journal, anticipating the twenty-nine-year-old spinster Valancy Stirling in *The Blue Castle*, who makes no bones about the fact that living means the opportunity to enjoy sexual contact with tawny-haired Barney Snaith.

In 1919 Montgomery illustrated her journals with photos (see Higgins 101), and this visual/textual matrix, in particular, is a rich space for constructing embodied autobiographical selves, as theorized by Sidonie Smith and Julia Watson (*Interfaces* 1–46). Providing a rare visual glimpse into her erotic fantasy life, Montgomery illustrated her journal account, not with Herman's photo, as one might expect, but with a magazine clipping of an androgynous male (fig. 4.3) along with the slightly bi-

4.3   'As much like Herman Leard as if it were his photograph' – the journal photo as fetish. (L.M. Montgomery Collection, Archival and Special Collections, University of Guelph Library.)

zarre caption: 'Picture cut from magazine. As much like Herman Leard as if it were his photograph' (*SJ* 1:232). The toy-boy in the clipping, a mixture of pretty boy and altar boy, has Herman's deep-seated eyes and sensual lips, and discloses aspects of sexual desire which she cannot fully articulate verbally. His eyes are closed so that the viewer's gaze can travel unimpeded down his face, his white skin and sensual mouth inviting the viewer's caress. His features are feminine and soft, while the white officer's uniform loudly asserts his masculinity and upper-class origins. Herman's skin wouldn't have been white, given his outdoor work; his hands would have been calloused from handling the pitchfork. Judging from her fantasy male, for Montgomery, her lover's putative femininity (she describes him as 'boyish' with 'lashes as long and silken as a girl's') is a key to her own sexual responsiveness. It was his soft androgyny and perceived inferiority that made him safe, safe enough, that is, for Montgomery to enter the danger zone of sex.

She asserted that Herman Leard was 'impossible, viewed as husband' and explains: 'He had no trace of intellect, culture, or education – no interest in anything beyond his farm and the circle of young people who composed the society he frequented' (*SJ* 1:210, 209). Yet Waldron Leard rejects the portrayal of Herman as 'a fool.' As he explains: 'The Leards were well read. They believed in education' (telephone interview, 2003); in fact, Montgomery's journal confirms that Herman did read novels (*SJ* 1:210). Moreover, by refusing to replay Herman's verbal banter in direct quotes, she renders him silent and wordless, thus heightening the intellectual inequality between the lovers. Her unflattering portrait explains some of the rancour unleashed among Leard family descendants since the publication of volume one of the *Selected Journals* in 1985. Still, Montgomery was not interested in biographical accuracy but was working to claim herself as an embodied, desiring subject. By reducing the affair to the purely physical, and by claiming Herman as 'a very nice, attractive young animal' (*SJ* 1:209), the usually reticent Montgomery was able to proclaim her sexual competence in her journal: her ability to yield passionately to the arms of a man. As she was contemplating marriage, she was labouring to give birth to a new self – her sexual self.

Edwin Simpson: 'a mysterious repugnance'

The timing of her mad fling, in November 1897, speaks to what was likely the profoundest sexual crisis in her life. Physically, Montgomery was not a very demonstrative person. According to her journal, she eschewed physical contact, and photos rarely show her touching friends; although she does express contact comfort in her mock love poetry to Nora Lefurgey – 'I'll put my cold feet on your feet, Nora' – and in her fond recollection of 'crawl[ing] into a warm bed beside Nora who speedily thawed me out' (see chapter 1). In 1931 she boasted that she had had beaux galore since age fifteen, but she also confessed that she had found kissing boring, silly at best and nauseating at worst

(*SJ* 4:145), suggesting a discomfort with sexuality. Moreover, her journal demonstrates a pattern of denigrating the few men she was sexually attracted to. For instance, she confesses a queer unaccountable attraction to Alf Simpson (1874–1952), Ed's brother, yet dismisses him as homely and uncouth (*SJ* 2:205). Her cousin Oliver Macneill kindled 'a devastating flame of the senses' while she was engaged to Ewan Macdonald in 1909, yet is not able to inspire in her 'one spark of real love or even admiration' (*SJ* 1:359). Conversely, there is no mention of even a single passionate kiss with Ewan Macdonald, the man she did respect and marry in 1911. The gaps in her journal, and the obvious penchant for triangulations, indicate that physical relations belonged to the realm of the foreign other.

To fully appreciate the extent of her sexual crisis in 1897, let us step back a few months in her journals to Belmont Lot 16 at Malpeque Bay, PEI, home to the proud Simpson family. If this were a Jane Austen novel, we would be entering Pemberly and meeting the dashing Mr Darcy: Montgomery's second cousin Edwin Simpson (1872–1955), a beau who shares important features with that other fictional male paragon, Gilbert Blythe. When she illustrated her journals in 1919, she inserted Ed's photo as the embodiment of the ideal man and the tangible emblem of her marriageability. In the journal photo (*SJ* 1:199), the bespectacled student of theology looks finely groomed and confident. The high forehead and full lips evoke an intriguing combination of cerebral and sensual qualities. His steady gaze suggests that he knows where he is heading. This ambitious man was very much like Montgomery, yet was he perhaps too close for comfort? The photo's glamour fiercely clashes with the journal's verbal text, in which Ed is unmasked as Mr Wrong. On 30 June 1897 she confessed an uncharacteristic clumsiness in accepting his June 8th marriage proposal: 'I managed to stammer out that I thought I cared for him and that I would be his wife' (*SJ* 1:188). Although she did enjoy the intellectual sparring with this Belmont beau, already a day after the engagement she catalogued his imperfections. She was what psychologists call a high self-monitoring type, always watching, observing, and controlling her own behaviour, and she found herself paired with someone who was not. She was irritated by his volubility, his inability to be still, his hands, fingers, and feet constantly moving, tapping, twitching.

Yet far worse was to come, as her journal's courtship tale morphed into a messy sexual de-initiation story. On the night of Thursday, 17 June 1897, Ed had stepped inside the house to say goodbye to her, yet when he tried to kiss her, she was shocked by her impulsive bodily reaction, recorded in hyperbolic language: 'I was suddenly in the clutches of an icy horror. I shrank from his embrace and kiss. I was literally terrified at the repulsion which quivered in every nerve of me at his touch' (SJ 1:189). The fairy tale prince at her side was regressing into a moist frog, whose wet kiss drove Montgomery into chilling terror. Besides her sexual aversion, the delicate and soft-spoken Maud soon displayed visceral anger – enough to blow to bits the iron mask of politeness that was her usual armour. Her physical reactions – pushing his arms away, unresponsive coldness, outbursts and clenched hands – were harsh and crude. The carefully constructed decorum of her life was collapsing, as the writing subject was becoming unhinged. Looking in the mirror of her journal, she now faced an unsettling reflection: Maud the sexual ice queen who was unfit for marriage. She fought like a Spartan to keep her self-command and refused to break her engagement. For almost nine months, she masqueraded as Ed's fiancée, conscious of playing a fake role from the first day on: 'I can never marry him – never, NEVER,' she had admitted to herself after leaving Belmont for Cavendish in early July (SJ 1:201). Questioning her sexual responsiveness, she held onto her mask as the only way of controlling the crisis. This unresolved conflict explains why this intensely controlled woman would plunge into a mad fling with Herman and record every single kiss and caress in her journal with the meticulousness of an accountant. She had something to prove to herself.

Her sexual aversion can be explained by Victorian society's hostility toward sexuality (the Puritanical Macneill side) and by interpersonal dynamics (her incompatibility with Ed), but perhaps the most important reason is relegated into the margins of her journals. Montgomery's written confession seems consumed with only one thing, her complex love life, yet the Lower Bedeque year was an intensely productive period during which writing and publishing were central in addition to her full-time teaching. In fact, Herman's thirteen-year-old sister, Mae, one of Montgomery's students in 1897, told her daughter, Jean, that Montgomery often neglected to teach the class and 'used quite a bit of time in school to do her own writing' (MacFarlane, 'Summary' 2). Also, as Montgomery notes almost as an afterthought at the very end of the 8 April entry, Herman accused her of being too ambitious: 'he seemed to hate my ambition.' This information is pivotal, for, as she admits, it was the 'real barrier between us' (SJ 1:220). The implication of this barrier was too close to be explored in detail in 1898. It would take two more decades before this conflict between the social demands of marriage and her drive to pursue a writing career could be centrally ex-plored in her autobiographical fiction, the *Emily* trilogy. In 1898, Mont-gomery was careful to protect her hard-earned identity as a writer, which marriage might have threatened. She had shown iron discipline in building her career and, in psychological lingo, was terrified of being dethroned. Unlike Anne, she was not willing to sacrifice her ambition for her man. Yet she was also careful to mask this conflict in her journals by using the hyperbolic language of passion and the dramatic story of the two suitors as a rhetorical tool.

Indeed, like an actress, she wore an impenetrable mask for her suit-ors. For someone so adept with words, there was astoundingly little real talk with the suitors in her life. Unlike Austen's Eliza Bennett, who confronts the arrogant Mr Darcy with the truth of her perceptions in an impassioned and no-holds-barred confrontation, Montgomery summons the rhetoric of passion in her journals, yet equivocates with strategic evasions, delays, and half-truths in her communication with Ed. If she was afraid of commitment, she was equally afraid of making her true feelings known, acting more like a cagey marriage broker than a lover or friend. Likewise, there was something cold in her behaviour as she ruthlessly blocked any expression of sentiment in her fling with Herman, as seen in the episode when she refuses to meet his eyes:

> To meet Herman's eyes was something I could never do. I remember that day, as I was furtively watching *his* flushed cheek, his long dark lashes, and dusky curls, he suddenly looked around and our eyes met – met and locked. What flashed from one to the other I do not know but when I dragged mine from that fascinated gaze he still looked down at me and finding that I would not look up again he shook my wrist until I did. (*SJ* 1:214)

Refusing to recognize their reciprocity, her walls remained tightly in place. No words of love could ever be spoken to Herman Leard.

Ironically, then, the mad affair with Herman allowed her to test herself as a sexual being without losing control, even as she donned the costume of the woman possessed by love: 'I *loved* Herman Leard with a wild passionate, unreasoning love ... a love that in its intensity seemed little short of madness' (*SJ* 1:210). The affair also had a catalyst effect in liberating her from the unwanted strings of marriage. In early March, she finally told Ed that the engagement was off. Simpson eventually became a minister in Green Bay, Wisconsin, and, according to PEI genealogical records, would marry Minnie Robinson in 1908 and Mary Fiske in 1937. Yet, like Gilbert Blythe, who was patiently waiting for Anne after she had refused his proposal, so Ed continued to nourish hope for many years. His letters are partially quoted in her journals and suggest that he never received a satisfactory explanation (*SJ* 1:336). He makes routine appearances in her journals and scrapbooks (see Epperly in this volume), as when she muses more than twenty years later, on 28 December 1919:

> [Ed Simpson's] wife is a clever, talkative woman, quite a dab at public speaking. They have no children. This must be a disappointment to Ed. But he would never have had children, no matter whom he married, I believe. When I was engaged to Ed I did not know enough of men to realize what was lacking in him, but I know now that there *was* something lacking and I believe that was why, though I did not understand it, I felt such a mysterious repugnance to him. (*SJ* 2:361)

By 1919, Ed's lack of offspring and putative infertility had become an elegant rationalization for her own mysterious repugnance twenty years earlier. It is a sexual aversion which she remembers well as a shameful moment but which she never truly confronts in her journals. In 1919, her proud role as mother of two sons allowed her to exhibit a new masquerade of her sexual normality.[2]

Ettie Schurman: '... mine, all mine in death'

As we have seen, Montgomery's feminine masquerade required a strategic withholding of information from her suitors, readers, and even herself. Such gaps are not unusual or sinister, as I have shown in *Confessional Politics* (1–10), for the autobiographical subject negotiates her comfort level in exploring and revealing her intimate self. Yet Montgomery's journal entries and the memories of others conflict in a more flagrant fashion regarding a certain Elma Louetta Schurman (1881–1909), Montgomery's teenage rival of Central Bedeque. By 1897, according to Raymond Leard, it was public knowledge that 'Herman was spoken for by the red-haired Schurman girl that lived up the road' (W. Leard, telephone interview, 2003). The attachment is corroborated by Nancy MacFarlane's report, which states for the same period: 'Herman was publicly engaged to Elma Louetta Schurman' (2). The literary love triangle identified by Buss as central to the journal's love story may in fact cover up another triangle in which Montgomery was the third-party intruder. Ettie, as she was called, was born 27 January 1881 and was seven years younger than Montgomery. A photo of 1894 reveals that Ettie and her sister Priscilla were students in Al Leard's class (see fig. 4.2). A photo of circa 1900 (fig. 4.4) shows Ettie in a strikingly sensual pose very different from Montgomery's poses: shoulder thrust forward, her body making physical contact with the person behind her, her eyes looking at the camera with a languid expression, inviting the viewer's engagement. Ettie was the daughter of Peter Jesse Schurman and Elizabeth (Libbie) Callbeck of Central Bedeque, and thus related to Catherine Callbeck, PEI's first woman premier and senator. A hard-working and industrious farmer, Ettie's father, a redhead, was known for his temper (MacFarlane, interview, 2002) and for his sometimes cruel jokes (Boswall, interview, 2003). That Montgomery figured as the infamous other woman, the Jezebel, in this unspoken, and potentially explosive, second triangle helps explain the hyperbolic guilt expressed in her journal and her need to heap shame and penitence on herself: 'I cannot express the self-contempt I feel when I think of my folly. I am in a gulf of self-abasement and humiliation and remorse' (*SJ* 1:193). The depths of self-abasement anticipate the other drama queen Anne Shirley in her false apology to Mrs Rachel Lynde: 'I am a dreadfully wicked and ungrateful girl, and I deserve to be punished and cast out by respectable people for ever' (*AGG* 82). Montgomery, too, was revelling in her wickedness, and one wonders whether the memory of the red-haired Schurman girl was projected into the other Island redhead, Anne Shirley, given the coincidental phonetic similarity in the beginning of the last names Shirley and Schurman.

When Montgomery, at age twenty-three, recorded the 8 April 1898 confession of love for Herman Leard, she was writing just two days after her mother's birthday of 6 April. Montgomery performed the death of her old self by summoning her mother's, Clara Woolner Macneill's, death from consumption at age twenty-three in the image of the eroticized dead girl popular in Victorian visual art:

> My mother [see fig. 11.1] had been beautiful and Death, so cruel in all else, had spared the delicate outline of feature, the long silken lashes brushing the hollow cheek, and the smooth masses of golden-brown hair.
>   [...] I reached down and laid my baby hand against mother's cheek. Even yet I can feel the peculiar coldness of that touch. The memory of it seems to link me with mother, somehow – the only remembrance I have of actual contact with my mother. (*SJ* 1:205)

4.4   Ettie – 'that red-haired Schurman girl' (left). Back: Beatrice Ramsay, Priscilla Schurman, Emma Wright. Front: Ettie Schurman, Annie Gardiner, Belle Wright. (Courtesy of Elizabeth [Wright] Boswall, Prince Edward Island.)

The description of Clara's 'long silken lashes' anticipates the nearly same wording regarding Herman Leard ('lashes ... long and silken') just a few paragraphs later (*SJ* 1:208), so that mother and lover are curiously cathected in the same journal entry. The coldness of her mother's cheek is a symbol for the lack of affection in Montgomery's young life, a coldness temporarily exorcised in the flooding warmth of her affair with Leard. This mirroring of mother and daughter in a triangle that includes Herman allows Montgomery to write her love story as an elegy, a staging of death as a prelude for her performance of a new self.

Montgomery staged the birth of a new self in a visual self-portrait with the caption 'Myself in 1898' inserted in the 8 April entry (fig. 4.5). 'The self-portrait photograph performs a kind of visual autobiography, promising to deliver a particular "subject"' (69), writes Amelia Jones, who documents that 'self-performance in self-portrait photography has a particular force for women artists, who struggle to articulate themselves as "authors" rather than "objects" of artistic creation' (69), a point eloquently illustrated by Montgomery. Scholars have puzzled over the photo's exact composition date, for Montgomery used the same photo in her entry of 13 November 1901, which describes her arrival in Halifax (see *SJ* 1:277). My research suggests that the photo was in fact taken in the spring of 1898 immediately following her separation from Herman Leard. A postcard of the photo held in the Fall Collection in the University of Prince Edward Island Library identifies the Westlake Brothers in Charlottetown, not a Halifax studio, as the photographers. Also, in late March she had promised Herman to have her portrait taken, and by 10 July she was able to record receipt of his thank-you note for the photo (*SJ* 1:224). But most telling is the iconography of her self-portrait, in which she performs herself as, what Jones would call, a conscious object of viewing, that is, as a subject who purposely poses for the other (69–74). The velvet of the dress evokes the sensuality of her relations with Leard. Posing in a *tableau vivant* with ostrich-feathered hat, slim-belted waist, and gloved hands, she has adopted a wistful victory pose; the left side of her face is shadowed, giving this picture an aura of mystery, as does the veil she holds in her gloved hands. With the mournful expression, there is a bit of a widow's pose in the picture. As we contemplate this pose of triumphant single-hood, Montgomery's journal entry of 8 October, expressing her grief about Herman Leard's loss, provides the matching sound track: 'She has a "past" and its shadow falls ever across her path. She has looked below the surface and seen strange things' (*SJ* 1:226).

4.5 'Myself in 1898' – L.M. Montgomery posing for Herman Leard. (Photo by Westlake Brothers, Charlottetown, PEI, 1898. Fall Collection, University of Prince Edward Island Library. Courtesy of the L.M. Montgomery Institute, Prince Edward Island.)

So theatrical and artful was her staging of her self that Herman responded, not with his own photo, but with a cautiously formal thank-you letter. In her school-marm pose, she chastised – 'There were some visible lapses of grammar in it; the writing and expression were rather crude. There was nothing in it at all the world might not have seen' – only to continue in the voice of lovesick teenager:

> But never in all my life did I get a letter that was more welcome or that pleased and moved me so. I re-read it until I knew it by heart. I slept with it under my pillow for a week, waking often in the darkness to draw it out and press my lips to it as passionately as I would have done to Herman's had he been there! (*SJ* 1:224)

This letter perhaps best encapsulates Herman's role as fetish in Montgomery's life. Years later, she replays the painful separation with a comic spin in *Anne of Green Gables*. When Anne has to part from Diana – 'Diana and I are parted forever. Oh, Marilla' (*AGG* 143) – Anne exchanges secret love letters with Diana, writing in her postscript, 'I shall sleep with your letter under my pillow tonight' (151), just as the adult Maud had slept with Herman's letter under her pillow. Just as Herman had made grammar errors, so Anne apologizes for spelling mistakes. Just as Maud's reconciliation with Leard in March 1898 is commemorated in a blissful sleigh ride in her journals ('With a little sigh of happiness I nestled there during our drive over the gleaming marsh and through the snowy woods' [*SJ* 1:219]), so the narrator evokes the 'gleaming white spaces and dark glens of spruce' and the 'tinkles of sleigh-bells' [*AGG* 161] in the description of the reunion of Diana and Anne. In safely defused form, this girls' novel repeats love and marriage vows, as in Diana's love declaration for Anne ('If you love me as I love you / Nothing but death can part us two,' drawn from an innocent keepsake album verse [*AGG* 162]) – the very words which Maud and Herman were never able to speak to each other.

A little over a year after the end of her affair, on 30 June 1899, Herman died. There was no telegram informing Montgomery of his sickness or death (she learned about it in the newspaper), underscoring her distance from his suffering (when Helen died in 1930, Alf did send her a telegram [*SJ* 4:89]). Nancy MacFarlane's report supplies the details:

> Herman [had] pneumonia, seemed to have recovered from it, but infection settled in his appendix, which burst. During his last illness his sister

Helen looked after him. He wasted away from infection all through his body. It was more than 8 weeks from the beginning of his last illness until the end. ('Summary' 3)

Herman Leard was buried on a Sunday, 2 July, the day of his twenty-ninth birthday. His interment was 'one of the largest funerals seen in that vicinity for years, there being over 100 carriages in the procession' (Obituary in *SJ* 1:244). One wonders to what extent Herman figures in Matthew Cuthbert, the other gentle bachelor-farmer, who was also for 'the first time ... a person of central importance; the white majesty of death had fallen on him and set him apart as one crowned' (*AGG* 315). Anne's white narcissus flowers, the June lilies on PEI and Montgomery's favourite spring flowers, put Matthew's death in June, the same month in which Herman passed away. Anne's romance with Matthew also begins with the unforgettable buggy ride along the red clay roads of PEI, replaying Montgomery's journal romance with Herman in safely displaced form.

Yet for Montgomery, the sting was gone from her mourning of his actual death, and she notes in her journal on 24 July 1899: 'It is easier to think of him as dead, mine, *all* mine in death, as he never could be in life, mine when no other woman could ever lie on his heart or kiss his lips' (*SJ* 1:240). There is an odd possessive note in this thought, as if she were locking Herman in the mausoleum of her memory, snatching him away from the clutches of Ettie Schurman, who was publicly mourning at his grave as his rightful bride. The old folks vividly remembered Ettie's trips to the graveyard, where Ettie would sob inconsolably (MacFarlane, interview, 2002). In the rivalry with Ettie, Montgomery had finally won, as she could set her love an epitaph in her journal. Ironically, the life of the unmentionable Ettie was even shorter than Herman's, as Elizabeth Boswall, a distant relative of Ettie's, recounts her story. In 1904 Ettie married Singleton Muncey of Central Bedeque, and they moved to Lloydminster, Saskatchewan, where they had a daughter, Doris, in 1905. Aged twenty-eight, Ettie died of consumption in 1909 and was buried in the Lower Bedeque graveyard on the very road that Herman and Maud had travelled in 1897. The fate of Ettie's daughter, Doris, was strikingly similar to Montgomery's. Only four years old when her mother died, Doris returned to Central Bedeque to be raised by her maternal grandparents and aunts; her father stayed out West, remarried, and later served overseas during the First World War (Boswall, interview, 2003). Doris became a teacher.[3]

As for Montgomery, she enshrined Leard in her journal as a fetish lover. Like Browning's Duke in 'My Last Duchess,' who hoards the picture of his dead wife behind a curtain, so Montgomery's fetish is an artful memory, which only she can access. Not even her closest friend, Frede Campbell, knows the secret shared with her journal, her silent and most secretive confidante, as she writes on 12 November 1918, after a visit to Summerside:

> At sunset we left. As we walked up and down the station platform while waiting for our train we saw a most wonderful sunset on Summerside Harbor. And *I* – I looked away across to the dim, twilit shore of Lower Bedeque. I saw the old warehouse at the wharf and up beyond it the spruce grove behind, which was the house where Herman Leard lived and where I suffered hell – and heaven. Dead memories stirred in their shrouds as I gazed at it – memories whose ghosts have not walked for many a year. That winter of love and agony seems like a dream now – a dream that some one else dreamed. I have been free from its thralldom this many a year. If Herman Leard were living now and I were to meet him my heart would not beat one iota the faster. And yet – the old memories *did* stir uneasily as I looked across the purple harbor to that shadowy shore. Frede did not notice my silence or my long gaze. She knows that I once loved and that the love was a tragedy. She does not know who the man was nor where he lived. Not even to Frede have I ever named his name ... (*SJ* 2:275)

Recording this event on 12 November, she was also marking an anniversary, since it had been on 11 and 12 November, twenty-one years earlier, that Herman had first put his arm around her. In 1918, just one day after the armistice that ended the First World War, the memory of her love is clothed in elegiac language, as 'dead memories stirred in their shrouds.' After seven years of marriage with Ewan, the Lower Bedeque memory had become the melancholy reflection of passion locked in the past, the gap in her journal indirectly alluding to the staleness of her own marriage bed. For the entries concerning her husband are consistently desexualized, a rigid self-censorship suggestive of the complexity of her sexual life in marriage. In November 1918, she was also concerned about Frede's state of marriage.

Again a decade later, in 1929, more than thirty years after she had first arrived in Lower Bedeque, in the same month of October, Montgomery, the celebrity author, returned to visit Helen Leard MacFarlane, now a grey-haired matron with ten children, living in Fernwood in a house overlooking the Northumberland Strait. Montgomery is picked up by Herman MacFarlane, Helen's son, named after her late brother. In contrast to Herman Leard, who knew when to be silent, Herman MacFarlane was loquacious, and without the burden of having to contribute to the conversation, Montgomery is able to let her thoughts drift as they motored by the Central Bedeque places that were filled with old memories:

> ... in the autumnal gloom of twilight, we passed the Baptist church and graveyard where Herman Leard is buried.
>
> For years Herman Leard has been – or has seemed – but a name and a memory to me. When the menopause took away from me the impulses and desires of sex, the thought of him ceased to have any physical influence on me. Sometimes I have even wondered incredulously if it could ever have been *I* who lived through that searing ordeal of passion and pain. I knew we would pass the graveyard but I did not suppose it would affect me at all. And then this thing happened: –
>
> My heart turned over in my breast!
>
> ... I had the oddest feeling of that Herman Leard *was reaching out to me from his grave* – catching hold of me – drawing me to him. The feeling lasted only a few moments but it was gruesome and terrible.
>
> Then we were past – Herman MacFarlane was talking unbrokenly on – he is a great talker – and I came to myself with a gasp. (*SJ* 4:19)

Menopause – or even more likely the abstinence in a physically passionless marriage – has long dulled Montgomery's sexual feelings, yet her sensations return with startling force. The Baptist Church, the departure point for her late-night buggy trysts with Herman, symbolizes her sexual awakening. Still visible from the street today, Herman's white tombstone (fig. 4.6), with the inscription 'G. Herman, Son of Cornelius & Amy J. Leard. Died June 30, 1899, AE t. 29,' is a reminder of the burial of a part of herself. That night, sleeping under Helen's roof, the almost fifty-five-year-old author once more dreamed of Herman. In the dream, she was seeking him through endless corridors and empty rooms but without ever finding him (*SJ* 4:20). The emptiness may well refer to the erotic emptiness of Montgomery's sexual life and to the lack of pleasure in her marriage. The memory of Herman ultimately illuminates aspects of her marriage too unsettling to put in words. Looking

4.6   'Herman Leard was reaching out to me from his grave' – Herman Leard's gravestone, Baptist Graveyard, Central Bedeque. (Photo by J. Paul Boudreau, Ontario.)

back on her love life in 1931, she confessed with a mixture of nostalgia and implicit critique that 'the first touch of Herman's lips on mine made me his forever, as I have never been any other man's, not even the man's whose wife I have been for twenty years and whose children I have borne' (*SJ* 4:145). Montgomery is like Gretta Conroy, the unfulfilled wife in James Joyce's *The Dead*, who has locked the passion for her youthful dead lover in her heart.

Epilogue

The spirit of yesteryear is still alive in Lower Bedeque. Even today wild rosebushes adorn the paths of this quiet south shore community, its pastoral atmosphere contrasting with the busy tourist sites of Cavendish. The gabled farmhouse once owned by the Leards, orchard-embowered and set away from the street behind a long grassy lane, looks a lot like Green Gables. The owners, Anne and Jim Nichols, raised their large family in it and lovingly restored the nearby one-room school where Montgomery taught during 1897–8. Pictures of Montgomery decorate the walls of the school, along with group photos of Lower Bedeque students, but there is no photo of Herman. When the Nicholses wanted to display his photo, members of the Leard family objected, disputing the veracity of Montgomery's portrayal of Herman Leard. 'Herman never indicated that he was interested in the boarder,' said Raymond Leard to his son Waldron (W. Leard, telephone interview, 2003).

On the pages of the journal, the figure of Herman came to assume a central role in Montgomery's imagination – the fantasy lover who confirmed her erotic responsiveness and capability for intimacy, yet also its tragically unrealized potential in her life. Erotic love, as the journal suggests, had been short in Montgomery's life, a memory of furtive and secret pleasures attached to the name of Herman Leard. The unconsummated relationship and his early death further facilitated his transformation into fetish. The affair gives us a glimpse into what the tightly corsetted author felt she had missed in life and the price she paid for never relinquishing control. The wild masquerade as a woman in love was confined to one brief moment in her journal, and the pose she liked the best was the widow's pose, the woman who had once loved and lost. As for Herman, he was the silent counterpart. He was immortalized as fetish, the frozen lover, arrested and immobilized in the past.

NOTES

My thanks to all those who generously provided information and help for this essay, including Elizabeth Boswall, J. Paul Boudreau, William Callbeck, Waldron Leard, Nancy MacFarlane, and Anne Nichols.

1 While Montgomery is selective in what she chooses to reveal, it is very unlikely that she would fabricate a quotation and attribute it to Leard.
2 Coincidentally, as PEI genealogical records indicate, his brother Alf's marriage with Dora Peters also remained childless. For Montgomery, sex and fertility are inseparably intertwined; see Gammel, 'Safe Pleasures.'
3 According to Waldron Leard, Doris Muncey refused to talk about her mother's engagement with Herman Leard. Also, since she was only four years old when her mother died, she would have had little first-hand information.

5

Veils and Gaps: The Private Worlds of Amy Andrew and L.M. Montgomery, 1910–1914

Mary McDonald-Rissanen

'I think labour has begun,' [the nurse] said. The next day, Sunday, July 7, at 12.40 my little son was born.

L.M. Montgomery, 22 September 1912, *SJ*, 2:100

A very dull day baby born
quarter past twelve awful sick

Amy Andrew, 5 April 1913

A few years ago, in looking through my mother's belongings, my sister and I discovered a diary in the top drawer of my mother's dresser. It belonged to my grandmother Amy Andrew, a woman farmer with little education but with great endurance, who had passed away in 1966. Some of the events recorded in the diary are family stories she told as we were growing up in Summerside, Prince Edward Island; some events seemed unfamiliar, appearing in the sparse text of the diary instead of the familiar voice of my memories. Amy's diary was kept in a small black leather book with golden text on the cover, reading 'A Line a Day.' The next page, called the 'Prefatory,' has the following instruction for keeping the diary: 'Jot down a line or two most worthy of remembrance / a record of events, incidents, joys, sorrows, successes, failures, things accomplished, things attempted.' This Amy did for five years from 1910 to 1914, religiously, except for a four-month period in 1912. Inside the front cover, she has written her name three times on the pale blue page. Her final scrolling, 'Amy Tanton St. Eleanor's,' carries a strong resemblance to her first lines on 1 January 1910, a young woman in her prime, full of happiness and joy when she wrote: 'a beautiful day ...'

To me, a native of Prince Edward Island and a scholar of life writing, the diary was a gift. I was captivated by its format, so different from the polished literary diaries I was used to reading, including the journals of L.M. Montgomery, Amy's more famous Island sister, whose works I had studied and admired for their aesthetic value. But I was also captivated by the contrast in this pair of Island women diarists. Despite the fact that they lived about thirty miles from one another in Prince Edward Island at the turn of the century, Amelia Darby Tanton Andrew (b. 1881) and L.M. Montgomery (b. 1874) likely never met. Their families were not related, they went to different churches, they moved in different social circles, and Montgomery was seven years older. As the epigraphs suggest, Amy Andrew's minimalist language, juxtaposed with Montgomery's dramatic outpourings in her diary, may initially appear barren of detail and emotion. Yet this essay is an invitation for readers to enter the world of an ordinary woman writer and delve into the extraordinary daily chronicle written, not for publication, but for herself, to be handed down to her daughter – a diary which remains in its most intense privacy cryptic and full of gaps. It is intriguing to juxtapose this sparse diary with the voluble and yet highly controlled journal writings of Montgomery, who despite her loquaciousness also left significant gaps. By juxtaposing these two different records, we are entering the very fabric of the writers' lives and gain insight into their strategies of veiling.

In her collection of essays *Confessional Politics: Women's Sexual Self-Representations in Life Writing and Popular Media*, Irene Gammel has documented that women are careful and strategic in disclosing their intimate lives, often leaving gaps or resorting to indirection, for there are risks in exposing the self. This argument can be extended beyond the realm of sexuality. There is always a danger that a private diary can be discovered by unwanted readers and the writer penalized for her thoughts, as Cecily Devereux explains in chapter 10. In Amy's case, gaps resulted from the limitations of language; the most glaring gap is the missing first-person pronoun 'I' in most entries in Amy's diary. In poring over this minimalist diary, I realize that lives can never be fully revealed in language, and yet the omissions and indirections themselves speak eloquently to what is being veiled. In the following, I will focus on the quotidian and mundane – the *weather* and the *physical body* – to make the silences speak and to show that life paradoxically can be laid bare through gaps and indirection. By introducing the work of this unknown Island diarist, I also hope to contribute to an understanding of the veiling in Montgomery's journals.

'Aunt Carrie came to make us a visit'

Islanders like Amy Andrew and L.M. Montgomery were born Canadians. Their ancestors had been residents of Prince Edward Island since the late eighteenth and early nineteenth centuries when they emigrated from England, in Andrew's case, and Scotland, in Montgomery's case. Both grew up in communities where their ancestors had acquired land, and throughout their lives they continued to strengthen their ties with their ancestors' institutions, the Church of England and the Presbyterian Church respectively. Between 1910 and 1914, both Amy Andrew and L.M. Montgomery were married, left their childhood homes, and had their first children, their lives following a relatively conventional pattern for women at the turn of the century.

Born on 30 April 1881, Amy Tanton Andrew was in her late twenties when she started to keep her diary in 1910. She was living at home with her mother, father, brothers Stan and Fred, and her sister, Marion, on their farm in St Eleanor's, a small community a few miles from Summerside, also home to Nora Lefurgey.[1] Coincidentally, my mother told me that Nora Lefurgey, who taught in North St Eleanor's from 1904 to 1907, was a good friend of Amy's, although we know little about the specifics of the friendship. A large network of relatives and friends came into Amy's life on a daily basis, and the family travelled almost every day to the nearby town of Summerside to shop and visit friends and relatives. In addition to farming, they collected taxes (Amy helped her father in this) and were active in the church and the community. Andrew's daily work would have been instrumental in the operation of the farm: her diary reports gardening, making jam, sewing, preparing meals for the harvesters, and spring cleaning. She was also active in the church: she played the organ for services, choir practice, and weddings.

During this same period, L.M. Montgomery was also keeping a journal, as she had been since childhood. She was thirty-six in 1910. Following her training at Prince of Wales College in 1894, she had taught school in several Island communities and at one point left the Island to work as a journalist in Halifax. She returned to the Island to be with her ageing grandmother after her grandfather's death in 1898, and by 1910 she had been living with her grandmother for twelve years. Although she had written poetry and stories since she was a child, Montgomery had only achieved real success with the publication of *Anne of Green Gables* in 1908; *Anne of Avonlea* was published in 1909, and during the

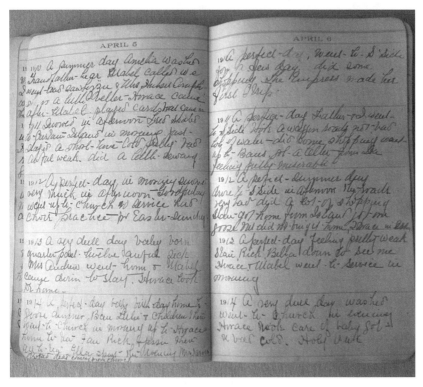

5.1   Amy Andrew's diary, 5–6 April 1910–1914. (Photo by Hannu Vanhanen. Courtesy Katherine [née Andrew] McDonald, Prince Edward Island.)

period that this chapter focuses on, Montgomery published four more books. Following the death of her grandmother and her marriage to the Rev. Ewan Macdonald, she took up residence in Ontario. Her first son was born in 1912, and her second son died at birth in the summer of 1914.

During the five years she kept a diary, from 1910 to 1914, ending shortly after the beginning of the First World War, Amy married Horace Andrew, a farmer. Each page of the diary provides five lines for recording the events of a day over a five-year period (i.e., opening the diary at random to 5 April, we find entries for the years 1910, 1911, 1912, 1913, and 1914 [fig. 5.1]). The text offers two main reading strategies: one can read from day to day, through one year at a time, in a horizontal or chronological reading; or one can read the same day over a period of five years, a vertical or thematic reading. Both strategies are used in this study, the first to get an overview of the people and events in Amy Andrew's life, as well as to become familiarized with her writing style, and the second, thematic reading to understand the seasonal rituals and rhythms of her life and the development of specific events. The book itself thus structures the recording of events: the introduction stipulates that it be written daily rather than when the urge takes her, yet it is limited in space. Amy Andrew plays within these constraints. Her lines occasionally cannot be contained in the space allotted for that day; her text runs outside the borders of the day. At other times, she appears to be hardly able to scribble a word, and the yellowing page, absent of ink, arrests the reader entirely; these gaps raise questions in the minds of her reader: why this, now?

Montgomery's journals raise different questions. She started keeping a journal at the age of nine, but destroyed the earliest ones. The journals in the possession of the University of Guelph consist of ten legal-sized volumes that begin at age fourteen and cover the period until her death in 1942. However, even these are not the originals: from 1889 to 1918 she wrote in 'blank books' that were recopied into these legal-sized ledgers at a later date, and we do not know whether, or to what extent, Montgomery altered the entries as she recopied them (she says she did not). Montgomery's entries in these journals appear to be far less structured by the organization of the books themselves. They are, as Rubio and Waterston observe, blank books (*SJ* 1: xxiv), so that entries are not subject to the manufacturer's direction. She gave herself more freedom in terms of when she wrote, what she wrote about, and the length of her journal entries. Entries might be as short as one line or as long as a dozen or more pages, and no matter how much time has passed, the next entry begins where the previous one finished. She used her journal as a deposit of her dreams, as the genre's form or formlessness gave her inner feelings a place for expression, as she noted on 9 June 1893: 'It's such a beautiful day and such a beautiful world that I must "bubble over" to someone, and you, old journal, are the only one I dare bubble over to' (*SJ* 1:90). The more than two million words she wrote in her journals have been edited and published as *The Selected Journals of L.M. Montgomery*.

In contrast, the small black book with the golden text on its cover is the text Amy Andrew inscribed and left intact as it now is with its 395 manuscript pages. Neither Amy herself nor any editor rewrote or edited what she had written, and in this way it is a complete and authentic document. Amy Andrew, as the author, selects the characters, sequences the events, and makes linguistic choices from her repertoire to bring forth the story of these five years of her life, but the narrative of the self is woven in with that of the others, as the self was primarily defined in terms of the others. She simultaneously constructs and exposes herself through these social relations. The repeated appearance of the same people and events in the diary, whether the text is read horizontally or vertically, contributes to the narrative's development: 'Uncle Tommy Murray died,' and then a few pages later, 'Uncle Tommy Murray buried.' Her long friendship and eventual courtship with Horace Andrew, and the accounts of his brothers, sisters, and parents, regularly enter the pages of her diary: 'Horace came in for a few minutes,' she writes on 23 January 1910, and, two years later, 'Horace called we went for a long drive' (14 February 1912).

Within the report of the main event of each day, 'went to church' or 'sewed most all day,' Amy Andrew generally eliminates herself as subject and instead implies that the subject is the self-evident 'I,' the author of the diary. 'Sold a pig' indicates the family sold a pig, and that for events surrounding herself, as well as her family, the subject is implied and does not need to be revealed or repeated. Yet the subject, 'I,' is blurred, downplayed. There is an assumption that 'I' and 'we' stand for the same, which can be problematic when trying to identify Andrew's voice among the others. Often one is left to draw the conclusion that Andrew feels that 'I' and 'we' are synonymous, and that life for her was a series of common endeavours in which the household, family, and extended family were more important than she as an individual was. She minimizes her own role in events, but when writing of other actors, she clearly makes them the subject: 'Aunt Carrie came to make us a visit,' or 'Horace took care of baby.' The cohesion in the diary comes in the reporting, which involves the repetition of people's names, places, events, and activities. The great number of people who enter her daily life, and the variety of activities she mentions throughout her diary, indicate the richness of her life and the importance of these people and events to her. She writes about herself as a person constructed from interaction with family and friends, and in her empathy with the family and community she finds and relates her self, her subjectivity. The social interaction, on a day-to-day basis as well as at times of crisis, provides grist for her entries more than any specific reflection of her mental or physical state, as is the case in L.M.

Montgomery's journals. Yet in everything, she describes the materiality of life with a certain literalness – the talk about weather, which is central in the diary, is literally about the weather, and yet it also contributes to constructing the diarist's subjectivity.

'I think the weather is largely responsible for my blues'

Amy generally initiates a diary entry much like a conversation, by referring to the weather. Then she continues by taking up events which are a consequence of the weather. The overall pattern of the entries can be described as an opening or declaration of the weather conditions, followed by a report of the events of the day, with an occasional closing. Thus, on 13 July 1910 Amy wrote, 'very warm all day very heavy shower in evening,' whereas four years later she wrote simply, 'fine but cold.' On 13 October 1913 her only entry was, 'poured rain all day.' Not a day goes by that she does not refer to the weather in the opening and sometimes in the body of the entry, where the weather may be linked with the day's activities.

Through her choice of theme, Amy's experience opens the daily entry and often resonates throughout. Given her choice of words in her openings, it appears that a 'perfect day' could be warm or cold, depending on what was appropriate for the season. The twentieth of December, 1911, was 'a perfect day cold,' but in other entries when she writes about how the wind blew, the absence of positive adjectives like 'perfect' (7 June 1911), 'beautiful' (4 April 1910), or 'fine' (10 June 1911) suggests she considers it less agreeable: 'a very cold day & blowing a hurricane' (20 Dec. 1912). When the weather was disagreeable, Andrew refrains from using a negative attribute and reserves attributes for the weather she appreciates. Her text implies that a cold north wind is not a good day and that 'a fine day but awful cold' is one that is clear and quite cold in Island English. Again, she simply reports the weather and refrains from directly giving an expressive value judgment. The absence of positive and negative attributes about the weather suggests the inevitable stance farmers must take toward the climate. They are forced to live and act in accordance with the weather.

Through the subtle nuances of weather discourse, Amy Andrew recorded her responses to her natural milieu. During a succession of days of bad weather, from the 18th to the 21st of November 1914, she wrote on each day a limited amount of text:

A regular snow storm got
storm doors on. (18 Nov. 1914)

Still storming banking
house awful cold. (19 Nov. 1914)

Rain & sleet   churned. (20 Nov. 1914)

The gaps on the page increase with each day's worsening weather, and at the same time the cohesion between the weather and its consequences alters. On the 18th, the use of 'got' creates a connection of agency between the storm and the installation of the storm doors. With each day of threatening weather, her syntax is reduced, so that the third day's entry is written as word-&-word-gap-word: 'Rain & sleet   churned.' She could hardly have said less. Her text was limited as though she herself were paralysed by the cold and unable to do more than try to cope, and keep the house warm, and fulfil her commitment to 'jot a line.'

The cumulative effect of Amy Andrew's choice of words and their sequence, as well as the processes within her text, reflects how she responds to nature. The weather, as storm, rain, or sleet, creates the conditions that force the family to act – to put the storm doors on and bank the house – and then the weather allows her to resume her normal duties, such as churning. The lexical items, the weather and the activities associated with hard weather, are the processes, and the actors are those responding and caught up in the weather. Yet her diary entry does not mention the actors, suggesting a self-evidence of characters and a predictability of their response to the situation, which repeats itself year after year. Nature is all-powerful and the actors operate within the dictates of nature; they do not attempt to harness or control nature. By their absence in the text, Amy Andrew's self and her family are invisible in the face of nature. These entries reflect her most dramatic responses to nature – that is, she could not freely choose what to do on these days as she did on a daily basis when she sewed or visited, but on these days her actions were determined by nature.

When the weather turns milder, Andrew resumes her domestic chores with a sense of relief, indicating that there is more to life than fighting the elements. Throughout most of her passages, she is actively experiencing the weather; her mood and text flow with its variations. The weather and the seasons influence what jobs were to be done, and there is the sense of satisfaction and great delight which she derives from these routines. Compared to her cryptic winter text above, her spring text covers the five lines with considerably more cohesive text. The weather and the seasons provide the setting for the events of the day, whether it be fine weather and the spring cleaning; a bad harvest and consequently her dismay from a poor crop of potatoes; or the return of spring and the pleasure she conveys from her first bouquet of mayflowers.

Montgomery, too, often began her journal with a reference to the weather: for example, on 11 September 1910 she began, 'To-day was very beautiful. We had service in the morning ... (*SJ* 2:12). (On the same day, Amy Andrew wrote, 'A perfect day very warm, went to church ...') Yet Montgomery, unlike Amy Andrew, often attached emotional values to a bad day: for example, on 26 December 1910, she wrote, 'Yesterday was Christmas – a very dreary day. It rained heavily from dawn to dark' (*SJ* 2:34). While Amy denies herself the possibility to express negative feelings or unpleasant emotions, Montgomery is far more open. Montgomery appears to think of her journal as a private space where she can write things she wanted no one else to know. However, it also suggests a very different relationship with the natural world. In the farming families, weather directly influenced people's work and social agenda, and subsequently their health and spirit. Andrew was materially dependent on nature for her family's sustenance. However, Montgomery was emotionally dependent on nature for her psychological and intellectual well-being. She also lived in a rural community, but was not involved in farming and was therefore less dependent on the weather for her livelihood. Instead, nature and its manifestations determined mood and invited reflection. 'It has been a disagreeable spring – cold and dull,' she notes on 12 April 1903 during a period of extended melancholy and depression: 'I think the weather is largely responsible for my blues. When the sunshine comes again I shall find life quite tolerable – yea even pleasant. Not an ecstatic, rapturous affair at all but something one can jog along very comfortably with. In sunlight the soul of me shines out and conquers the flesh' (*SJ* 1:287). The day of 12 April had brought a spring snowstorm after two weeks of rainstorms. Such entries support Janice Fiamengo's suggestion that Montgomery may have been prone to seasonal depressions (see chapter 6).

At the same time that she recorded her weather blues, for Montgomery, in the Romantic tradition, nature was a point of departure for discovering consciousness, as well as for defining and exercising her identity as a woman artist through her beautiful other. Growing up without a mother, and raised by undemonstrative and dour grandparents, Montgomery's early life was starved for affection. In the absence of her true mother, she formed a surrogate bond with her natural kingdom, visiting and writing her way into a relationship to fill the void. Her emotional starvation was abated by books and nature, with an ever-increasing fusion of these themes in her writing. She wrote, 'I had ... then as now, two great refuges and consolations – the world of nature and the world of books. They kept life in my soul' (*SJ* 1:301). Her writing was a location for recording and reflecting on her encounters with nature. Her love of nature was fed and cultivated from many sources, from her familial relationship with her geraniums – 'Dear things, how I love them! [...] I believe that old geranium has a soul' (*SJ* 1:1) – to longer, more sustained relationships with familiar landscapes. The cumulative effect of her greatest pleasures, to play in the woods and revisit the same places in her adult years, to walk in Lover's Lane, and through the old orchard, and taste the wild strawberries, all figured in her conceptualization of her love of place. Her textual account of nature was not only an account of place but also of her interaction with the spirit and soul of nature, as embodied in, for example, the 'breeze that blew over the clover fields [...] the very water of life to me' (*SJ* 3:342). Through nature she experienced a symbiosis with the family she never had, and the continuity of life which nature symbolized: 'I shall always be grateful that my childhood was passed in a spot where there were many trees – "old ancestral trees," planted and tended by hands long dead, bound up with everything of joy and sorrow that visited the lives in their shadow' (*SJ* 2:37). Thus Montgomery's engagement with nature in her journals does not avoid emotional response as Andrew does, but rather invokes, explores, and interrogates it, for it is where she constructs her very identity.

Montgomery thus wrote more openly about the particulars of her life, the mental anguish of the rejection of her early manuscripts, and the eventual struggles with her publishers. Her journal was her 'grumble' book. In contrast, Amy Andrew stoically refrains from fretting over herself and instead resorts to an attitude of spunkiest perseverance, having faith, and being optimistic. Thinking or behaving otherwise could bring about devastation. For both women, life writing was a means through which they talked themselves through their lives, giving pep talks to the self as a means of survival. Their diaries and journals thus document the struggles in their building of character and a fine location to return to in order to gaze upon themselves, a site for self-reflexive textuality. Of course, Andrew did not have the discursive options a woman like Montgomery had.

Amy Andrew's text seldom reflects on events other than those of the past day. Often the verb, like the subject of the sentence, is omitted, which allows her more space to crowd in the five lines the sometimes eventful days without causing any incoherence in her text. A few times this technique causes confusion as to who is the subject. Often there is a string of verbs in the past tense:

> Started to make a dress
> Made my fruit cake   a beauty
> [outside the five lines:] The largest steamer Titanic sank   with 1707 lives.

Both the temporal and spatial qualities of Amy Andrew's life are obvious in the above diary entry from 15 April 1912. She writes out of the immediate past and prioritizes the events that take place in her locale, rather than the tragedy of the *Titanic,* which took place off the Canadian coast (Montgomery does not mention the event at all). Those events close to home were primary in Amy's life, and she makes little reference to places beyond her community and the neighbouring one. Other locations are mentioned only when a family member departs for a faraway destination, or when she receives a letter from a relative living away. The simple language conveys the helplessness of the sorrow, but is utterly lacking the detail and emotion of Montgomery's retrospective account of the death of Tillie Houston:

> Tillie took measles. I had known she was ill and very ill with them; but a letter from Margaret two days before had said she was over the worst and was recovering. Therefore this message was a horrible shock.
>
> To this day I am not any more reconciled to Tillie's death than I was then, and I *cannot* become reconciled to it ... Tillie was in the prime of life, happy, useful, beloved by all. Her death has made in my life a blank which can never be filled ... She was one of the few Cavendish people who really mattered to me, one of the few people in the world whom I deeply and intimately love. (*SJ* 2:62)

The bitterness and injustice of Montgomery's loss are palpably and articulately expressed in this entry, which is fairly long. Amy Andrew's diary does not provide the space for such length, and yet the lack of adjectives to describe the emotion cannot be entirely explained as a question of space. It appears that Andrew did not allow the immediate expression of emotion. Her emotional state must be read through the conventions associated with events. Any extremes in Andrew's expression of misfortune or sorrow, like those of joy and happiness, are not highlighted textually with adjectives, or with any clear linguistic structure. Supratextual features such as the quality of her handwriting and anecdotal evidence hint that whatever Amy Andrew did write, had other unscribeable dimensions.

'... make his birth safe and painless for me'

Montgomery was, from an early age, acutely aware of language, as she aspired to become a writer. Girls were encouraged to keep diaries during the transition from childhood to adulthood, but as Valerie Raoul notes 'once married, writing about themselves was perceived as an unjustifiable self-indulgence, a theft of time more profitably spent (on others)' (58). There is an almost one-year hiatus in Montgomery's journal, following her marriage to Ewan Macdonald in 1911. Amy Andrew's silence in her diary for a period immediately after her marriage in 1912 can partially be explained by the fact that diary writing was perceived as a selfish activity that took time away from the common good of her new family. Once married, she didn't have the personal space to move in, as she once had when single. Her private space had diminished, so that her diary was one of the few sites for privately assembling her life.

Unlike Montgomery, in writing down her life, Amy consistently uses positive attributes and refrains from expressing anything negative. Three obvious ways in which the diary avoids negative expression were, firstly, to resort to gaps – that is, not to mention the issue at all; secondly, to make a topic shift – that is, to refocus her attention on a cheerful subject; or thirdly, to resort to neutral word choice, such as she does with the word 'sick' to refer to the labour she endured in childbirth. After all, why did she want to dwell on the miseries of life, weather, or suffering, when she could divert her attention to something more positive, or say nothing at all? Helen Buss, in *Mapping Our Selves* (1993), describes Susanna Moodie's similar predicament. In Moodie's *Roughing It in the Bush; or, Life in Canada* there is no indication of a suffering woman, but through private writings, her letters, one is able to decode the message of a woman alone in the wilderness with her anguish (85). When reading Andrew's text there is no supplementary text from which to get a different version of her life. Instead, sections of her text must be read intertextually and questions raised at even the slightest hint of divergence.

The entry from 5 April 1913 (see fig. 5.1), the day on which Amy Andrew gave birth to her first child, exemplifies her writing strategy, by eschewing any reference to pain. Her entry focuses not on herself but on other people who witness the event. Mrs Andrew, Mabel, Amy's husband, Horace, and the doctor are the clearly named actors:

A very dull day baby born
quarter past twelve awful sick
Mrs. Andrew went home & Mabel
came down to stay. Horace took
Dr. home.

Again our attention is drawn to what is not being said. In contrast with the contemporary view that motherhood brings happiness, there is little direct reference to maternal bliss. Entries preceding the actual birth and immediately following it indicate that Andrew was not her usual self. Her text contains more references to her physical state – 'a awful sore back' (27 March 1913), 'took sick after I got home' (4 April 1913) – and she stayed closer to home on the days before the birth. After the birth, the days are filled with accounts of numerous visitors, after the usual reports of weather or road conditions. There is only the occasional mention of her mental or physical state:

snowed & roads very bad
nothing happened but be in bed
& (?) legs very weak (7 April 1913)

Ten days after the birth, Andrew mentions her own baby for the first time:

A perfect day got up for the
first – put the clothes out – Mrs
Richardson went over to see Leo
baby weight – nine lbs. (15 April 1913)

For the woman giving birth and for those attending her, the commentary on pregnancy and birth is limited, and absent in it are the emotions often played up in advertisements on the female function, motherhood and happy homes, in the press of the time. Giving birth was a real risk for a woman and her child at the beginning of the twentieth century. Andrew, while confined following her child's birth, mentions, 'Mrs White's baby died' (9 April 1913), and then, 'Mr White's baby buried Horace went / to funeral...' (11 April 1913). Death was never far off. Rural women at the turn of the century silently witnessed their own, and their neighbours', struggle to come to terms with the inevitability of death. Entries anticipating the birth and lamenting the death of farm animals, crucial to the welfare of the farm, are charged with emotion seldom recorded when a similar fate occurs among humans.

For an urban woman, as Montgomery was when she gave birth for the first time in July 1912, living in Canada's most urbanized area, Central Ontario, the situation was somewhat different. She recorded her pregnancy two months after conception: 'Early in November [1911] I began to suspect that what I had intensely longed for was to be mine and now I knew it. I am to be a mother' (*SJ* 2:90). She wrote about her confinement two months after the birth, recording that she had suffered more pain with toothache than the actual giving birth. It was her fear for the survival of her self and her child that haunted her most, as she remembered on 22 September:

> In the dead, dim hours of night fears and gloomy dreads came to me. I put them resolutely away, but always they lurked in the background of my mind. Would I escape with my life? ... These and a score of other fears haunted me. And not the least dreadful among them was the quiet, persistent, secret dread that I would not *love* my child when it came. (*SJ* 2:99)

By the time she writes this account, the birth has passed safely and mother and son have formed a close bond. Nevertheless, her analysis of her first birth reiterates belief in the power of mind over body: 'A few years ago I read Hudson's "Law of Psychic Phenomena." Ever since I have had a strong belief in the power that the subconscious mind can exert over physical functions. Every night, as I was dropping off to sleep, and frequently through the day I repeated over and over the command to my subconscious mind "Make my child strong and healthy in mind and body and make his birth safe and painless for me"' (*SJ* 2:101). Montgomery was, with the distance of time, putting together a story of how an early twentieth-century urban woman could take charge of the process of becoming a mother by using both medical and psychological teachings. As a professional writer, she constructed a narrative to record her experience in the past tense, in retrospect. Amy's record conveys a far stronger sense of the immediacy of anticipation, fear, discomfort, and satisfaction accompanying the birth experience, for all its unpolished style. For rural women like Amy, the day was prefaced with a series of physical symptoms and social events that subtly hinted that new life would enter her world. Family and friends assisted and witnessed this event, and gradually the community came forth to greet its new member.

On one level, Amy Tanton Andrew's diary can be read as filling the gaps in local history, while on another level, her writing is read as the story of a woman writing herself, and her kind, into history. In some cases, the discursive strategies she employs in the telling of her story suggest the obvious comfort she found from the rhythms in her life. Her diary entries follow the pattern she establishes in her first entry, namely, describing the weather, and then the happenings of the day, generally with no particular ending to the entry, and only the occasional closure-like comment, such as 'had a perfect time' (19 Oct. 1910). By providing an emotional outlet, Montgomery's free-form journal allowed her overtly to articulate both her need to express her emotions and her lack of any other audience for them. Amy Andrew's more structured diary does not seem to have offered her space for such an overt expression of her self and her needs. Nonetheless, her handwriting, in both its calligraphy and orthography, reveals the rhythms of her life. The free-flowing handwriting of her early entries, during 1910–12, when she wrote out the established routines in the security of her family home, contrast with the cryptic text of the later years full of responsibility and stress. During the period 1912–14, Andrew and her young family faced sickness, uncertain weather, and financial insecurity.

Finally, there are a limited number of texts where one can get a glimpse into how women lived their lives at the beginning of the century in rural Eastern Canada, and even fewer documents which give readers a woman's view of the early decades of this century on Prince Edward Island. Amy's diary is one example of a discourse seldom exposed to public scrutiny. While L.M. Montgomery's journals have received more critical attention because of the writer's status as an artist, Amy Andrew's 'A Line a Day' diary is rich in its reference to the spatial, temporal, and textual confines of a rural woman at the turn of the century. Over a period of five years, she indicates how and where she spends her time among home, relatives, and activities in the immediate and neighbouring communities. Within those entries, she provides extensive evidence of the social relations and patterns within her family, extended family, and the community at large. Much of the emotional information surfaces only in the gaps of her entries. Yet through all her accounts, readers are constantly reminded that the subject is a woman, doing a woman's work, experiencing a woman's pain, and in a minimalist way, relating it in five lines a day.

NOTE

1 North St Eleanor's has since been incorporated into the city of Summerside.

6

'... the refuge of my sick spirit ...':
L.M. Montgomery and the Shadows
of Depression

Janice Fiamengo

> What a comfort this old journal is to me! It is my one outlet for my dark
> moods. Into it I pour the bitterness which might otherwise overflow and
> poison other lives.
>
> L.M. Montgomery, SJ, 1:287

Reflecting in October 1908 on the critical reception of *Anne of Green
Gables*, L.M. Montgomery noted: 'One of the reviews says "the book
radiates happiness and optimism." When I think of the conditions of
worry and gloom and care under which it was written I wonder at this.
Thank God, I can keep the shadows of my life out of my work' (*SJ*
1:339). A first-time reader of Montgomery's journals is likely to be
struck, as Montgomery was, by the contrast between the sunshine of
Anne and the 'shadows' of the life presented in the journals.[1] From 1903,
when she co-wrote the comic diary with Nora Lefurgey, until the time
of her marriage in 1911, Montgomery recorded periods of debilitating
sadness and anxiety. During these times, she had trouble reading and
working; at the worst, she could not sleep or eat and had 'a morbid
horror of seeing anyone' (*SJ* 1:342). Feeling trapped, hopeless, and
restless, she dreaded the future and even longed for death, recording on
one particularly miserable day in March 1904, 'I just wish I could die! I
hate the thought of living – of the miserable night before me – of getting
up tomorrow to another dull lonely day' (*SJ* 1:294). Yet despite such
misery, these were very productive years for Montgomery, during which
she launched her literary career and began to create a much-loved
public persona. In the pages that follow, I consider what this public/
private dichotomy reveals about Montgomery's self-creation in the journals she intended for posthumous publication. I argue that, in articulat-

ing the sadness she kept secret from the world, Montgomery found a powerful means not only of describing, managing, and understanding her depression, but also of justifying her life-writing project and confirming her identity as a creative artist.

Helen Buss has preceded me in noting the severity of Montgomery's black moods and the attention she paid them in her journal. Contrasting Montgomery's diary to the success story recounted in *The Alpine Path* (1917), Buss notes that the diary 'reveals a darker side' of Montgomery during the years she was caring for her grandmother and becoming a famous author (*Mapping* 165). Buss interprets the depressive episodes as 'an artist's reaction to all the silencing mechanisms of the familial and societal world in which she lived' (167). At the time a male artist would have been escaping convention to discover himself and his voice out in the world, Montgomery was shut up in her grandfather's house, a prey to unspeakable frustration. Read from a feminist perspective, Montgomery's depression was 'the result of her never having been allowed a place of her own, literally and figuratively, as woman or as artist' (167). Buss's comments are pertinent, but they move in a different direction from the one I wish to pursue here. Whereas Buss focuses on the depression as stark evidence for the conflicts that bedevil a creative woman in a patriarchal society, I am interested in the depression as a problem – and ultimately, for Montgomery, a strategy – of representation. Depression was a fact of life for Montgomery, but it also became an important discourse through which she created her life narrative.

As Laura Marcus makes clear in *Auto/biographical Discourses* (1994), life writing has generated a good deal of theorizing and debate, especially in the last two decades, because of its paradoxical positioning on the shifting border between public and private, fact and fiction, spontaneous confession and artful construction.[2] Montgomery's record of sadness invites consideration of these unstable oppositions because Montgomery was aware of herself as a public figure hiding a secret life and because she intended her journals as a contribution to the public record. Questions of genre, subjectivity, language, and intention come to the fore as we consider what exactly Montgomery is telling – and why – when she reports on her black moods. The problematic identity of the autobiographical 'I' is of particular urgency, for the 'I' who writes of depression is not the same as the suffering subject who cannot write (*SJ* 1:343): depression's moment of articulation is always after the fact, emotionally removed from the extreme state – of paralysis and despair – being described. The problem of language complicates the issue: all emotion exceeds or escapes language to some extent, but depression is often the ultimate negation, denying the sufferer not only appropriate words but even the necessary faith in or capacity for naming and describing. Montgomery tells us, 'I cannot describe how I felt and it is puerile to try' (*SJ* 1:343). Moreover, despite its visceral force, depression is intensely cultural, overlaid with moral, religious, and social dimensions even as it seems to insist on its bedrock grounding in feeling. Adding another layer of complexity is the fact that Montgomery's journals are multiply mediated and removed from the moment of experience, 'a complex process of re-reading and re-writing,' as Margaret Turner has emphasized in her article on Montgomery's autobiographical process (94). Written, rewritten, and edited in multiple versions, the truth of the journals is a carefully shaped and circumscribed one throughout. Thus even as I offer some tentative thoughts toward defining Montgomery's experience of depression, I remain aware that representation rather than definition is the issue at hand.

'... out of tune – nothing but jangling discords ...'

Periods of deep unhappiness are a feature of Montgomery's journals: in the aftermath of her engagement to Edwin Simpson and during her hopeless passion for Herman Leard during 1897–8 (see chapter 4); following her father's death in January 1900; following Frederica Campbell's death in January 1919; and in connection with her husband's mental illness, which began in the summer of 1919 and caused torment for Montgomery throughout their life together. My focus here, however, is the eight-year period of debilitating sadness recorded in the second volume of her journals. Beginning in 1903 and worsening in intensity from late 1907 until her marriage to Ewan Macdonald in 1911, she suffered a despondency that seems to surpass in intensity and duration these other periods of loss and distress. Particularly in the winter, to which she looked forward 'with inexpressible dread' (*SJ* 1:310) as a time when she was 'afraid of the dark and the wail of the wind' (*SJ* 1:294), Montgomery's journal became a record of 'moans and groans' (*SJ* 1:307). She frequently felt 'like a sick, frightened baby with no hope or strength or courage or – anything' (*SJ* 1:294). She was plagued by feelings she claimed were indescribable, asserting that 'if I could drag them [the feelings] out and put them into words it would help me. But I can't – I can't describe or define them' (*SJ* 1:294). At such

6.1 '…life…was so bitter' – journal entry of 11 February 1910. (Manuscript page. L.M. Montgomery Collection, Archival and Special Collections, University of Guelph Library.)

times, she felt her entire being to be 'out of tune – nothing but jangling discords' (*SJ* 1:304).

Was Montgomery suffering from what we would now term a mood disorder or simply from ordinary unhappiness, to use Sigmund Freud's phrase, brought on by difficult life conditions? Undoubtedly she had reasons to feel sad. She often complained, for example, of soul loneliness (*SJ* 1:255), the aching sense that she lacked a close friend with whom she could share her worries and concerns. She chafed under the strain of living with her grandmother, who became more unreasonable and exacting as she grew older. Winter frequently left Montgomery a snowbound prisoner, cut off from intellectual and physical outlets. No wonder, then, that she became 'depressed, tired, broken, a prey to indescribable and unconquerable unrest' (*SJ* 1:340). Yet her descriptions suggest a sadness more profound than ordinary frustration or loneliness; on 31 October 1908, for example, she described an 'absurd and reasonless dread which I cannot control or banish' (*SJ* 1:341). 'In so far as I can express it in words,' she wrote in 1907, 'I feel a great and awful *weariness* – not of body or brain, but of *feeling*, coupled with a heavy dread of the future – *any* future, even a happy one – nay, a happy one most of all, for in this strange mood it seems to me that to be happy would require more effort, more buoyancy, than I shall possess' (*SJ* 1:333). In after years, this period in her life became the standard against which all future suffering was measured, a unique event to which Montgomery looked back with horror and shuddering.[3]

One needs to exercise caution when defining the medical or mental condition of a writer. As Hermione Lee mentions when discussing Virginia Woolf's depressive episodes, to diagnose is to affix a label and make someone into a category when what matters is what the writer did with his or her experience: 'To name the illness is to begin a process of description which can demote [the writer's] extraordinary personality to a collection of symptoms, or reduce her writing to an exercise in therapy' (176).[4] Yet given that Montgomery devoted a significant portion of her journals during these years to describing her symptoms in detail and attempting to communicate her experience exactly, she seems to have believed her sadness worth recording, assessing, naming, and analysing. The terms and contexts she chose for her depression provide a fascinating glimpse of her cultural and personal frames of reference.

Montgomery believed that her suffering stemmed from a medical condition for which she would have sought advice had she known a competent doctor (*SJ* 1:342). She did not call her suffering *melancholia*, the nineteenth-century term for depression, probably to avoid the associations with mental disease attached to the term. (Certainly her description of her husband's religious melancholia ten years later was very pejorative.)[5] Yet she wondered on one occasion (3 May 1908) whether she was fitted to 'undertake the responsibilities of marriage' (*SJ* 1:334), a query that suggests concern about her mental health, and she mentions on a few occasions that she thought she came close to mental imbalance during her suffering.[6] Her names for her plunging moods were various: she referred to the blues (*SJ* 1:287); dark moods (*SJ* 1:287); nerves (*SJ* 1:304); a dour gloom (*SJ* 1:333); unrest (*SJ* 1:340); a nervous disorder (*SJ* 1:342); nervous prostration (*SJ* 1:392); a nervous breakdown (*SJ* 2:240); the change (*SJ* 1:343); 'terrible attacks of gloom and restlessness' (*SJ* 1:361); 'an utter breakdown of body, soul, and spirit' (*SJ* 1:392); and hell (*SJ* 1:393). Frequent references to nerves and nervous unrest (*SJ* 1:343) point to the discourse of neurasthenia, a word Montgomery used in a 1910 entry (*SJ* 1:393). Ewan's advice in 1908 that she do no writing for a month (*SJ* 1:342) reflects the classic medical response to neurasthenia, as pioneered by the famous American neurologist Silas Weir Mitchell, who forced neurasthenic women to stop intellectual pursuits. Her self-diagnosis of neurasthenia, the disease of refined and intelligent women in the late nineteenth and early twentieth centuries, reflects Montgomery's sense of herself as possessing an unusually sensitive temperament.

In the late nineteenth century, neurasthenia was a widely used term for a general psychiatric illness that Montgomery, who frequently consulted medical books, would certainly have known well.[7] Thought to be a disease of advanced societies, it was prevalent among women 'of high culture and refinement' (quoted in Showalter 140), similar to the class status of consumption, as discussed by Melissa Prycer in chapter 11. Neurasthenia was characterized by symptoms such as headaches, weeping, difficulty concentrating, worry, irritability, and neuralgia; the latter referred to acute facial pain caused by a disorder of the facial nerves and is often mentioned by Montgomery.[8] The illness was thought to be related, in women, to overly intense mental activity (Showalter 134–40). Given that one of the symptoms of neurasthenia was depression, we can see that it was a catch-all illness closely related to other, more serious, disorders such as hysteria and melancholia.

For the twenty-first-century reader, Montgomery's anxiety, sleeplessness, self-loathing, and groundless despair would probably be diagnosed as depression.[9] Her symptoms of lowered mood, loss of appetite, insomnia, psychomotor agitation, poor concentration, and thoughts of death correspond to the depression symptoms listed in the *Diagnostic and Statistical Manual of Mental Disorders* (Hales 20), and the onset of her first episode, in her late twenties, is considered medically typical of depression. 'At such hours,' she described her depressive episodes, 'I am bankrupt in hope and belief. I become convinced that I am a creature whom no one could love' (*SJ* 1:333). On Christmas Eve in 1909, she wrote that her condition was alarming: 'I feel so bitter and vindictive. I can't even cry – it would be a relief if I could' (*SJ* 1:363). During these periods, she was often 'physically ill from lack of sleep and utter inability to eat anything,' but most disturbed by the 'hideous nervous distress' and certain she would 'rather die than go through such a time again' (*SJ* 1:343). Complicating a diagnosis of depression is the fact that the episodes were relatively short-lived and confined almost exclusively to the winter season, suggesting a version of seasonal affective disorder, though Montgomery was not convinced that winter triggered her distress.[10] Certainly, the episodes interfered with her normal functioning. In later years, she was often to refer to the pain of this period, to 'those dreadful attacks of neurasthenia' (*SJ* 2:401), which undeniably played a major role in her self-conception.

One of depression's worst symptoms, for a writer, is the sense of meaninglessness that makes any communicative or artistic enterprise seem futile and empty. Montgomery refers frequently to the 'awful weariness' (*SJ* 1:333) she came to dread during these times, the 'hopeless' and 'played-out' feeling (*SJ* 1:334) that stifled initiative and creativity. 'I cannot do anything – not even read – with pleasure or satisfaction,' she recorded on 31 October 1908 (*SJ* 2:340). As Hilary Clark explains, using Julia Kristeva's work on semiotics and depression, depression is often 'experienced as a breakdown in signification: the depressive loses a sense of the power of the signifier, having difficulties with thinking and speaking' (191–2). Montgomery's determination to articulate her moods even during some very bad times signalled her refusal to lapse into silence, and her journal record constitutes an act of resistance to the debilitating effects of despair.

The problem of writing about depression was to find a language for an ineffable state of being. A close examination of Montgomery's entries on depression suggests that she moved in two discursive directions at once – the denotative and the figurative. Often she was starkly literal, stressing the monotony of sleeplessness, pacing, nervousness, dread. This insistence on the literal may have been a way to manage the chaotic subjectivity of depression through the sane orderliness of the measurable. Montgomery itemized and counted, recording the number of hours pacing the floor or lying awake. She recorded her episodes with exactitude, detailing how many days she suffered, noting whether her anxiety increased or remained constant, identifying the moment at which the mood lifted. She chose simple sentences and bare parallelism. On 31 October 1908 she wrote, 'I compel myself to work, read, sew, talk – and under it all I am nervous and tense with this absurd and reasonless dread which I cannot control or banish' (*SJ* 2:340–1). On 1 December 1908 she listed precisely the succession of suffering days: 'Wednesday evening. ... I felt the most intolerable nervous unrest, coupled with an equally intolerable dread of coming disaster. I could not sleep at all that night. Thursday was worse. I could not do anything – read, work, or eat. Thursday night again no sleep. Friday, still worse – Friday night, no sleep. As for Saturday, it was indescribable' (*SJ* 2:343). An episode in February 1910 (when, as she later revealed, she believed she was dying of cancer) was the worst ever: 'The days were only one degree less hideous than the nights. I could not eat; every mouthful had to be forced down. I could not work or think or read or talk. I was possessed by a very fury of restlessness, only to be endured by walking the floor until my limbs failed' (*SJ* 2:392).[11] Such minimalist precision suggests her belief that the quality of her suffering deserved to be communicated. The record mattered, not because pain was thereby lessened, but because itemizing it helped her resist emotional disintegration.

In addition to this literal accounting, Montgomery also used metaphors to describe her suffering. Whereas literal language worked against her erasure as subject by insisting on the 'I' who felt dread, forced down food, and compelled herself to talk, metaphorical language articulated her alienation and self-alterity. Such metaphorical language drew on two contemporary discourses of mental illness, psychiatric and religious. In one series of metaphors, she described her state of mind as an access of the irrational: the plunge into depression was an encounter with some other self, an alien yet self-engendered being. Her image of the mind here emphasized subterranean depths and recesses where dark thoughts hid, waiting to ambush her: 'Every hateful thought that ever came across my mind creeps out of its lurking place like some slimy hateful thing to which I had given birth' (*SJ* 2:333).[12] In this description, she is at once responsible and helpless, victim and author of an attack from within. She emphasizes the stubborn unreason of her moods, convinced, while in their possession, that she can never feel any other way and figuring her illness as a fretful conversation between alienated parts of herself: 'It is no use to tell myself that I have often felt so before and got over it. "Yes, those moods passed away but this will be permanent," is the unreasonable answer suffering consciousness makes' (*SJ* 2:333). A sense of impending doom assails her, which 'has no foundation in fact but reason has no effect on it' (*SJ* 1:340). Injustices and slights done to her in the past are remembered and bitterly cherished 'as if they had been churned up from some lower depths by some disturbance in my inner consciousness' (*SJ* 2:341). The language of depths, shadows, and hidden places marks her sense of the division between her knowable self and the dark, frightening non-self that assaults and overtakes her during these moods.

Montgomery also cast her self-estrangement in religious language, referring to her black moods as evil and demonic. She described walking the floor 'like one possessed of devils' (*SJ* 2:392). After a particularly bad bout of mental suffering, she felt exhausted, 'as if I had just passed through some severe struggle – a wrestling with "principalities and powers" of evil and darkness' (*SJ* 2:340). In a burst of fury, she blamed God as her tormentor, stating that she felt 'utterly rebellious ... as if God were indeed the cruel tyrant of Calvin's theology, who tortures his creatures for no fault of their own at his whim and pleasure' (*SJ* 2:363). Her hateful, bitter thoughts were 'like some foul brood engendered in darkness' (*SJ* 2:363). After a later episode, she reflected, 'I have heard hell defined as "a world from which hope was excluded." Then I was in hell for those three weeks' (*SJ* 2:393). When a dark mood finally passed, she felt 'as if I had been released from the grasp of an evil thing' (*SJ* 2:364). Work was 'blessedness' (*SJ* 2:393) when she could manage it because it took her out of thoughts of her suffering, but at her worst she 'could not work or think or read or talk' (*SJ* 2:392) and wanted only 'to die and escape life!' (*SJ* 2:392). Repeatedly, she psychologized hell to emphasize her possession by darkness and dispossession of hope, stressing the horrifying split between a self blessed by grace and one cast into eternal darkness.

Montgomery's Secret Life

As she crafted a language for her depression, Montgomery was also struggling to make sense of her suffering in relation to the practice of writing. Not unusually for a creative artist, she came to see a close and mutually reinforcing relationship between writing and suffering. The journal was a necessity, she believed, not only because she had to write but because she had to write out her pain. 'Temperaments such as mine must have some outlet,' she explained, 'else they become morbid and poisoned by "consuming their own smoke"' (*SJ* 2:1). During the years of suffering, the journal became 'the refuge of my sick spirit in its unbearable agonies' (*SJ* 2:1). Only writing made her 'able to endure' (*SJ* 2:4) a suffering so intense she occasionally feared it would unsettle her mind. In short, depression seems to have solidified and intensified Montgomery's conviction that she could not live without writing, that it was essential not only to her well-being but even to her sanity and survival.

Thus, during the time when she was reflecting on all that seemed to have been stolen from her during her early adulthood, Montgomery was also formulating a compensatory belief in the sustaining power of her life-writing project. Living with her tyrannical grandmother, for whom any mark of individuality was unacceptable – even such innocuous departures from orthodoxy as a light on at night or a bath in the evening – Montgomery began to believe that her true self only really lived on the page. The rest of her life came to seem like a sham constructed according to the dictates of her family and society while the truth lay in the pages of a journal no one else could read. In the late winter of 1903, she reflected on her private pain:

> Life has been a sorry business for me these past five years. I don't think anybody suspects this. To those around me, even my most intimate friends, I am known as a 'very jolly girl,' seemingly always light-hearted 'good company' and 'always in good spirits.' It makes me laugh rather bitterly to hear people say this. If they could only see below the mask! I am thankful they cannot. I don't want to be pitied. And pain would not be any the less because it were known – nay, it would be – for me, at least – far greater. (*SJ* 1:287)

In this passage, Montgomery both desires that her secret suffering be known (as shown in the hypothetical construction of 'If they could only see below the mask!') and rejects self-revelation ('I am thankful they cannot'). The contradiction is key to her autobiographical project, becoming one of Montgomery's most potent personal myths. She needed her journal because she needed to unburden her private self while maintaining strict privacy. Furthermore, in the process of emphasizing the division between her public and private selves, she was also hypothesizing a time when public and private would become one, imagining an ideal community of readers who would, in some obscure future, know her as no contemporaries could.

Although Montgomery had not yet explicitly stated her intention that a version of the journals be published (which appears in the entry for 16 April 1922), we can see her formulating an understanding of the journals as a record directed to a future generation. That such had long been her intention is suggested both by her careful revisions and by the aesthetic structure of the journals, which in their extensive use of narrative techniques such as character description, scene setting, flashbacks, and foreshadowing show Montgomery intensely 'alert to the concerns of an audience,' according to Lynn Bloom the hallmark of the public diary (Bloom 28).[13] Writing about her depression seems to have intensified Montgomery's sense of the journal as a testimony in reserve. Such a testimony would be, among other things, a posthumous self-tribute, in which she could reveal her pain, not in order to be pitied, but to be understood as the woman who bravely hid (and creatively articulated) a secret life that was both devastatingly painful and artistically necessary to her writing. This sense of the journal's eventual public audience allowed Montgomery to speak at once to no one ('I cannot say this to *anyone*' [*SJ* 2:399], she claimed frequently) and to the world. To borrow Paul de Man's term, Montgomery imagined her autobiography as a form of *prosopopeia*, an address from the dead, in which readers of the journals after her death would activate her 'voice-from-beyond-the-grave' (77), speaking to them of what she could tell no one while alive.

Preserving a text of suffering for readers not yet born, the journals enact the circular relationship between secret self and discursive record that has long fascinated critics such as de Man who see in autobiography the ultimate deconstruction of the writing subject. On one level, Montgomery's secret self created the journals because she had to write out what she could not otherwise tell; the journal became 'the outlet of pain and bitter experiences which none shared with me and which I could tell to no other confidant' (*SJ* 2:349). But on another level, the secret self was produced in and through the process of writing the journal; it was an effect rather than cause of the particular discursive and material circumstances of Montgomery's life-writing practice. A complex identity-in-process, Montgomery's suffering generated her lifetext and was itself textually generated as self-defining.

Montgomery's suffering was a lived experience, but in her autobiographical practice it also became an enabling fiction, a trope of self-presence and authenticity. Montgomery often found solace in the thought of how surprised her acquaintances would be to catch a glimpse of the real self she hid from them. On 31 December 1923 she recorded that a friend had remarked at dinner that few people saw 'the funny side of L.M. Montgomery.' Montgomery, in turn, commented in her journal, 'There are a good many of L.M. Montgomery's sides they don't see!' (*SJ* 3:154). There was a satisfaction in growling in her journal while reminding herself and her imagined audience, 'Nobody ever hears me growl outside of it' (*SJ* 3:160). During the years of her depression, Montgomery took pride in the depth of her reserve, which came to stand for her complexity and multi-facetedness. On 10 November 1908 she was suffering from a 'feeling of dread' and 'morbid horror of seeing anyone' (*SJ* 1:342). When she received a request from a Toronto journalist to provide details of her life, she reflected grimly: 'I'll give him the bare facts he wants. He will not know any more about the real *me* or my real life for it all, nor will his readers. The only key to *that* is found in this old journal' (*SJ* 1:342). While the experience of depression threatened to obliterate meaning, the textual sign of depression became the guarantor of the real.

In addition to marking the 'real *me*' of the journals, depression came to signal artistic creativity. During a prolonged period of dour gloom, Montgomery reflected that depression was 'the fatal shadow of the imaginative temperament. "The gods don't allow us to be in their debt." For all their so-called gifts they make us pay roundly' (*SJ* 1:333). If pain was a form of payment to the gods for unusual ability, it was also its sign, the 'fatal shadow' that conferred artistic legitimacy. Elizabeth Waterston has discussed how Montgomery's schooling in Romantic poetry influenced her verse, and undoubtedly it also contributed to her belief that mental suffering and creativity were connected, that artists had to suffer.[14] In 'Resolution and Independence,' William Wordsworth seemed to offer a prescription for the poet's life in claiming: 'We Poets in our youth begin in gladness; / But thereof come in the end despondency and madness' (48–9). Montgomery knew Wordsworth well and had probably read Samuel Taylor Coleridge's 'Dejection' and John Keats's 'Ode on Melancholy.' All three poets associated melancholy with acute perception and imaginative sensitivity. As Kay Jamison has observed in *Touched with Fire* (1993), poets of the Romantic period emphasized their deep suffering in order to differentiate themselves from non-artists. This discourse of poetic melancholy provided Montgomery with a powerfully self-confirming lens through which to view her black moods. As she commented in her entry for 31 January 1920, 'One cannot have imagination and the gift of wings, along with the placidity and contentment of those who creep on the earth's solid surface' (*SJ* 2:369–70). It was better to fly, even if pain was the price.

Montgomery had always understood herself as set apart from her fellows, distinguished from ordinary people by her imagination and affinity for language. During the period of her depression, she also came to see herself as set apart by pain. As she looked back upon her years of particular suffering, she felt that they had changed her irrevocably, deepening her character and teaching her life lessons. They were not lessons she would have chosen, but having experienced them, she emphasized their formative importance. On 23 January 1921 Montgomery reflected on her childhood friendship with Laura Pritchard. Recently, Laura and her husband had suffered financial losses necessitating their move to Saskatoon, yet Montgomery declared that she could not be friends with Laura again because Laura had not suffered as she had. She reveals an egotistical insistence on her greater pain, refusing to believe that others could have experienced equivalent losses. 'No, I don't think Laura would satisfy my demands on friendship now,' she concluded, 'not after having had my soul seared in sorrow and pain and passion for thirty years while Laura has walked only the hedged paths of happy, protected girlhood and wifehood. She would not know my language and I should have forgotten hers' (*SJ* 2:400). Montgomery's insistence that pain gave her a language others could not know reveals her understanding of suffering as a profoundly self-defining and exclusive experience.

As time went on, secret sadness became the primary rhetorical vehicle for Montgomery's articulation of her identity as woman, writer, and wife. In each case, her sense of self depended on an unknown struggle, first as a young woman fighting to resist emotional breakdown, then as an author striving to keep personal sadness out of her art, and finally as a wife covering for her morbid and suicidal husband. So exclusive, in fact, was her focus on self-defining private pain that Montgomery's account of her husband's mental illness tends to figure it, not as his own malady, but as a grotesque externalization of her personal hell. Though more severe, Ewan's illness was not dissimilar to Montgomery's earlier depressive episodes: both sufferers experienced weakness, sleeplessness, restless anxiety, headache, despair. Reason had no effect on their dread. Ewan, as Montgomery had done, 'walked the floor ceaselessly' (*SJ* 2:329). Yet Montgomery's reaction to Ewan's illness seemed to deny its terrible separateness as his, almost as if her appropriation of pain as a discourse of self-identity left no room to imagine the suffering of another. She declared in the midst of his breakdown in 1919: 'The very hardest part of my trial was this same lack of sympathy on Ewan's part' (*SJ* 2:324). She saw Ewan's illness as a trial that she suffered, during which once again she had to hide her pain from the outside world, covering her anxiety with cheerful conversation. She described him as a burden to shoulder, his presence 'an incubus' (*SJ* 2:325) causing 'horror and repulsion' (*SJ* 2:340). Isolated by pride, need, and social convention, Montgomery figured Ewan's mental anguish as an extension of her own.

So convincing has been Montgomery's writing of her painful story, in fact, that some readers of the journals have tended to accept her characterization of Ewan (see fig. I.2), discussing him unsympathetically as an uncongenial partner and seeing his illness as a drain on his wife's time and energy. Buss, for example, regrets the time Montgomery had to spend as caregiver and describes Ewan as 'a husband who, if the diaries are any indication, saw his wife's talent, when he noticed it at all in his increasing self-absorption in his illness, as secondary, as adjunct, to their real lives as clergyman and wife' (169). If we were studying a male diarist recounting his wife's failures of sympathy, would we be so willing to accept his version of the story? Would we be so flippant in dismissing a partner's mental illness? Mary Rubio and Elizabeth Waterston are more cautious about accepting Montgomery's portrait of Ewan, but in their introduction to the second volume of *The Selected Journals*, they do report as fact that he 'provided scant intellectual companionship' and 'did not respond to beauty in nature or to any kind of aesthetic experience' (*SJ* 2:xiii). By the time the third volume was published, their introduction raises the question of Montgomery's objectivity: 'Does she reshape the man in order to strengthen the image of herself as long-suffering, ingenious in hiding his malady from the world?' (*SJ* 3:xii).[15] We need to recognize more fully how Montgomery's characterization of her suffering may have affected her portrayal of her husband's illness. Indeed, a new sub-discipline of autobiography studies now focuses on personal accounts of illness, considering their function as 'both "cure" and consolation' (Smith and Watson, *A Reader* 40) and emphasizing their complex narrative shaping.

Montgomery herself concluded that she had overemphasized pain in the second volume of her journals, shaping an excessively 'bitter and tragic' story (*SJ* 2:1). Looking back at the volume as she began a new one, she stated that it gave a false impression 'of a morbid tempera-ment' (*SJ* 2:1). She had written only of the bad times, omitting the periods in between when she 'was quite tolerably happy, hopeful and interested in life' (*SJ* 2:1). Still, she did not revise her account of the period. A decade later, on 30 January 1921, she reflected of that time when 'what should have been the best years of my life were years of such ghastly, long-drawn-out loneliness and suffering as make me shud-der in the recollection' (*SJ* 2:401). She saw the period as a watershed in her development as a person and as a writer. Out of that time, she forged a language and created a compelling and troubling personal myth. She mined her suffering for symbols and meanings: it came to define her complexity, validate her secret testimony, and justify her need and ability to write. Lacking 'the spur of pain,' she reflected, she might not have 'climbed so high' (*SJ* 1:393).

My focus on depression as a discourse rather than a biographical fact may appear to ignore the truth of the author's experience, making Montgomery's pain into a mere rhetorical effect, but such is not my intention. Reading the pain-filled journal entries, a reader vividly en-counters Montgomery's secret self even while conscious of the rhetori-cal means by which such a compelling interiority was created. Montgomery's writing of depression is never merely a fiction; rather, it is a complex process involving self-disclosure and self-construction that must have required remarkable determination and courage. In insisting that 'the worst as well as the best must be written out' (*SJ* 2:1), Mont-gomery crafted an autobiographical 'I' whose record of private pain had the power to shatter and rebuild her public identity; in turning pain into a strategy of self-articulation, she successfully resisted depression's sentence of meaninglessness and despair.

NOTES

1 For a fascinating account of readers' hurt and anger in response to the journals, see Rubio's '"A Dusting Off": An Anecdotal Account of Editing the L.M. Montgomery Journals,' 71–4.

2 Marcus provides an excellent overview of recent auto/biographical theory, especially concerning the autobiographical subject as debated by human-ist, formalist, and deconstructive critics (179–228).

3 On 18 March 1917 she reflected on 'how terrible' the winters were before her grandmother died, stressing that 'I am often – very often – tired and

worried. But I never have any of the terrible days or hours of nervous agony I suffered then' (*SJ* 2:212). She repeated the comparison on 30 January 1921: 'Life is strenuous enough still and holds many baffling and perplexing problems yet; but at least I do not have to wrestle with such periods of nervous agony' (*SJ* 2:401).

4 On the question of writing as therapy, however, see Hilary Clark's persuasive account of how writing poetry for Anne Sexton 'functioned as a temporary stay of self-execution' (204), helping her to find meaning and positive identity in the face of suicidal depression. Montgomery wrote because she felt she had to, and although her writing should not be seen solely as a form of self-healing, it seems inarguable that writing helped her cope with her depression.

5 When referring to her discovery of Ewan's illness, her language is that of nineteenth-century degeneration theory: she reports that she is horror-stricken that 'I had married, all unknowingly, a man who was subject to recurrent constitutional melancholia, and I had brought children into the world who might inherit the taint. It was a hideous thought' (*SJ* 2:323). After persuading Ewan to see a nerve specialist in Toronto, a Dr Garrick, Montgomery was relieved to be told 'that Ewan's malady was simple melancholia' rather than 'manic depressive insanity' (*SJ* 2:330).

6 On 7 February 1910 she wrote, 'I thank God I do not come of a stock in which there is any tendency to insanity. If I had I believe that my mind would have given way hopelessly' (*SJ* 1:392).

7 See, for example, her hunting up of 'all the "doctor's books" in the house' (*SJ* 2:240) when she fears she has found a tumour in her breast; also, she immediately consulted a medical encyclopedia when Ewan told her of his damnation fears, finding that 'he had every symptom given in the encyclopedia on that type of insanity' (*SJ* 2:322).

8 She refers to 'neuralgia in my face' on 10 November 1908 (*SJ* 1:342) and, again, 'facial neuralgia' on 7 February 1910 (*SJ* 1:392).

9 For a comprehensive overview of the symptoms of depression, see Schwartz and Schwartz, 5–22.

10 She is contradictory on this point. On 12 April 1903 she wrote, 'I think the weather is largely responsible for my blues' (*SJ* 1:287), but on 10 November 1908 she reported that the days 'have been cold, wet and dull; and though this is not the cause of my suffering it aggravates it' (*SJ* 1:342).

11 See the entry for 25 February 1918 for an explanation of her cancer scare (*SJ* 2:240–1).

12 That Montgomery had a conception of the subconscious is clear from a number of entries, for example, that of 19 July 1918, when she explains

table-rapping as a product of 'that mysterious part of it [the mind] known as the subconscious mind' (*SJ* 2:256).

13 Whereas private diaries written solely for personal use tend to be terse, decontextualized, and lacking in narrative shape or interpretative comment, diaries intended as public documents are 'artfully shaped to accommodate an audience' (Bloom 28).

14 See also Epperly's *Fragrance* (1992) for a very illuminating discussion of the influence of the Romantic and Victorian-Romantic poets on Montgomery's fiction (3–14).

15 Rubio explores this question of objectivity fully in reference to Montgomery's scathing accounts of careless maids ('"A Dusting Off"' 66–70).

PART 3

WRITING FOR AN INTIMATE AUDIENCE

The earlier essays in this book have demonstrated Montgomery's performative flair in writing and imaging herself. Part 3 amplifies and expands this focus on drama but documents, more specifically, that the theatre of life writing involves the engagement of an audience. The audience may be a 'fictive reader,' that is, an ideal confidante projected into the journal, a listener who does not talk back or pass judgment, but sympathizes. Indeed, as Sidonie Smith and Julia Watson have noted, autobiographical texts, whether diaries or self-images, are always performative, 'situated addresses that invite their readers' collaboration in producing specific meanings of the life' (*Interfaces* 11). In the essay opening this section, Elizabeth Epperly discusses the scrapbooks as a form of visual life writing and proposes that in this self-portrait collage, Montgomery imagined for herself a community as a counter to loneliness. The second essay, by Joy Alexander, returns to the journals to argue that Montgomery's conversational style not only was designed to establish a relationship with the implied audience but also underlies all of Montgomery's writing. In the third essay, the audience discussed is no longer fictive but literal, as Paul and Hildi Tiessen investigate Montgomery's epistolary relationship with Ephraim Weber, a lifelong friend and pen pal; even he, the essay suggests, was stylized as an ideal reader. In considering the role of the intimate audience in Montgomery's personal writings, then, we realize that the writing self cannot be understood as a fixed self involved in a purely narcissistic, mirroring relationship with only itself. Rather, the self addresses an intimate – if imagined – community.

7

Visual Drama: Capturing Life in L.M. Montgomery's Scrapbooks

Elizabeth R. Epperly

... this afternoon I was in the attic looking over some old scrapbooks ... the ghostly charm of the old books seized hold of me and I stayed longer than I should ... turning over their yellowing leaves.

L.M. Montgomery, *SJ*, 3:314

When so much of our consciousness is visual, or nonverbal, how much of it can we convey through the limited medium of words?

Jill Ker Conway, *When Memory Speaks*, 3

Always an avid record-keeper as well as shaper of stories, L.M. Montgomery kept personal scrapbooks from (at least) age nineteen until her early sixties, roughly from 1893 to 1937. Most of the time that she was taking photographs, writing long letters, filling volumes of diaries, and collecting clippings of her own published poems and stories, she was also keeping personal scrapbooks.[1] These six scrapbooks, especially the early ones, are filled with mixed-media collage and arrangements of pressed flowers, magazine cut-outs, cats' fur, greeting cards and invitations, photographs, jokes, secrets, and souvenirs. Packed with images, both collected and created, the scrapbooks capture parts of Montgomery's internal and surrounding dramas that the letters and journals often do not cover or only just mention.

The scrapbooks are an intimate form of autobiography, filled as they are with the remnants and mementoes of daily life Montgomery chose to preserve. Neither straightforwardly chronological nor fully annotated, the scrapbooks tease and suggest, celebrate and obscure. Studying the scrapbooks offers surprises and affirmations about Montgomery's sense of humour and tragedy, and about her need to construct an enriching context for herself and her work. Most of all, perhaps, the scrapbooks suggest Montgomery's passion for drama.

It can be argued that Montgomery is always telling and reshaping her own story, whether she is writing letters, journals entries, or indeed poetry or fiction. Even her photographs suggest stories about herself and her context. Whether she is describing Anne's raptures over the White Way of Delight or photographing the enticing keyhole of light around the bend in the path of Lover's Lane, Montgomery is suggesting to us a (late Victorian-Romantic) story about how she sees and feels (Epperly, 'Visual'). In the letters and journals, we experience direct forms of autobiography, and in them we find Montgomery artistically revising materials, altering personae, and shaping events to suit an imagined or real audience and to paint herself as heroine of her own story. In their scholarly work with the journals, Mary Rubio and Elizabeth Waterston have been offering us for years insights into Montgomery's creative refashioning of events as she shaped the story of her career with herself as beleaguered but resourceful artist (*SJ* 1:xix–xxiv; *SJ* 2:ix–xix; *SJ* 3:x–xxv; *SJ* 4:xi–xxviii; *Writing a Life*, passim; and see their essay in this collection).

Even before Montgomery became famous and determined that she wanted her journals to be published after her death, she was creating personae to tell her story in the most favourable light. When she wrote her first letter to George Boyd MacMillan, for example, she recreated herself as a twenty-six-year-old woman, when she was already twenty-nine (*MDMM* 2). She passed herself off to MacMillan as becomingly diffident – even offhanded – about the acceptance of *Anne of Green Gables,* calling it '... a juvenilish story of and for girls but I rather hope some grown-ups will like it, too' (*MDMM* 35), when she had confessed to her diary a month before that the realization of her dream of writing a book and having it published 'is sweet – almost as sweet as the dream!' (*SJ* 1:331). When Montgomery began to recopy the journals in 1919, we strongly suspect she recast earlier parts of her story so that events would conform with her later responses to them. This reshaping is perfectly consistent with the patterns of women's autobiography, in which, Sidonie Smith reminds us, the woman 'constructs a narrative that promises both to capture the specificities of personal experience and to cast her self-interpretation in a timeless, idealized mold for posterity' (*A Poetics* 45). This 'idealized mold' involves creating a complex persona, what Smith calls a 'narrating "I"' and a 'narrated "I,"' and then 'fracturing the narrated "I" into multiple speaking postures' (47). This complex 'I' suffers daily during the First World War, is the (sincerely) inconsolable artist when her muse and soulmate (Frederica) dies, is the righteous victor in the eight-and-a- half-year lawsuit with the Pages, and is the domestic martyr of her husband's illness. By casting herself as the heroine of her story, a story she has determined will become public, Montgomery claims her voice and her place as artist. She rehearses this public telling of her own story in *Emily of New Moon* (1923), giving Emily much of her background and many of her feelings and challenges (Epperly, *Fragrance* 145–207), and even ending the novel with the words she meant to be a joke for the knowing reader years later. Emily writes in her Jimmy book, 'I am going to write a diary, that it may be published when I die' (*ENM* 355).

Ribbons and Robins, Wallpapers and Worsteds

What about the scrapbooks? How do they share the heroic and shaping 'I' of the letters, journals, and fiction? The scrapbooks, like Montgomery's photographs, offer direct access to images she created and collected from a context she was determined to appropriate and enrich. Montgomery fed her visual imagination with scenes from nature, some of which she captured in photographs and certainly transformed into poetry and poetic description. She also fed her imagination and her passion for colour through looking at magazines from her time. Dozens of them passed through her hands in the Cavendish kitchen post office; she was able to share annotated lists of these with young George Boyd MacMillan, who also aspired to publish in new journals.[2] The illustrations, poems, stories, lithographs and engravings, and coloured advertisements in these magazines made deep impressions on her. She cut out images from them and arranged them in her scrapbooks, sometimes in the early years using her own deep-blue cyanotypes to accompany magazine clippings.

As in the journals, with their pasted-in pages replacing razored-out ones, Montgomery replaced some images in the scrapbooks years later, perhaps obliterating earlier interests or making the old pages speak to more recent events in her life. For example, the very last page of the first volume of the scrapbooks has a newspaper drawing of a bride with its headline announcing, 'I was a bride in 1903,' and close to it, a tiny clipping containing the wedding notice of Laura Pritchard, of Saskatchewan schooldays, to Andrew Agnew (fig. 7.1). On the same

7.1   'I was a bride in 1903' – wedding notice of Laura Pritchard. Last page of the first Island scrapbook. (CM67.5.15. Courtesy of the Lucy Maud Montgomery Birthplace. Digital image by the Confederation Centre Art Gallery and Museum.)

page, she pasted three small, rectangular souvenir Canadian National Railway photographs with minute identifying labels. Looking at these quickly, and recognizing them as belonging to the same series of souvenir photographs found in several other pages in the scrapbook, I assumed they belonged to Montgomery's trip to Prince Albert in 1890. I suspected they were Notman images (which the pictures of the railroads may well be), possibly belonging to the Maple Box Portfolio prepared after the Prince of Wales visited Canada in the 1860s (see Skidmore). A closer look, however, shows that one of the three last-page photographs has the tiny caption 'Mt. Edith Cavell, Jaspar National Park' (USB, CM67.5.15. IBC). The National Park Act was not in force until 1930, and Edith Cavell was the British nurse who became a heroine and martyr of the First World War when she was executed by the Germans in 1915. Obviously at least one – if not all – of these souvenir cards dates from the 1930s and was probably obtained on Montgomery's trip to Saskatchewan in 1930, when she visited Laura Pritchard Agnew to renew old ties. Perhaps she even took the old scrapbook with her to share with Laura and replaced old photographs or mementoes with new ones. The faded and fragile condition of the scrapbook pages makes it difficult to tell if and when some images have been changed, although there are a few places where a photograph or clipping has been placed overtop of the glued and printed remains of an earlier and now unrecognizable piece. Over time, in the two early scrapbooks at least, flowers and souvenirs have simply crumbled or fallen out. In any case, it should come as no surprise that the scrapbooks, like the recopied journals, were edited by Montgomery.

If the heroic story developed in Montgomery's collective journals sometimes resembles what Sidonie Smith calls the more 'androcentric genre' (*A Poetics* 52) of public memoir, then perhaps it is in the scrapbooks where we may find glorious gynocentric play. With very few words, the images capture and suggest stories, using great splashes of colour, lush magazine bouquets of flowers, fashion plates, and mementoes glued to cards that bear sentimental or humorous quotations and mysterious inscriptions or series of initials. There are ribbons and robins, wallpapers and worsteds. The variety of materials is itself revealing, as are the arrangements of them. In the scrapbooks, we find the things of daily life given a new significance as they form parts of Montgomery's visual story of her (inner) life.

The scrapbooks are indeed a visual chronicle of Montgomery's imaginative life, taking the form, in the Cavendish years especially, of exuberant play with colours, paper, fabrics, scissors, and glue. Just as the photographs offer ways to see Montgomery seeing the world around her, so the scrapbooks offer ways to see her collecting and recreating from the Island world, but also from the larger world she wished to claim as her context, her imaginative community. The scrapbooks borrow quotations and images from other writers, and as you read through them, you feel that Montgomery is creating in her scrapbook pages a community of her own that claims kinship with such writers she admired as Scott and Burns, but also with those she knew and corresponded with: Frank Monroe Beverley, Ephraim Weber, George Boyd MacMillan, Miriam Zieber, and Lucy Lincoln Montgomery. In the diaries, she fashions the events and reading of her life into a heroic story, and in the scrapbooks, she creates, in effect, postcards from a larger world – preserving the colours, the literary bits, the fashion, in an imaginative home for her writing self.

More than just storing images, the scrapbooks – like the journals and letters – tell, conceal, and suggest stories. Studying the scrapbooks made me realize how much and in how many ways Montgomery experienced drama. Montgomery played with scenes all her career, sometimes making the volumes of journals seem like one long, long drama. Perhaps it is no accident that as early as 1898 she compared talking about Lower Bedeque without mentioning Herman Leard to 'the play of Hamlet with Hamlet left out' (*SJ* 1:204). Then she crafted for the diary those unforgettably steamy scenes with Hamlet very much in (*SJ* 1:208–18). The scrapbooks create glimpses of scenes. In the early years, Montgomery even covered little white cards with comic bits of dialogue snatched from the gatherings she attended.

In fact, perhaps we may read Montgomery's life as one great (performed/recorded) drama. I suggest this passion for drama, together with her powerfully visual imagination, makes the scrapbooks especially rich life writing. In an essay entitled 'Mimesis: The Dramatic Lineage of Auto/Biography,' Evelyn Hinz describes the elements of, and impulses in, autobiography that I suggest can help us to see Montgomery's scrapbooks as rich sites of visual drama. Hinz talks about 'pictorial metaphors' ('Mimesis' 196) used in autobiography, hence the use, as in this collection of essays, of 'self-portrait' for various forms of life writing. According to Hinz, autobiography, rather than being akin to narrative and thus to prose fiction, is really dramatic and finds its sister art in drama. She outlines the three elements that many autobiographies have in common and then identifies these with drama, finding the best definitions in Aristotle's *Poetics*. Autobiographies, she says, share: 'an element of conflict and dialogue, a sense of performance / or spectatorship, and a mimetic or referential quality' (195). This definition fits Montgomery's journals well, and it also fits the scrapbooks. The 'conflict and dialogue' of the scrapbook pieces may be found in their juxtapositions and in their reflection of other written pieces by Montgomery; the 'sense of performance / or spectatorship' is everywhere apparent since the scrapbooks must rely on the arrangement of materials for their visual drama to work – and in some places, Montgomery's annotations are even written as though for someone else to enjoy; and the scrapbooks are 'mimetic' in their constant references to life and real-life actions, composed as they are of artefacts commenting on or representing life around Montgomery.

Leaving aside explicit treatment of the sense of spectatorship and the power of the mimetic in this essay, I would like to address this question: how do the scrapbooks visually suggest, create, and capture dramatic 'conflict and dialogue'? Montgomery arranges the images themselves so that they sometimes seem to speak to and among each other. Sometimes the images may even form part of a dialogue among Montgomery's own texts – between or among journal entries, letters, her fiction – or between Montgomery and the newspapers and magazines she read. We can no more go to the scrapbooks on their own to interpret Montgomery's life than we can rely entirely on the journals, letters, photographs, or fiction on their own to explain fully how Montgomery felt about or saw events. Yet among these we gain a sense of the complexity and tenor of her responses, if not a clear picture. Even without clear references – a form of dialogue – among the texts, we can appreciate something of the individual dramas and conflicts the images suggest.

Of the hundreds of suggested dialogues and conflicts creating visual drama in the scrapbooks, let me describe four: the first involves a conflict bemoaned in the journals and referenced in the scrapbook by an ironic placement of images; the second involves images that make a startling statement because of their placement side-by-side, even without a possible explanation in the later published journals; the third involves a concentration of images and artefacts unexplained in the published journals and made clear only through an unpublished diary; the fourth involves a mass of images scattered through dozens of pages that collectively amplify considerably a story sketched in the published journals and later transformed into fiction. In all four cases, the scrapbooks' images on their own are arresting, and their recreated contexts make their tensions and conflicts speak.

Mount of Venus at High Court

First, the ironic reference. From her journals, we know that after Montgomery broke her engagement to Edwin Simpson, she continued for several years to be disturbed by his letters or his presence. It was especially difficult to see him when he came to Bay View and preached in Cavendish in August 1903 since Maud felt so self-conscious around him and feared many were whispering about their suspected earlier relationship (*SJ* 1:288–9). Simpson shows up in these early scrapbooks through several clippings and coded messages, but the single most visually arresting placement of items on a page involves clippings, an odd piece of stitching, and a diagram. What attracts the eye immediately on this page with several clippings are three contiguous items: a small square of white cloth with a chicken roughly stitched in black yarn; beneath it a magazine cut-out of a palmist's diagram of the areas to be read on a palm; and beside them both a clipping about a public gathering with the prominent headline 'High Court of Foresters at Tignish: An Interesting Session Closed' (USB, CM67.5.12, p. 11). The comic chicken and the palm are directly lined up, with the chicken centred above the fingertips of the hand; the most prominent part of the palm, the base of the thumb, is labelled the 'Mount of Venus,' and this right thumb seems to be pointing to the headline of the centrally placed headline 'High Court.' These three items suggest a comic story of some kind, with Venus involved and the court session finally ending, 'An Interesting Session Closed.' On closer inspection, one notices that immediately beneath the palm, placed squarely and deliberately below the wrist as though it is a cuff, is a very small clipping that reads 'Rev. Edwin Simpson of Illinois and Burton Simpson of Acadia College are visiting in Bay View. The former occupied the pulpit of the Cavendish Baptist Church on Sunday evening.' Interestingly, another coded reference to this same Cavendish visit is found thirty-three pages later in the scrapbook. There, on a page of poetic pieces and a calendar for March, Montgomery glues in a calendar for August, on which she has circled Monday, August 12th. Below the small inserted calendar she writes, 'August 12, 1903 Trial by Fire' (USB, CM67.5.12, p. 44). What appears in the published journals that reinforces the notion of drama captured in the scrapbooks is actually a small scene, stage-crafted by Montgomery. On 23 August 1903 Maud sets up a scene, with stage directions and dialogue, as a sample of the torturing moments she has endured about Ed's visit:

> **Scene:** Mrs. Alec Macneill's parlor. Mrs. A. Macneill, crocheting in foreground. Maud, in centre of stage, netting. Lu to right, Fannie to left, slightly in background, embroidering pillow shams.
>
> **Mrs. Alec:** Were you up to hear Mr. Simpson preach last Sunday evening, Maud?
>
> **Maud:** Oh, yes. (Misses a loop in her netting.)
>
> **Mrs. Alec:** Isn't he just a splendid preacher?
>
> **Maud:** Very good. (Feels Lu and Fannie exchanging significant smiles behind her back.)
>
> **Mrs. Alec:** And I think he's very fine looking, don't you?
>
> **Maud:** Oh yes. (Nets furiously and says 'Darn' under her breath.)
> (*SJ* 1:288–9)

Reading the journal entries together with the scrapbooks shows Maud envisioning her ordeal as a drama and taking pains to record her 'centre of stage' martyrdom with wry humour. Twenty-three years later when she records in her journal an afternoon of looking over the old scrapbooks, she singles out the tiny article quoted above about Simpson's visit to Cavendish, and says this: 'A very harmless, commonplace note. Yet there was much behind it for me of unpleasant emotions. I often wonder when reading similar notices in the papers today what is behind them all of human passion and joy and fate. It would not be a bad idea for a series of stories, eh?' (*SJ* 3:316).

The second example (fig. 7.2) of compressed drama is striking even without reference to the journals. Two items stand out on this page containing several small clippings and (another) magazine picture: the large headline of a newspaper column and a large black-and-white magazine cut-out (USB, CM67.5.12, p. 53). The clipping concerns Montgomery's elderly cousin, the father of Amanda, William C. Macneill. The long, large headline reads: 'A Sad Suicide: Victim Was William C. McNeill [*sic*] of Cavendish: Body Was Found Last Night Lying Face Downward in Clark's Pond, in a Foot and a Half of Water.' Beside the column of print is a large, black-and-white magazine photograph of a widely grinning Lewis Morrison as Mephistopheles from a production of *Faust* – the very actor we assume Montgomery saw years before in

7.2   'A Sad Suicide: Victim Was William C. McNeill of Cavendish' – clippings that appear side-by-side in the second Island scrapbook, p. 53. (CM67.5.12. Courtesy of the Lucy Maud Montgomery Birthplace. Digital image by the Confederation Centre Art Gallery and Museum.)

1895 in Halifax, since she pasted the program with his name in it into her earlier scrapbook (USB, CM67.5.15, p. 68). It is possible that the photograph came to hand just as she had reached this page in her scrapbook, but that seems unlikely. It is intriguing to speculate on what this arrangement meant to Montgomery and when she actually assembled the page. Perhaps she saw some parallel between Goethe's play and the circumstances of William C. Macneill's death. Interestingly, there is nothing in the published journals about the suicide of 3 May 1907 until 27 September 1917, when Montgomery recorded her dismay over the unhappily married Amanda's complaints about her husband:

> If she would control her own diabolical temper he would be good enough to her. If she does *not* control that same temper she will end up as her wretched old father did in insanity and suicide. Shall I ever forget that night after his death and the way Amanda behaved! It was enough to make one believe the old legends of devil possession. (*SJ* 2:225)

By 1917, Montgomery had been living in Ontario for six years and had moved into the fourth volume of scrapbooks. She may have edited the early scrapbook page when she wrote the journal entry about Amanda's temper, but it is more likely that, in thinking about Amanda, she hunted up the early scrapbook entry with the suicide article and picture of Mephistopheles, and this earlier coded drama may have inspired her to use 'diabolical' and 'devil possession' to describe William C. Macneill's daughter, Amanda.

The page and the arrangement become even more suggestive when we look closely at two other items lying close to these central, commanding two. Oddly, glued right to the bottom of the suicide article, so that at a glance it seems almost part of the same piece, is the wedding announcement of Montgomery's cousin Laura McIntyre to Calgary native R.B. Aylesworth. And beneath the suicide/wedding article and also beneath the large photograph of Morrison's Mephistopheles is a magazine photograph of Prince Albert, Saskatchewan. One wonders if the photograph of Prince Albert has any relationship to the contiguous photograph of Mephistopheles or to the suicide. Perhaps the connection is as whimsical as this: at her father's home, Eglinton Villa in Prince Albert, Mephistopheles was the name of one of the cats; his fur is preserved in the first volume of the scrapbooks (USB, CM67.5.15, p. 37). In any case, the two items that capture the eye on this page speak loudly to each other and suggest many possible levels of complex internal and community drama.

The third example involves several pages that correspond roughly to Nora Lefurgey's time, 1902–3, teaching in the Cavendish school. In the early pages of the second Island scrapbook there are numerous items I was at a loss to explain using the published journals as a guide. Why was this bit of stick put into a greeting card next to a squashed green velvet rose, and what did the annotations for both of them mean (USB, CM67.5.12, p. 23)? On another page close to this one, who was the woman in the cyanotype (see fig. 7.3) standing outdoors in the snow, and what was the significance of the coin and the straw bow? Most of all, I puzzled over why Montgomery had taken a small white card and written on it, beside a piece of yellow ribbed satin pasted there, a heading 'Lost, Stolen, or Strayed' (see fig. 7.3), beneath which she added:

Chap. I   A mysterious disappearance
Chap. II   A disconsolate girl
Chap. III   A long-suffering girl
Chap. IV   The lost is found (USB, CM67.5.12, p. 19)

It was not until, with the help of Jennifer Litster, I located in the Guelph archives the unpublished typescript of the secret diary Nora and Maud kept (see chapters 2 and 3) that I knew the comedy to which these intriguing items belonged. While younger schoolteacher Nora boarded at the Macneill farm for the first six months of 1903, these women created their own hilarious fun by writing in a joint diary about their mock triumphs and tribulations, competing for the attention of men, quarreling about Nora's supposed theft of Maud's yellow garter, and borrowing each other's cameras to take pictures that turned up surprises in the darkroom for the unsuspecting victim (hence the cyanotype of Nora in the snow). From the diary, I found out that Maud and Nora competed to 'swipe' things and Maud stored some of her loot in the scrapbook, no doubt to the pretended envy and scorn of Nora (we do not know if Nora kept her own scrapbook). Among the mementoes Maud preserved, we also find many white cards, some of them comic minutes from the Cavendish Literary Society meetings and some of them bits of coded dialogue and jokes referred to in the secret diary. The lively pages concerning Nora's and Maud's activities must have furnished Maud with many a laugh and sigh as she looked back over the evidence of and recreations of comic scenes.

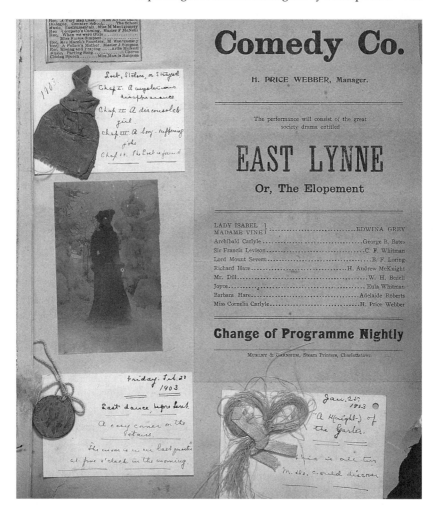

7.3 'Lost, Stolen, or Strayed' – the yellow garter (top, left); Nora Lefurgey in the snow, cyanotype (middle, left); 'A K(night) of the Garter' (bottom, right). (Courtesy of the Lucy Maud Montgomery Birthplace. Digital image by the Confederation Centre Art Gallery and Museum.)

On 30 July 1905, when she would have been immersed in the writing of *Anne of Green Gables*, Montgomery looked back through her old scrapbook and found pictures of puffed sleeves that she may have found inspirational (*SJ* 1:309); perhaps she looked back at the comic, secret diary and the comic souvenirs of the scrapbook when she created the high spirits of Anne and her chums in *Anne of Avonlea* and *Anne of the Island* or of Emily and Ilse in *Emily Climbs*.

The fourth example of visual drama is scattered over many pages in the Guelph red scrapbooks (USB, X25 MS A002). It is not until one views all of the pages concerning the First World War together that one sees a particular drama emerging, the story of the heroism of Col. Sam Sharpe and of the 116th Ontario County Battalion he raised and commanded. Several of the Leaskdale and Uxbridge parish youths joined the battalion,[3] and Montgomery, including some of her own photographs, described the 116th's final route march in the journal pages. At the same time, she was also keeping a record of clippings, photographs, and mementoes in her scrapbook. The large cluster of clippings concerning Col. Sharpe's death made me go back over the pages several times and to look at them with the journal entries in mind. The story of Col. Sharpe is more prominent in the scrapbooks than in the journals, as though Montgomery is creating parallel stories with different emphases.

Montgomery mentions MP Sam Sharpe of Uxbridge several times in her diaries. She watched his battalion, though she does not name him, march past her front door in 1916, photographing Chester under the arch that was erected right at their gate for the soldiers (*SJ* 2:184); she voted for him for Parliament when she was able to cast her very first ballot (*SJ* 2:235); she attended his military funeral after his tragic suicide in 1918 (*SJ* 2:247); she had tea with his widow (*SJ* 2:308). The scrapbooks capture a much more involved and powerful story. Since Mrs Sharpe's calling card appears among the wedding and honeymoon pages, we assume Mrs Sharpe called on the new minister's wife when she first arrived in Leaskdale. Maud Macdonald would have had fairly frequent contact with the Sharpes' circle of Uxbridge elite through the Hypatia Club, for which Montgomery served as honorary head (the Guelph scrapbooks preserve many of the Hypatia Club programs). The scrapbooks have dozens of clippings involving Sharpe – including election returns and articles announcing the formation of the 116th Ontario County Battalion. There are pictures in the scrapbook that she did not paste into the journal – one shows Sharpe's soldiers as they march uphill in Leaskdale. There are postcards of Sharpe's house in Uxbridge, probably made when he was an electioneering MP and before he was the commander of the battalion he led overseas. Scattered through the pages, one finds clippings about the 116th Battalion while it is overseas. Even these pages alone suggest that the story of Col. Sharpe had far more prominence in Montgomery's life than the journal entries describe. If Montgomery was among the crowd waiting at the station in May 1918 to meet Col. Sharpe returning triumphantly from his years overseas and in an English hospital recovering from shell-shock, then she heard the telegram announcing to the horrified crowd that Sharpe had leapt from the window of a Montreal hospital while supposedly taking a rest on his journey home.

Montgomery does not say in the journals how she felt about the death of the man she had probably met many times. The scrapbook suggests that his death was big news for his community and his constituency. The Uxbridge-Scott Museum has a photograph showing a huge crowd of mourners standing and waiting outside the Sharpes' home for the private funeral service. Columns of clippings and stories in the scrapbooks tell differently the same story again and again – of Sharpe's heroism under fire, of his confidence in his men, of his gallantry and bravery generally. The Uxbridge-Scott Museum's large binder of articles about Sharpe shows his prominent and successful political career as well as his military one; Uxbridge's war memorial features Col. Sharpe, heading the list of the 116th Battalion's dead from the community. Sharpe was a local hero, and Montgomery's scrapbooks show us a vivid part of Sharpe's career that the journals do not describe. Similarly, the journals do not tell us that Mrs Norman Beale, who was Montgomery's friend in Uxbridge and later gave so many elegant society teas for Montgomery in Toronto, was Col. Sharpe's niece (McGillivray 61).

Montgomery scanned her scrapbooks, knowing how, as Paul John Eakin suggests in *Fictions in Autobiography*, 'materials of the past are shaped by memory and imagination to serve the needs of the present' (quoted in Hinz, 'Mimesis' 198). Just as Montgomery probably drew on her scrapbook recollections of hilarity during her Prince of Wales, Bideford, and Halifax days (as well as with Nora in Cavendish) to enliven her portraits of female friendships, so she no doubt drew from the scrapbooks, as well as the journals, to enrich *Rilla of Ingleside* and her presentation of heroism during wartime.

Certainly, Montgomery did make use of Col. Sharpe's 116th Ontario County Battalion march in *Rilla*, having the Ingleside folk witness the stirring sight of Island men parading as they prepare to leave for Europe. In her journal, Montgomery used her own photograph of the memorial arch outside her gate and said this on 19 May 1916 of Col. Sharpe's men:

> This was quite a day in the annals of our little village. The 116th Battalion which has been training in Uxbridge all winter and to which many of 'our boys' belong made a route march through the township and passed here at noon. We had several arches erected for them and treated them all to fruit and read them an address. Poor fellows. I wonder how many of them will ever return. (*SJ* 2:184)

In Rilla's diary in the novel, dated 20 June 1916, the march becomes intimate and personal, with names and stories of the local soldiers:

> It was wonderful and heartbreaking to see the battalion marching past. There were young men and middle-aged men in it. There was Laurie MacAllister from over-harbour who is only sixteen but swore he was eighteen, so that he could enlist; and there was Angus Mackenzie, from the Upper Glen who is fifty-five if he is a day and swore he was forty-four... Everybody cheered as they went by, and they cheered Foster Booth, who is forty, walking side by side with his son Charley who is twenty. Charley's mother died when he was born, and when Charley enlisted Foster said he'd never yet let Charley go anywhere he daren't go himself, and he didn't mean to begin with the Flanders trenches. (179)

In the scrapbooks, over several pages, we find long clippings, with bold headlines, describing the length and the events of the march, and photographs of the arch and of the soldiers. In the Virtual Museum of Canada exhibition, which I discuss below, I focused on a Guelph scrapbook page that suggests some of Montgomery's war efforts at a glance. There are four images on the page: a Leaskdale Presbyterian Church recruitment program of 19 December [1916?], chaired by Ewan Macdonald, features Mrs E. Macdonald as a reader; below the handbill is a photograph of the Zephyr Presbyterian Church, where Montgomery spent so many anxious days and evenings; beside the handbill is a the printed program of the Lindsay Presbyterial Society's third annual Women's Missionary Society meeting in Sunderland on 16 June 1916, where Montgomery no doubt observed first-hand some of the parish politics she caught so well in *Rilla*; below the WMS program is one of

Montgomery's own photographs of the 116th Battalion soldiers marching uphill in Leaskdale. We can imagine the drama suggested by Sunderland and Zephyr on the page, but the images that stand out for the eye are the bold headlines of the recruitment poster/program and the vertical photograph of the marching soldiers. It is easy to imagine Montgomery reading through her journals to create the outline of scenes for *Rilla* and then, in writing the scenes themselves, refreshing her memory with the vivid pages of the scrapbooks.

Montgomery does not merely paste into the scrapbook items from the everyday or even from preferred publications. The scrapbooks are not merely page-size files for haphazard arrangements of materials. Instead, even on the very first page, we find Montgomery conscious of her role as orchestrator of the new arrangement of items, as though she knows she will draw from them later, just as she uses the pages of her own journals as both trials and sources for her later fiction and poetry. Evidently, just as she enjoyed the physical act of writing, she also enjoyed the play of placing the materials in relation to each other. The first two scrapbooks, in particular – those from 1893 to 1909 – are full of thoughtful play. The first two (red) University of Guelph scrapbooks, at least for the years 1910 through 1918, while not so exuberant as the very early Island ones, also show many pages crammed with images and colour. Interestingly, this playful, creative arranging seems to disappear in the two (later) black scrapbooks. In these later scrapbooks, Montgomery still collects memorabilia – ticket stubs, photographs, and name cards – but the old time-consuming and playful arranging is not in evidence. In fact, the two black scrapbooks in Guelph are predominantly clippings pasted in rows. These clippings often tell directly about Montgomery's life, whether she is giving readings or being guest of honour at numerous social teas. The play of the scrapbooks gradually turns from visual drama into chronicle.

A Counter to Loneliness

Hinz describes autobiography as a 'counter to loneliness' ('Mimesis' 209), which Montgomery's journals and letters certainly were, and which the scrapbooks may also have been. Hinz also claims that creating autobiography is a way of constructing a sympathetic community which may be lacking in real life (208). The scrapbooks show us Montgomery's imagined, embracing community. Early and late, Montgomery is constructing a context and community for her imaginary and imaginative life. Particularly in the years before the publication of *Anne of Green Gables*, Montgomery may have used the ritual of composing the scrapbooks to create an imaginary context in which to enjoy them, drawing from admired publications to create her own theatre, her own community of favourite people and images. Later in life, she drew from the publications that name her as heroine, preserving evidence perhaps that the imagined community is now indeed hers. Next to clippings about herself, she enthusiastically gathers clippings about a new form of absorbing drama – movies. Early and late, she is the heroine of her autobiography/drama, while the created stage changes from the vivid colour of an imaginative assemblage of artefacts to the black-and-white clippings of her own social doings – set alongside notices of her favourite (black-and-white) movies. Scanning, in imagination, all six scrapbooks together is like seeing Montgomery's imaginative community change from the colourful pieces she can draw from her everyday world and can claim from publications she admires, to a global community where she has become an acknowledged player, but where she has no time or inclination – perhaps no need – to create the bright collages of her youth. I hope others will explore further what Montgomery's passion for movies suggests about her need for an imaginative community, her love of images, and her desire to discover, witness, and record drama. It seems sadly fitting that the very last scrapbook entry is a 1937 newspaper item sent to her presumably by MacMillan concerning a movie star cat: the comic article is about an enormous whiskey-drinking cat whose name is Matthew of Greengables [sic] but who answers to the calling name of Marilla (USB, X25 MS A002). Montgomery's imaginative community has stretched far indeed.

If the scrapbooks can be viewed as drama, and if we accept the argument that drama involves ritual that creates community (Hinz, 'Mimesis' 208), then we may see Montgomery's scrapbooks as forms of community-creating life writing, places where the drama Montgomery preferred is enacted simultaneously with – and enlarges upon – the journals and letters. The audience for Montgomery's visual drama is no longer Montgomery or an imagined Montgomery, but includes all of those who have the privilege of viewing the images for themselves, re-enacting, but differently, the acts of reading and interpreting the pieces of her surrounding culture Montgomery chose to claim for her own dramatic mosaic. Montgomery draws from her scrapbooks, transforming their drama into the drama of her fiction.

Since Montgomery's scrapbooks need to be seen to be appreciated, the Virtual Museum of Canada Partnership was formed in 2001 to create an on-line exhibition to display selected pages from the scrapbooks and to offer commentary and opportunities to interact with the material.[4] As curator of the exhibition, I selected a small sample of the Island and Ontario scrapbooks – nineteen full pages and some two hundred individual images – to suggest the range of images and kinds of stories captured in them. 'Picturing a Canadian Life: L.M. Montgomery's Personal Scrapbooks and Book Covers' was launched in August 2002 (http://lmm.confederationcentre.com). If the worldwide Web is meant to make a global community in which information and images are freely shared, then it seems fitting the Web should make available for study and enjoyment a portion of the created community of Montgomery's scrapbooks, the created context for her imaginings and the miniature reflection and re-creation of the dramas from her surroundings and in her living.

The journals, photographs, and scrapbooks speak to each other, offering in combination excellent sites for appreciating Montgomery's gift for visual drama. Often using what Irene Gammel calls 'retrospective disclosure' (see the Introduction), Montgomery brings before us vivid scenes that suggest a larger drama unfolding. Alice Van Wart describes this strong visual element as one of the hallmarks of women's autobiography. Whereas the male mode of life writing, she says, may involve a 'framed, contained, and closed thinking,' '... the writing in women's diaries generally proceeds by indirection and reveals female thinking to be eidetic (presented through detailed and accurate visual image reproducing a past impression), open-ended, and generative' (22). The scrapbooks use images as markers of experiences, and we see through them how Montgomery compressed stories to record or commemorate with an artefact that would stimulate the 'past impression.' A piece of Dr Anderson's desk from Prince of Wales College, a mashed green velvet flower she 'swiped' from a lapel, a photograph of J.M. Barrie's Den of Kirriemuir – these all captured moments of vivid drama for Montgomery. Her very arranging of the images and mementoes begins to look like a kind of ritual, a ritual to which drama belongs. Perhaps, in viewing the scrapbooks, we provide an audience for the play of images and also for Montgomery playing and creating the play. We may never be able to decipher her many secrets or uncover the stories she signals, and this is part of Montgomery's continuing appeal. Characteristically, in the scrapbooks Montgomery creates a dramatic form of life writing that celebrates images, preserves her memories in code, and invites and baffles our seeing.

Montgomery loved mystery stories, and one of the joys of doing research on her papers is that one's own sleuthing is often rewarded. Like the academic detective hero of A.S. Byatt's novel *Possession* (1990), the Montgomery scholar may trace clues and uncover secrets only half buried – perhaps even planted. I am convinced Montgomery imagined future readers looking on the backs of manuscript pages to see what she placed there, so that clues would not be lost (Epperly, 'Approaching'). It is significant that she did not destroy the scrapbooks, and while she commented even in 1926 that they were 'yellowing' (*SJ* 3:314), she kept adding to them at least until 1937. Unintentional and deliberate mysteries in the scrapbooks ensure that the drama of reading Montgomery's life writing will intensify as images become clues that make us envision new scenes in new contexts.

NOTES

I wish to thank Aliant Telecom for support for my work with the L.M. Montgomery Institute; the Social Sciences and Humanities Research Council of Canada for funds, made available through the LMMI, to study the scrapbooks; Canadian Heritage and the Virtual Museum of Canada Partnership for supporting me as curator for the on-line Montgomery exhibition; and the Smart Communities Program for support for research on Montgomery.

1 There are six personal scrapbooks in all: two (covering roughly the period from 1893 to 1909) are owned by the Lucy Maud Montgomery Birthplace and housed by the Confederation Centre Art Gallery and Museum; four (covering 1910 to 1937) are owned by the University of Guelph. In all there are some 562 pages. For a good overview of the scrapbooks, see Carolyn Strom Collins's 'The Scrapbooks.' For film footage of some scrapbook pages, see the CD-ROM *The Bend in the Road*. For sample scrapbook pages, in colour, see the Virtual Museum of Canada exhibition (http://lmm .confederationcentre.com), which is available on-line from August 2002 to August 2007. I am grateful to the Confederation Centre Art Gallery and Museum for providing me with digital images of Island scrapbook items.

2 The sample list at the end of the first letter to MacMillan (*MDMM* 4–5) is but one of several lists sent to him in the first years of their correspondence.

3 Six Uxbridge soldiers are listed in the honour roll of the dead published in the Adjutant's *The 116th Battalion in France*, 95–111.

4 The Virtual Museum of Canada Partnership was formed among Heritage Canada's Virtual Museum of Canada, the Confederation Centre Art Gallery and Museum, the National Library, the L.M. Montgomery Institute of the University of Prince Edward Island, the University of Guelph, the Lucy Maud Montgomery Birthplace, and the Heirs of L.M. Montgomery. The site contains several hundred images and some thirty-five thousand words of text. With permission, we borrowed the zooming architecture created by the (digital) William Blake Archive of the University of Virginia, so that viewers may enlarge, reduce, or see in actual size the images on the scrapbook pages for closer study.

8

'I hear what you say': Soundings in L.M. Montgomery's Life Writings

Joy Alexander

'Oh,' you said – didn't you? – '*now* I begin to see why you had a good time.'
Don't be impertinent, you journal, you!

L.M. Montgomery, 24 July 1891, *SJ*, 1:58

Oral culture prevailed in the late-nineteenth-century Prince Edward Island in which L.M. Montgomery grew up. She was a practised listener, and speech rhythms came naturally to her as she began to write; subtleties of movement and inflection and a living diversity of tone and tempo are such pervasive elements of her characteristic style that the reader scarcely notices them. Oral influences are evident in her account of her literary career in *The Alpine Path*: 'There were many traditions and tales on both sides of the family, to which, as a child, I listened with delight while my elders talked them over around winter firesides' (*AP* 12). She remembered that James Macneill 'composed hundreds of poems, which he would sometimes recite to favoured persons. They were never written down.' She heard her grandfather repeat many of them and recalls that they were 'witty, pointed, and dramatic' (*AP* 15). Aunt Mary Lawson, to whom Montgomery dedicated *The Golden Road*, was one of the formative influences of Montgomery's childhood: 'She was a brilliant conversationalist, and it was a treat to get Aunt Mary started on tales and recollections of her youth, and all the vivid doings and sayings, of the folk in those young years of the Province' (*AP* 16). Montgomery's biographers have also noted that as a small child 'Maud crouched under the post-office table listening to a shipwrecked sea captain tell of storm and stranding on Cavendish beach' and that Grandfather Macneill spun his tale in a memorable way (Rubio and Waterston, *Writing* 17).

The dominant literary influence on the young Maud was the spoken and heard (rather than silently read) word. In fact, while four pages of *The Alpine Path* are devoted to the topic of books and reading, Montgomery prefaces her comments by acknowledging that 'we did not have a great many books in the house' (*AP* 48). At the age of nineteen, in 1894, she recorded in her journal: 'I wish I could have lots of books' (*SJ* 1:114). Early reading consisted of magazines and appropriate Sunday reading, rather than novels, which were 'frowned on as reading for children' and of which she states that there were only three in the house, namely, *Rob Roy, Pickwick Papers,* and *Zanoni,* by Bulwer Lytton. Of these she claims to have known 'whole chapters by heart.' She speaks in similar terms of poetry, saying that 'its music was woven into my growing soul and has echoed through it, consciously and subconsciously, ever since' (*AP* 49). Her own first publication, proudly reported in her journal on 7 December 1890, was a poem, a rhyming retelling of one of those oral tales of the Cavendish coast. Already, however, by 1890 she had been regularly writing up her new journal for more than a year. The strongest formative guide as L.M. Montgomery found her literary style through life writing was her oral background. She had the advantage from an early age of a well-developed auditory imagination, the faculty described by T.S. Eliot as 'the feeling for syllable and rhythm, penetrating far below the conscious levels of thought and feeling, invigorating every word' (Eliot 108). It came naturally to her from the very beginning to conceive of the writer as a speaker and the reader as a listener.

My basic contention in this chapter is that L.M. Montgomery is a writer who writes with the ear. The voice of the narrator, and indeed the voices of the characters, are of notable significance in her work; her words therefore require 'an epireader' who will listen with attentiveness and sensitivity, attuned to the living voice contained in the printed page. There are certainly many literary texts which are written with, and appeal to, what T.S. Eliot called the auditory imagination. Far more prose than we realize is intended for the ear as well as the eye. This is particularly true of children's literature, which frequently constructs the reader as a listener, whereas life writing does not necessarily entail a listening reader. Her journals enabled Montgomery to construct her own voice as a writer and to cast her imagined readers as listeners. Having internalized this frame of mind when writing, it became an embedded aspect of her subsequent literary style. Her early journals were the training ground for writing with the ear.

The literary critic Denis Donoghue, in his book *Ferocious Alphabets*, deals at length with what he terms epireading and graphireading. His concern is to describe and evaluate two kinds of readers – those who read with the eye and those who read with the ear. Graphireaders rely principally on their visual sense: 'The graphireader deals with writing as such and does not think of it as transcribing an event properly construed as vocal and audible' (Donoghue 151). Primacy is given to the word on the page, to the text. To the epireader, by contrast, the auditory sense is all-important. Words presuppose a voice, a speaker. Writing is not text; it is dialogue and conversation: 'The only require-ment in epireading is that reading be construed as a personal encounter, the reader enters into a virtual relation with the speaker' (99–100). The reader is engaged in the reconstruction of the dialogic nature of the text. The words on the page are experienced as voice, whether they are those of the author or diarist or the speaker (in a poem) or a character (in fiction). The voice of the author may be foregrounded, as Henry James's voice is so often in his novels, or a character's voice may monopolize the ear, as, for example, Molly Bloom's in *Ulysses*. Certain texts demand to be vocalized.

Denis Donoghue's discussion of epireading is a persuasive reminder that listening is an important part of reading, more necessary perhaps for some texts than for others, but to ignore it may be to miss out on a significant aspect of the text's richness. Walter J. Ong has been foremost among those who have tracked the development of language from an oral culture, to a print culture to modern digital culture and in so doing he has given impetus to a consideration of literature as something written to be heard – if not actually uttered aloud, at least attended to with the inner ear. In an article the title of which states its main thesis, 'The Writer's Audience Is Always a Fiction,' Ong demonstrates that when the medium through which authors expressed themselves changed from orality to print, a move that L.M. Montgomery made on the small scale, writers had to project or construct – fictionalize – their audience. Ong writes as follows of life writing:

> The audience of the diarist is ... encased in fictions. To what self is he talking? To the self he imagines he is? Or would like to be? Or really thinks he is? Or thinks other people think he is? To himself as he is now? Or as he will probably or ideally be twenty years hence? ... The history of diaries,

I believe, has yet to be written. Possibly more than the history of any other genre, it will have to be a history of the fictionalizing of readers. (Ong 20)

This string of questions is based on two premises which are probably true of most diarists. The first is that the self who writes a journal addresses a supposed reader who is also the self. The second is that diaries, to a greater degree than most other forms of imaginative writing, are *not* written to be read aloud; they provide a private, intimate sphere in which the writer is allowed to talk to herself, or rather, to whisper, or better still, to communicate thoughts in dialogue.

In her journals (fig. 8.1), Montgomery characteristically is not talking to herself but projects another whom she can address; the substance of the journals is more akin to conversational speech than silent musings. She constructs her reader as a listener and practises life writing as conversation. In her early diary writing, she conceives of it as a form of address – to someone other than herself. It was only later that what she wrote appears more as performance, an evolution that coincided with her sense of a more public audience for her journals. Having established her style in her journal, L.M. Montgomery's attitude as writer with regard to the page and to the reader passed on into her story writing in a way that became one of the finest and most effective features of her style. I will draw principally on early journal entries since in them the voice was not only at a formative stage, but gives the appearance of being more artless, authentic, and spontaneous. In later years, the journal was more consciously composed for posterity, for an audience more tangible than fictive, existent rather than created. I shall then discuss an early novel to show how the journal style carried into and helped to form the story-writing style.

'Do you know, journal mine ...': Conversing with the Journal

Speaking of what she memorably described as her 'great soul loneliness,' L.M. Montgomery at age twenty-six described her circumstances in 1900: 'I love bright, cheerful companionship, laughter, sparkling conversation. I get nothing of them' (*SJ* 1:255). This lack was supplied by her journal, whose necessity to her she admitted in a comment on the epigram 'It is the lonely people who keep diaries': 'When I have anybody to "talk it over with" I don't feel the need of a diary so strongly. When I haven't I *must* have a journal to overflow in. It is a companion' (3 Jan. 1904; *SJ* 1:292). Thus the diary becomes for her a person, and the

8.1 'When I have anybody to "talk it over with" I don't feel the need of a diary so strongly' – L.M. Montgomery's journal entry on Sunday, 3 January 1904. (L.M. Montgomery Collection, Archival and Special Collections, University of Guelph Library.)

words she writes are a conversation. She speaks of 'this dear old journal, which I love as if it were a living friend' (30 July 1905; *SJ* 1:308) and refers to it as a 'real old friend and confidant' (7 Feb. 1910; *SJ* 1:393). The style is dialogic, the writer is a conversationalist with craft, and the reader is constructed as an intimate listening friend.

There are numerous examples of L.M. Montgomery naturally falling into conversational mode in her journal:

> Well, journal, this is the last day of the old year ... Good-bye, dear old year. (31 Dec. 1889; *SJ* 1:8)

> Do you know, journal mine, I may take a trip out west to see father this summer. (22 April 1890; *SJ* 1:19)

Many times it is apparent that as she writes she assumes a listener:

> ... – rather risky topic, say you? ... (9 April 1891; *SJ* 1:48)

> Mustard actually *mustered* – oh, forgive the pun. It just *made itself* – up enough courage ... (1 July 1891; *SJ* 1:55)

> ... – and guess who else! (19 Dec. 1891; *SJ* 1:70)

> Very dreadful, do you say? (20 Jan. 1896; *SJ* 1:156)

> I do not think I have grumbled to you – or anyone about it. (25 June 1909; *SJ* 1:357)

Oral turns of phrase are used, though they might properly be deemed too informal for the journal genre: 'By the way I believe ...' (26 Jan. 1891; *SJ* 1:45). More than once, L.M. Montgomery says she is writing in her journal 'for comfort because I feel a bit lonely' (9 Aug. 1890; *SJ* 1:25). It provided her with someone with whom to converse. In 1894 she professes her love of letter writing, despite the fact that 'all my correspondents are not equally interesting. Some are dull and it is rather tedious to write to them' (*SJ* 1:118). By contrast, her journals allowed her to write to a supposed ideal correspondent.

Aspects of her journal style are distinctly odd unless they are construed, not as memorials for the self to read, but as speech directed at an imagined listener. For example, most diaries present conversations in reported speech, whereas L.M. Montgomery quite frequently records, or more accurately recreates, conversations in direct speech (for instance, Lem McLeod's declaration of his affection for her [22 Oct. 1894; *SJ* 1:121–3]). Another oddity is the lack of the lacunae so commonly found in diaries. Details, filling in, explanations are not required when we are only writing for ourselves. That Montgomery's journals are now readable at all is principally because she did not adopt this shorthand characteristic of a private diary-style. She tells real narratives with immense particularity and garrulous attention to detail, just as a story would be filled out and embroidered when told to a friend.

On the other hand, what might be called the set pieces which she favoured draw attention to themselves because they are *not* in conversational style. They would form an interesting study in themselves. I mean the many passages such as these egregious examples, with their Romantic anthropomorphisms and archaisms:

> Sunday evening, as we drove out, was perfection – clear and sparkling, with lemon lights in the west and one great lucent evening star gleaming like a liquid jewel on the hectic cheek of dying day. It grew darker as we drove along over the white fields – the velvet sky was powdered with stars, and the spruces took on their mystic gloom! (18 Feb. 1895; *SJ* 1:134)

> Yesterday was a dream – a poem – a symphony – a what you will so that your definition expresses the ethereal revel of colour, the thrilling glory and splendor of the wonderful day that came in roseate and golden across frost-rimed hills and crept away at night in an elf-land of moonlight. (18 Jan. 1897; *SJ* 1:176)

These descriptions appear to be written – or, rather, overwritten – for the page, and so with the eye only. They are the notebook exercises of an apprentice writer. Even here the conversational tone breaks through: the exclamation mark and the dashes in the punctuation; 'as we drove out'; 'your definition.' However, this is suppressed by the content, so heavily dependent on adjectives and clotted with imagery. The verbosity leads the reader away from reality into linguistic display. It was when Montgomery learned to introduce sound, and thus implicitly life and movement, into these inert visual spectacles that they become more grounded and real and emerge from the surfeit of words such as *hazy, ethereal, balsamic, pearly, shroud*, and *shimmer*. This happened as her experience as a writer grew, as in this description of

Lover's Lane recorded on 8 October 1899:

> ... the wind sweeps through the swaying spruce tops with a sound as of surf breaking on a far distant shore ... sloping down into the heart of a peaceful hush ... The brook purls softly by and the old firs whisper over it as of yore ... the low murmur of a hidden brook ever in our ears. (*SJ* 1:243)

Another much later example is considerably more skilfully written. It is *about* the reality of remembered natural scenery ('Sam Wyand's field'), and it draws on the senses rather than on vocabulary to recreate that actuality:

> It has been so real to me that it has filled me with a bitter longing to be in those spots once more – to taste the inimitable flavor of the wild fruit, to lie amid the sun-warm grasses, to hear the robins whistling, to tiptoe through the lanes of greenery and fragrance in the summer mornings of those faraway years. (3 Sept. 1919; *SJ* 2:341–2)

The significant point about the set-piece compositions is that they conform to purely written conventions, and, to refer back to my earlier terminology, they force the reader from the pleasurable role of aural epireader throughout most of the journals to that of visual graphireader.

Reference has already been made to the oral background of L.M. Montgomery's childhood. It nurtured the style of the journals, which in turn was formative for her style as a writer. Oral literature was in her genes, inherited from Grandfather Macneill's brother James, a prolific oral poet, and also from his sister Mary, a gifted storyteller. The young Maud lived in an oral world, talking to her two imaginary companions in the glass doors of the bookcase, Katie Maurice and Lucy Gray, and even when looking at pressed flowers, 'it just seemed as if they *spoke* to me' (20 Oct. 1890; *SJ* 1:34). A perennial delight was 'getting up songs and recitations and dialogues' (13 May 1890; *SJ* 1:20) in school, for impromptu social events, or public concerts. The chief entertainments in her youth were the Literary Society with its program of 'lecture, debate, essay' (31 Dec. 1898; *SJ* 1:229) and the prayer meeting, where both sermon and prayer were oral forms of address. 'I like nothing better than a well-told ghost story,' Maud confesses (1 June 1909; *SJ* 1:351), and so she naturally adopts the style of an oral storyteller, so that the retelling of even quite ordinary incidents in the journal is shaped like a narrative.

There is evidence that L.M. Montgomery's method of composition as a writer was essentially oral. Her maid, Elsie Bushby, recalled her walking round Leaskdale Manse 'whispering or talking out loud to herself' (Heilbron, 'Memories' 5). Her second cousin Georgie Campbell remembered her visits to Park Corner:

> I would hear her talking to herself ... I was amused to death to see Aunt Maud talking to herself. And finally she laughed right out loud and she said, 'That's just what I'll put down.' So she picked out the little notepad out of her apron and started to write. (Heilbron, 'Memories' 23)

This picture of L.M. Montgomery is highly reminiscent of the heroine of *Kilmeny of the Orchard*, with her 'little slate that hung at her belt.' I will look at this early (third) book to demonstrate the transfer of style from journal to fiction, especially in the relation between storyteller/author and listener/reader.

First, however, to reinforce my point and to anticipate its full realization in her stories, I will briefly glance at the poems. In my view, the successful poems are few in number, but they are those in which L.M. Montgomery trusts her speaking voice rather than assuming a conventional poetic voice. The first verse of 'Midnight in Camp,' which I have selected virtually at random, is characteristic of her verse:

> Night in the unslumbering forest! From the free,
> Vast pinelands by the foot of man untrod,
> Blows the wild wind, roaming rejoicingly
> This wilderness of God;
> And the tall firs that all day long have flung
> Balsamic odors where the sunshine burned,
> Chant to its harping primal epics learned
> When this old world was young.

With their poetic diction, formality, and high-minded tone, these lines lack any freshness. Despite her liking for penning many such lyrics, for which there was a certain vogue and a ready audience, her literary reputation could never be derived from them. Nevertheless, a few poems do stand out. 'Home from Town' and 'Southernwood,' both in the first person, colloquial, and close to her own experience, work so well no doubt for these very reasons. In the former, the speaker talks to his horse, Doll, as he rides home from town:

And that little white thing there, a-standing close by his side?
It's my own little Mayflower, bless her! And of course she wants a ride.
And Kate and Ray are coming as fast as they can down the lane,
And wife's at the kitchen door – I can see her just as plain!
What a look she'll give when I show her the brand-new merino gown!
Down, Rover, old dog – be careful. Well, I'm glad to be home from town.

The conversational tone and the turns of speech lift the poem off the page. 'Southernwood,' though unexceptional, similarly originates in chat:

What is it you have in the heart of your posy, stranger?
Well, well, if it isn't a sprig of southernwood!
From the country, I reckon? They call it out of fashion,
But a whiff of its fragrance always does me good ...

It is a pity that L.M. Montgomery did not work more in this vein. The competition-winning poem 'Which Has More Patience – Man or Woman?' allowed her to use the congenial debate-form, which she further livened with humour and a jolly, springing rhythm. 'At the Dance,' first-person again, moves out of wistful memory toward present reality and the direct address of an imagined conversation:

Come, I promise to dream no more,
Look not up with reproachful glance,
Lightly drift we across the floor.
I am yours, tonight at the dance.

The tighter verse form together with the control necessary to manage the movement from present to past and back to the present rein in the tendency to meandering chat. It even permits the delicate rhetorical flourish of the final line, which is courteously formal without becoming stilted, as the speaker capitulates to the present moment, thus evading the treachery of time. Regular journal writing made possible this style of writing, with its immediacy and the inflections of conversation. 'The Watchman' is virtually a pastiche of Browning; L.M. Montgomery gives a voice to the guard who watches at Christ's tomb, just as Browning had done for Lazarus and St John (in 'An Epistle Containing the Strange Medical Experience of Karshish' and 'A Death in the Desert'). Nevertheless, it is admirably realized, and the dramatic monologue was for her, as for Browning – of whom she recorded that, among poets, 'I love him most' (4 Sept. 1909; *SJ* 1:358) – a form of expression *par excellence*. The style formed in her journal writing serves her well in her best poems.

The narration of *Kilmeny of the Orchard* is interesting and not untypical of L.M. Montgomery's storytelling style. After initial scene-setting, most of the first chapter gets the plot under way through a conversation between the male protagonist, Eric Marshall, and his doctor friend. The second chapter reproduces a 'letter of destiny,' which is presented as speech. In the third chapter, we have dramatic monologue, soliloquy – whatever you want to call it – what Eric thinks to himself as he walks to his lodgings from the schoolhouse, again presented as speech. Thus the familiar journal-style keeps reappearing, and, in fact, the story is mainly told in direct speech. When comparing the film version of *Anne of Green Gables* to the book, L.M. Montgomery acknowledged that some of her characters live in their speech and consequently are superfluous on screen: 'Now, these characters do little in the books but *talk* and unluckily talk can't be reproduced on the screen. Only the characters who *do* something can appear there' (18 Dec. 1919; *SJ* 2:358).

Also relevant to my thesis are the occurrences of that pivotal pairing in L.M. Montgomery's fiction of teller and listener: Mr Williamson is an 'amusing old gossip,' while his wife 'talked little as a rule; but, in the pungent country phrase, she never spoke but she said something.' Eric Marshall, with his 'glib tongue,' falls in love with mute Kilmeny, though there is a reversal here. She is a perfect listener as he reads stories to her, but he also delights to be a listener to her expressive speech-surrogate, the violin, which is also the objective correlative of her feelings. In the violin music can be heard 'a pitiful, plaintive cry as of some imprisoned thing calling for freedom and utterance.' This imagery runs through the book – two later chapters are titled 'A Prisoner of Love' and 'A Broken Fetter.' Utterance is freedom. Communication is intrinsic to humanity.

The central theme of the book is a set of variations on the view that speech and silence can be a curse or a blessing. In terms of narration, Kilmeny is not truly mute – that would surely be a limitation too far for L.M. Montgomery. The clumsy device of the slate allows her to participate fully in conversation. It is important to note that Kilmeny is not deaf – as though listening and hearing are fundamental, the *sine qua non* of the senses. Dumb, yes. And, in a way, blind too. We have to regard this story as a kind of fairy tale, if it is not to presume too far on our willing suspension of disbelief. We are asked to accept that Kilmeny has never seen herself in a mirror and believes herself to be ugly; consequently she is reclusive. Only once she has truly seen and accepted herself as she really is can the greater liberation occur which releases her into speech. She moves from being a private slate-writer into the public arena of speech.

This progression from listening to seeing to speaking was significant for L.M. Montgomery, too. It may even be that her rich oral experience in childhood, whereby she found her voice, was a necessary precursor of her journal writing, which allowed her to see and know and create herself, and that this in turn was a necessary precursor of the books she authored. Would there have been the books without the journal? Would there have been a journal without Katie Maurice and childhood recitations and debates and ghost stories? L.M. Montgomery's narration frequently implies a speaking voice rather than a writer putting pen to paper. The author-reader relationship is one of openness and trust. The conversational style and rhythms of ordinary speech create a sense of listening as much as of reading.

In her book *Tellers and Listeners: The Narrative Imagination*, Barbara Hardy links the narration of life writing and the narration of fiction. She says of 'the man in the street': 'Like everyone else, he is telling stories and scraps of stories every day of his life, assembling and revising the stories of his days into an informal autobiography' (Hardy ix). Literary artists heighten, pattern, and shape this quotidian discourse. For L.M. Montgomery, oral storytelling instinctively became the form of her life writing, and this developed into her narrative art, in all of which she is as aware of her hearers as she is of her telling. The motivation of the author should ideally be matched by a corresponding response from the reader. Hence it is fitting that Anne-with-an-*e*, the chatterbox orphan, Maud's alter ego, requires to be balanced and paired with Matthew, regarded by Anne as 'such a sympathetic listener,' in whose company she was 'sure of an appreciative and sympathetic listener.' Even so do storyteller-author and listener-reader form the bond which makes of them true 'kindred spirits.'

9

Epistolary Performance:
Writing Mr Weber

Paul Tiessen and Hildi Froese Tiessen

After thirty years of this paper conversing, we met. We almost called for
pen and ink! The face-to-face way wasn't the same thing.
                    Ephraim Weber, 'L.M. Montgomery as a Letter-Writer,' 304

L.M. Montgomery and Ephraim Weber enjoyed a zesty, forty-year relationship that they lived almost entirely by correspondence. He mailed
his first letter to her in 1902, a 'tentative note of old-world courtesy,
gentle and prim' (Eggleston, in Weber, B-Précis 435);[1] her last letter to
him was dated 1941. Their relationship began in letters and was sustained there. As they wrote for over a quarter of a century before they
ever met face to face, it was inevitable that they should become, to a
significant degree, creatures of each other's imaginations. Montgomery,
for example, would have projected, in her correspondence with 'Mr.
Weber,' a reader not readily distinguishable from the imaginary reader
of her personal journals. In fact, a correspondence such as theirs – as
rich and layered as it at times became – would have left so many gaps
that the correspondents' imaginative construction of the reader would
have been inevitable.

The ways in which an epistolary relationship such as Montgomery
and Weber's evokes the relationship between the journal writer and the
reader she constructs is instructive here. The American literary scholar
Sidonie Smith has commented on how a journal writer, as writer, creates of herself a 'rhetorical construct'; at the same time, she invents the
other as reader, or what she calls '"fictive" reader' (Smith, *Poetics* 6).[2]
In her journal and letters, Montgomery created 'fictive' readers who
included her imagined variants of herself. In light of Smith's com-

ments, we could say that Montgomery inserted herself into the gap left by the disembodied 'Mr. Weber,' whom she seldom saw or heard. That is, the audience of her letters to Weber included, strongly, both 'Mr. Weber' and herself. Montgomery's 'Mr. Weber' (the fictive 'other,' who for Montgomery was not restricted to the historical Mr Weber) became what Linda S. Coleman calls 'an empowering and sympathetic other' (1).

Surely the Weber who did engage her – stimulated her thinking, applauded her successes – confirmed Montgomery's most elevated sense of herself as a woman of intellectual and creative achievement. When he did challenge her ideological suppositions or otherwise put the products of her efforts in question, her quick response was to shake him off, to dismiss his remarks as if they could not possibly reflect the opinions of the reader she had made him out to be. The disembodied Weber – that is, the figure whom Montgomery encountered for the first quarter century only in paper and ink – was for her a reader who, like the projected reader of her journals, offered no threat to her. Such a reader, after all, had no opportunity to reach further into her life and thought than she herself was ready to permit.

On the other hand, insofar as Weber *did* exist independently of her 'fictive' projection of him, he challenged her thinking and her very sense of who she was. It was when Weber presented himself, not as 'fictive' reader, but as palpable interlocutor, that she was compelled to confront facets of herself she was not otherwise driven to engage. One could conjecture that she valued the encounters Weber's sometimes probing remarks precipitated, because they tended to objectify aspects of her world that she might not otherwise have bothered to examine. It is those aspects of their correspondence – where she would seem to take up cultural, ideological, and intellectual issues that she would not necessarily have addressed of her own volition – that are of interest to us here. She could, after all, readily control the 'Mr. Weber' who would, like any reader of her imagination, fairly placidly be entertained by or give assent to her vivid musings about daily life, landscape, and matters of general interest. It was the Mr Weber whom she could not control, who pushed her to articulate – and sometimes to examine – some of the givens by which she lived, who both intrigued and threatened her. And it is her epistolary engagement with him that illumines some aspects of Montgomery beyond those constructions of herself she created for the consumption of the diverse 'fictive' readers – private and public – for whom she wrote.

'... the lost and lovely art of letter-writing ...'

'Some day,' she had written in 1921, 'I shall ... meet you in the flesh – but know you none the better for that – perhaps not so well' (*MEW* 34–5). After the emotional paucity of each of their three face-to-face meetings in 1928, 1930, and 1935, Montgomery and Weber returned with relief and renewed pleasure to the imaginative richness of pen and ink, to the 'warm individuality of the human hand' (fig. 9.1). He later suggested that when the writer wrote as illegibly as Montgomery sometimes did, a reader like himself virtually folded himself into the lines of her letter and caressed its body: 'slow reading allows fond lingering on the lines' (Weber, 'Letter-Writer' 309–10). In spite of the success of their epistolary relationship, it seems unlikely, on the face of it, that Montgomery should have attached herself to the real-life Mr Weber, a homesteader and self-deprecating Prairie bard born in 1870, with roots in the Mennonite community in Waterloo County, Ontario. Weber himself puzzled over what she might have seen in him. In 1942, in 'L.M. Montgomery as a Letter-Writer,' the first of two *Dalhousie Review* articles that he wrote about her, Weber wondered why a writer so famous as she was had made so great an effort to maintain a lifelong 'literary' correspondence with him, by then a failed writer and disgruntled schoolteacher, and with G.B. MacMillan, a journalist in Alcoa, Scotland, with whom Montgomery had begun a correspondence in 1903, a year after her first letter exchange with Weber:

> [W]hy we two? Were we bolder to strain her good nature, or more patient to decipher her long letters? I hardly dared think we wrote *better* letters. I never found out. In any case, she could easily have squelched us with silence. Of the other survivor I am sorry to know nothing, but as for me, the exchange has been richly in my favor, aside from the honor of it. Surely a famous author needs no obscure schoolmaster. (Weber, 'Letter-Writer' 300)

Of course, as Weber might very well have guessed, he *did* write better letters than most others. Indeed, in his 1942 'familiar essay' on Montgomery and himself – what he elsewhere called this 'bit of intimate confession literature' (Weber, *Letters Home* 145; see also 100) – a lively and gallant Weber displayed something of the verve of his letters to her.

As for Montgomery, her remarks concerning Weber as correspondent leave little question as to why she persisted in writing him. As early as

9.1 'After thirty years ... we met. We almost called for pen and ink!' – L.M. Montgomery and Ephraim Weber, 1928. (L.M. Montgomery Collection, Archival and Special Collections, University of Guelph Library.)

1904, she said that back at the beginning of their correspondence in 1902 she had felt 'but little enthusiasm' in taking up an exchange with a would-be writer living in isolation in the West.[3] True, she herself was, at that time, an isolated and aspiring author, wishing for contact with any 'literary' people ready to exchange letters that might be 'helpful, interesting or amusing' (*SJ* 1:297). But she had had little good luck so far, and this Mr Weber did not at first appear to be any different from anyone else. However, she very quickly changed her mind, and on 14 November 1904, recorded in her journal:

> Mr. Weber turned out to be an ideal correspondent. His letters are capital. The man himself I rather think is a dreamy, impractical somewhat *shiftless* person, hampered also by delicacy of health. But his intellect is unquestionable. His letters are cultured, thoughtful, stimulating epistles to which I look eagerly forward. They are written from a lonely Alberta ranch but they sparkle from beginning to end. (*SJ* 1:297)

Weber not only wrote great letters, but he was also attentive. In tandem with her other pen friend, MacMillan,[4] he gave Montgomery a chance to think out loud – at least insofar as she was likely to 'think aloud' with a male stranger who came her way because he, too, had aspirations to be a writer. Fortunately for her, he was a Canadian who became increasingly conversant with Canadian literature and details of the Canadian literary scene, and from 1917 on, he was able to function as a particularly resonant and informed – and relatively detached – sounding board for Montgomery. He never wavered in his interest in her parade of literary activities and her stream of publications, and – never himself succeeding as a writer – he did not rival her on any front. Indeed, his marginality relative to the several layers of her world perhaps stood them both in good stead and contributed to making their relationship such an enduring one. Reflecting in her journal on the role both Weber and MacMillan played in her life of the mind, Montgomery wrote in the same 14 November 1904 entry:

> If I lived where I could meet with intellectually congenial friends I suppose these correspondences would not mean so much to me. But under my present limitations these unseen friends are of vital interest to me. In my letters to them I 'let myself go' – writing freely from my soul, with no fear of being misunderstood or condemned – or worst of all, meeting with a blank wall of non-comprehension. (*SJ* 1:297)

Weber served not only as 'fictive' reader but also as 'unseen friend' – his convenient immateriality, and only distant palpable reality, perceived as offering mostly support to a Montgomery so often beset by antipathetic forces so close around her. Weber gave Montgomery room to extend herself beyond the limits of her own social and cultural landscapes, and even beyond the closed circuit of her journal. He offered a milieu in which Montgomery, so often caught by 'all the silencing mechanisms of the familial and societal world in which she lived,' might try to explore, in a relatively safe space outside her journal, 'a place of her own ... as woman or as artist' (Buss, *Mapping* 167). Montgomery laid claim to both in the same breath: 'Between these letters and my journal I manage to keep my intellectual life tolerably wholesome. If I could not "write out" freely certain words, opinions and fancies they would remain bottled up in my soul and would probably ferment and sour and cause some acute disturbance' (*SJ* 1:297).

At an overt or manifest level, the journal written to herself and the letters written to Weber were of course quite different – even when their content might sometimes overlap. Montgomery's journal, though shot through with brilliance and light, chutzpah and hope, is steeped in anguish and insecurity, tragedy and dread. By comparison, her letters to Weber, primarily informed by her vigorous no-nonsense voice, her spirit of leadership, her sense of fun, and her love of friendship, are manifestos of self-confidence and success. If we find embedded at the heart of Montgomery's journal an inner voice 'so needy and so uncertain of herself' (Wylie 199), we find in her letters to Weber an outer voice of good cheer and exhortation. So, even if the letters offered Montgomery a place to 'write out' what she could not express in everyday life or in her romance fiction, they still share more nearly the spirit of her fiction than the much grimmer depths of her journal. Weber himself felt that there was a similarity in tone between her letters and her novels. 'The poetic descriptions that give the Montgomery stories such freshness and cheery imagery,' he wrote, 'make the letters delightful too' (Weber, 'Letter-Writer' 306).

But the vast difference between the repeated grimness of her journal and the only occasional sombre tone in her letters to Weber did not prevent Montgomery from feeling a continuity of subjectivity between these two vehicles of expression. For one thing, her journal did not talk back to her, and she appears to have expected from Weber similar tacit assent. However, it would seem that Montgomery's untrammelled and blissful 'literary' correspondence with Weber functioned at another register when his own critical voice entered into the terrain that she had come to see as a safe haven for her own assumptions and passions. Their 'intellectual companionship' (as Montgomery once described her letters with Weber) was threatened when Weber stiffly introduced some of his own fairly radical or subversive notions about contemporary culture into his otherwise polite, even slightly deferential, epistles. Montgomery, who could be, as Clara Thomas observes, 'mercurial, hypersensitive, idealistic' (204), was not particularly receptive to a critically active 'Weber' as a resisting reader. She had, after all, come to rely on 'Weber' as an obliging reader not much more threatening than the imagined audience of her journal.

Fortunately, Weber and Montgomery both made a point of writing letters that were entertaining to the other. From the evidence that is available – including Weber's letters to some of his other friends[5] – we can readily imagine that Weber's letters to Montgomery were carefully crafted pieces, exemplary instances of what Weber called 'the lost and lovely art of letter-writing' (Weber, 'Letter-Writer' 300).[6] Although Weber was quick to insist on the lesser significance of his side of the correspondence, a contribution based, he claimed, on 'more commonplace news and less adventurous lay expression' (310), he was overly modest in defending himself.

Of course, unlike Weber's letters, a great proportion of Montgomery's letters to him were drawn from a life of considerable adventure, often in high places. Her 'epistles' were invariably exceptional productions and should, said Weber, be regarded as 'classics' (Weber, 'Letter-Writer' 301). Her epistolary style, he said, 'carried her personality to her distant friends' (300). Lamenting (as we continue to lament today) that the age of great letter-writing had ceased, Weber claimed that in her many long letters Montgomery 'preserved the liberal epistolary ways of the Queen Anners and the Victorians' (303). 'Their style,' he said in 1942, was 'so facile and natural that you forget it isn't conversation' (310). In fact, Montgomery longingly and nostalgically lamented that by the time of the First World War, her letters no longer felt rooted in the lyricism of their earliest correspondence, which had been so 'full of leisurely dreams and graceful outlines of beautiful little things' (*MEW* 11).

As entertainer, Montgomery took the lead. She and Weber crafted their epistolary relationship largely in terms of her identity as successful performer, his as her appreciative audience and intelligent onlooker. Overall, as long as they were observing their respective hierarchical roles, theirs were largely ebullient and mutually sympathetic literary conversations. But Montgomery was not only a great entertainer; she was also a demanding one. Thus, when interruptions in their role-playing led to a defensive sparring for position, we are invited to find in her letters new strands of her personality at play. At that point, presumably feeling compelled to control Weber's place as speaker and as listener, writer and reader, she reveals what Clara Thomas calls her 'aptitude for both emotional hyperbole and hard-headed manipulation' (204).

Jockeying for Self-Validation

In letter after letter, the two of them, jockeying gently for some kind of self-validation with respect to their right to offer readings of the world around them, made Canada itself a point of reference. Weber tried to situate himself firmly within a distinctly Canadian cultural orbit, but he would find himself, time and again, almost irredeemably outside his country's approved social and cultural circles. 'Yes, I am Canadian born,' he had forcefully written to Montgomery in 1902. 'Are you? My parents are, too ... [Y]ou perceive that my name is German. At home amongst ourselves we speak [Pennsylvania German] but we are thoroughly Canadian' (Weber, Précis 2).

Once Weber had leaped onto academic high ground at Queen's University from 1910 to 1913, he gained some of the cultural capital he desperately desired. His change in circumstances and persona – from that of struggling homesteader and hapless scribbler, or of discouraged schoolteacher in the 1910 winter term, overcome by gangs of 'bench-smashing youths' (Weber, Précis 7/44), to highly lauded first-class graduate student at Queen's, anticipating entry to doctoral studies at Harvard or Chicago – very well might have tempted Weber away from Montgomery and what he described to others as her world, however remarkable, of girls' books (Weber, unpublished letter to Eggleston, November 1927).[7] However, Weber remained steadfastly loyal to Montgomery from his new perch as a student of modern and classical literatures and languages. Indeed, differentiating between himself and his professors, he sought to negotiate – in Montgomery's eyes at least – an enlarged identity as a magnanimous and loyal supporter of her successes. He suggested to her a couple times, in letters that he wrote to her in 1910 and 1911, that he translate her novels into German (Weber, Précis 6a). Further, he insisted that, unlike other intellectuals at Queen's – with their 'humbug and platitudes' and colonial attitudes (Weber, Précis 7/

44) – he was keenly interested even in what she might be writing for magazines: 'I have not yet cultivated the university sneer for "periodical trash,"' he calmly and coolly assured her (Weber, Précis 6a-7/42). But he was at the same time patronizing her, extending to her a kind of backhanded praise, even when he was happily forthcoming with the confession that there was a palpable gap between the academic writing with which he was now associated, and the world of popular literature to which she belonged: 'How pitiable are some university profs! Most of them. They couldn't produce anything readable by the general public to save their lives, poor grubbers!' (Weber, Précis 7/42).

As for Montgomery, her own attempts to inform Weber of her place as writer within what she regarded as an art-less age were strained and self-conscious. In conversation with Weber, a man who with some pleasure was ready to imagine himself as highbrow when he joined in the Monday-night meetings of the Athenian club in Outlook, Saskatchewan, in the early 1920s (letter to Eggleston, September 1921), Montgomery felt compelled to negotiate a space for herself between her unequivocal intolerance of new art forms and her growing complicity with an ethos defined by popular cultural forms that Weber, for the most part, explicitly resisted. When he tried to coax her into writing serious poetry or fiction – that is, to fulfil in her life what were his own greatest, but always unfulfilled, ambitions – her responses tended to be limp and self-deprecatory. As early as 1917, Montgomery replied to Weber's prompting by undercutting the very presuppositions of his request: 'You wondered in your letter if I still found time to write any "literature," now. Well, I should hardly call my productions literature – Canada you know has no literature!! – but such as they are I peg away at them' (*MEW* 9). Four years later, shortly after the publication of *Rilla of Ingleside*, she wrote to Weber – whom she aligned with a sophisticated reading approach – again in apologetic tones:

My tenth novel *Rilla of Ingleside* was published a month ago. I have a copy for you when I am sure of your address. It is really a 'story for girls' – the heroine being a young girl who lives her girlhood in the years of the great war and I wrote it as a tribute to the girlhood of Canada. So it's my only 'novel with a purpose.' Read it from the standpoint of a young girl (if you can!) and not from any sophisticated angle or you will not think much of it ... I wish I could get time to do some short stories and verse. They were my first loves and I've never been wholly false to them. I wrote a little sketch 'White Magic' for a new Canadian venture *The Woman's Century* lately and will send you a copy when etc. It doesn't amount to anything as I didn't put any thought in it. But I believe I could do some good short stories if I had the time. (*MEW* 29–30)

Weber was not prepared to let Montgomery abandon writing that might be read from a 'sophisticated angle.' So in 1923 Montgomery responded once again to his prodding: 'No, I haven't yet "tackled my adult novel." It is impossible under present conditions. I keep hoping I shall "have more time later on" but "later on" I have even less. It is all pretty well shaped out in my mind but I can not write it by fits and starts, as I do my *Annes* and *Emilys'* (*MEW* 52). In 1926 Montgomery responded to Weber's urging once again – this time with reference to *The Blue Castle*, which she dedicated to him as if, at last, to placate him on the matter of her finally taking on the serious work he had identified her with when they had begun their correspondence. And she added a comment about her efforts at writing poetry:

> But I have a book coming out in August – *The Blue Castle*. It is for adults but is not a serious attempt at a 'real' novel at all. It is merely an amusing (I hope) little comedy. For the first time I have left P.E. Island and have laid the scene in Muskoka. It will be more interesting to a girl than a man but I'll send you a copy.
>
> One of your questions 'Have you written any poems lately?' touched a real sore spot. Writing verse was my first love and I always hanker after it but I never can get time for it. I have written only three or four poems in as many years. (*MEW* 78–9)

Then, as she continued her letter, she turned to an old favourite topic of theirs: income from writing. As if to justify to Weber her persistent occupation with popular romance fiction, Montgomery sidestepped the issue of artistic integrity and made a point of her commercial success. 'Last summer,' she told Weber, 'I wrote a series of four stories for the *Delineator* ... For these four, 5000 word stories the *Delineator* paid me four hundred dollars apiece – $1600 in all' (79).

A little over a year later, in 1927, Montgomery revealed to Weber that her engagement with publishing in a romance-fiction market was developing along what we would regard now as predictable lines in this new age. She revealed how she had progressed from an interest in what we have come to regard as high art to an interest in the marketability of her work, and finally to a rather glib satisfaction with the value of literary prestige by association. Her most recently published work brought her satisfaction, she revealed to him, less for its inherent quality, or even for its market value, than for its ability to draw attention to her and her work: for its *'advertising* value' (*MEW* 98). She was, finally, once more bewildered – and only temporarily humiliated – at finding herself both fixture and victim of the art-less age she had so aggressively identified:

> Last spring Mr. Palmer wrote me again and asked me to do four more for him saying that the other series had been very popular with his readers. I was very busy and felt I could hardly take the time but the *advertising* value of being in the *Delineator* is great so I sat up o'nights and wrote the new series. Mr. Palmer was delighted with them, bought and paid for them ... In October came an upheaval. Loren Palmer resigned and a new editor a Mr. Oscar Graeves came into power. He promptly announced that the new policy of the *Delineator* was to use only 'highly sophisticated fiction' and consequently my stories could not be used!! (*MEW* 98–9)

Ironically, Montgomery at least now and again seemed prepared to express a good measure of contempt for popular romance fiction when she looked at her own literary success or, even more, when she detected in Weber the belief that she took seriously what she said to him were but her 'harmless pot-boilers' (*MEW* 9–10; see also 189,199). In fact, it seems that she had found in the potboiler a literary form that worked in her time, a form suited to the demands of the age. After she had published her eighth novel, she confided to Weber, who she knew had a strong preference for the classics, and who longed for the development of great contemporary writing in Canada too, that it was not literature at which she had been aiming. 'Literature,' she told Weber in 1917, had little chance at commercial success, given the world's current fashions; however, she hoped sometime to find the leisure to write 'literature,' even if her only reward should lie 'in the doing of it' (*MEW* 10).

But Weber's steady display of support for Montgomery and her potboilers – support mixed, it is true, with his intermittent calls for her to write the adult novel she kept promising to work on – was for him a mixed blessing. Ironically, his unabashed praise of her work provided a space for Montgomery to undermine Weber's very enthusiasm, even his taking her at her word in 1926 that *The Blue Castle* was, as she said, for adults. After he had applauded her – in his October 1926 letter with its 'far-too-kind "review" of *Blue Castle*' (*MEW* 92) – on finally having produced an adult novel, she must have surprised him by writing back a little severely in 1927:

> You say in your letter, 'Your adult book has materialized – .' I take this to be a reference to a long-ago confession of mine that I wanted some day to write a book for adults. Oh, no, this is not the book of my ambition. The *Blue Castle* was merely an accident – a short story that wouldn't stay short. 'The' book is still unwritten. Though I hope to write it still. (*MEW* 93–4)

Montgomery seemed to resent what she might very well have taken as Weber's patiently patronizing attitude. She seemed to find in his requests and observations about her work too much readiness to indulge her own naïvely romantic or sentimentally simplistic views.

In Weber's presence, Montgomery reacted with expressions of disdain for the world she kept in thrall. She openly asserted (as we find her doing in 1924) that she was playing a game in supplying an open-ended number of Anne and Emily books to a public and publisher who simply begged for more, once they had consumed the first book in the series: 'The publishers and public insist on it. So I do it – but I have lost interest in it, as I always do after the first volume ... I can't afford to damn the public. I must cater to it for awhile yet' (*MEW* 58, 60). In effect, Montgomery's blithe display of indifference, her deliberate show of condescension toward the public who devoured her work, represented a strong criticism of the other-worldly and intellectual Weber for his own endlessly tolerant alignment with the idealistic public on her behalf. When he ventured to ask her whether she had tried stories with unhappy endings, she declared that she had to keep on pouring out happy endings: 'The public *want* the happy ending,' she told the impossibly impractical Weber in 1936. 'The world *must* have its fairy tales' (*MEW* 168).

Weber is likely to have looked with wistful dubiousness at her chutzpah, as he did at the glib posture of the world itself in a statement that he registered with Eggleston just months before Montgomery died: 'I recall that you said in a letter you are sometimes very depressed about the future of civilization. As for me, I at least wish the prevalent optimism were not so wishfully shallow' (letter to Eggleston, December 1941).

'Fancy Achilles whizzing around Troy ...'

Montgomery and Weber engaged, in their own way, and often with reference to each other, in the debates that occupied so many artists and intellectuals during the years between the wars: about the impact of the new technologies, the merits of modern experiments in art, the future of religion, the struggle between a high culture increasingly reserved for an elite audience and a low culture broadly accessible. She carried on as though the age in which she found herself was a gap into which she might deposit whatever she thought it allowed; it was but a kind of hiatus between the old world she had loved and the new age that promised fantastic wonders.

There was a strained buoyancy in her vision that the stern Weber must have found galling. She seemed so prepared to live with conditions as they unfolded. Even her comment about books-made-into-movies could be flippant – not a rendering of sober judgment, but a casual and apparently worldly-wise afterthought about the ways of Hollywood. Thus she expressed no sign of real concern when she remarked in 1939 that R.K.O. studios, which had bought the film rights to *Anne of Windy Poplars*, would, as she put it to him, 'murder the book as per usual' (*MEW* 190). She concluded her next letter, what was to be her last long letter to Weber, by breezily conveying developments as she found them stated in the *Hollywood News*: 'R.K.O., after seeing the script of [*Anne of Windy Poplars*] has upped the budget and means to make it a Class A film instead of one of the general features' (*MEW* 201). She seemed quite ready to accept fairly uncritically the forces that defined contemporary popular mass culture and, whenever possible, to take advantage of them.

Again, Weber must have been baffled by her forbearance, her gestures proclaiming innocence. For him, popular entertainment provided too many signs that the present civilization, like civilizations in the past, would perish. He agonized, for example, over the fact that students and their parents, the primary players on the stage that, as a teacher, he knew best, persisted in their 'self-indulgent and pleasure-chasing' ways. He despaired, at the same time, that good teachers 'spill [their] souls trying to secure the intellectual salvation of youngsters who (as well as their parents) do not know that they are lost.' He complained further: 'The automobile is making the rising generation giddy, and the "movies" are making the solid books of our curricula intolerable' (letter to Eggleston, December 1922).

Montgomery rather enjoyed not only the movies but also the motor car, and in her letter of 7 June 1930 gently mocked Weber's anxiety by placing an image of the car and Weber's beloved Homer into a comic context: 'Fancy Achilles whizzing around Troy in [a motor car], dragging Hector tied to the rear axle' (*MEW* 122). After all, she added, he was trying to write a prose manuscript himself, called 'Westward Ho, Liz,' about his own adventures in his endearingly named automobile! As Sasha Mullally has remarked in an essay on Montgomery and the automobile, Montgomery was quite prepared to drift toward the 'cautious technological optimism' that characterized Canadian society of the post-war years (128). Motor car, motion picture, and commercial radio were, with some qualification here and there, sources of considerable pleasure. In 1931, after exclaiming in a letter to Weber that she had been presented with 'a new kind of *moving picture* camera' that included 'a new process for taking and reproducing moving pictures in *colors*,' she observed (alluding to Thomas Edison's death earlier that year):

> I suppose Edison and Henry Ford have done more to change the world and life in the world than any other two men since the dawn of history. Only the unknown genius who first conceived the idea of making a sign stand for a word on the shoulder blade of a deer can be classed with them as far as revolutionary changes go. (*MEW* 141)

Montgomery's evaluations of mass culture and its effects reveal multiple positions that would frequently seem to be in conflict with each other. She might allow herself, for example, to draw on the *success* of the popular as evidence of its own authenticity and authority, as in the case of what seemed to her to be the benignly natural grass-roots support for the First World War in Canada (e.g., in *MEW* 5–6, 10–12). In 1927 she lamented such developments in popular culture as what she called 'the commercialization of so many kinds of sport in the present day.' These were for her '*un*lovely' developments: 'Those big ball games! And those paid professional players! Ugh! We will have Nero back with us yet!?' (*MEW* 95). Yet, alongside this jocund criticism of sports, lay her capacity to accept the commodification of her own work, as we have noted.

In the 1920s and '30s, the Montgomery–Weber dialogue occurred partly in the context of his drawing – however paradoxically and unintentionally – on a tradition in some ways underscored and extended by the intellectual elitism identified with literary modernism, especially with what Montgomery sarcastically called its he-man forms (*MEW*

144). Weber remained for a long time disdainful of what critics have described as a 'feminine' popular culture pulsating everywhere in such forms for example, as movies and magazines (see, for instance, his *Letters Home* 122). For Weber, a gender anxiety, linked to the stereotypes raised by what he felt were the conventions of a popular girl culture versus the manliness of a serious literary art beginning with the Greeks, always lay in the background, at least indirectly affecting his and Montgomery's discussion. In that sense, it is ironic that Weber, in keeping with Montgomery, spurned much modernist literary production, from Morley Callaghan's 'sex novels' to 'free verse' shorn of the essential 'bondage to certain rules' (*MEW* 53). In 1932 Montgomery developed a delicious mock-attack on Weber for a philistinism in him that matched the philistinism that she claimed for herself in her rejection of the 'modern hysterics' of contemporary literature (*MEW* 109). Weber must have chuckled at the audacity he saw in her bringing himself as reader into triangular relation with her and Callaghan: 'I just *howled* when you called Morley Callaghan's book "wishy-washy"! Why you benighted Philistine, Morley thinks he is the only person writing real "he-man" fiction in Canada!!!! He is wild with bitterness because Canadians won't buy his books' (*MEW* 144; see also 117 for Weber's 1930 statement to Eggleston; and Pike, '(Re)Producing' 71, 74). Here Montgomery was delighting that Weber had a place in her camp, where books were being bought in large numbers by Canadians.

Today, our awareness of the relationships among the cultural forms addressed and also practised by Montgomery encourages us to applaud her resistance to the elitist (and masculinist) side of the highly educated, academically trained Weber. We see now the context in which Montgomery cautiously applauded the cultural legitimacy of work that women more than men writers were prepared to propose as options for artistic expression. It is an unfortunate consequence of arguments such as those she felt forced to make in front of Weber – that the world of the 1920s and '30s was in some way a frantic interlude between two great ages, when literature could not be written – that she may have contributed to 'serious' readers' deferring indefinitely a critical consideration of herself and her work.

Still, by corresponding with Weber, Montgomery had opportunity to write on important issues outside of herself, there testing her mettle, her conviction. She was particularly alive and alert when Weber put her up to some challenge, or when she was challenging him. Because she put her personal views into action in her performance with and for Weber, Weber lent her a means of transforming the often intimate text that she rehearsed in the solitude of her journal, and placing it in the dynamic of a conversation concerned at heart about the role and the future of intellectual and artistic life in the complex cultural landscape of their day. Along the way, however ambivalently she might have expressed herself, Montgomery – often with incredible humour and lightness of touch – prevented Weber from succumbing to the discouragement and despair he felt from his own failure as a writer in a world the cultural dynamics of which contributed to his feeling of estrangement and isolation. Entertaining, dazzling, teasing, she helped to make the world of popular culture – indeed, the world of books such as she was writing – safe for a man like him.

As for herself, Montgomery, in her sixty-second year, declared in 1936: 'I have spent my life making gardens and leaving them behind' (*MEW* 168–9). Her buoyancy could not sustain her to the very end, when she found herself without the necessary strength to hold off those forces that lurked always beneath the engaging voice of her public texts. Yet she had managed, for the most part, to conduct her performance of herself playfully for Weber, with a comic edge that gave her room to indulge in self-parody. 'Thus saith the Preacher' marked her closing of one polemic, when she gently ribbed Weber on the 'Lives – manners – morals – customs' of a generation rocked by vast tidal waves of contemporary popular culture: 'The present age is degenerate,' she confided to Weber in 1922, winking at him, trying to make him smile; 'The boys and girls are not as *we* were – sage, sensible youngsters that we always were!' (*MEW* 38).

Weber in the end recognized that hers had been an incredible performance in what – when in December 1940 she saw that she was dying – she called their 'long and true friendship' (*MEW* 202). Finally, in December 1941, in her last words to Weber, she wrote with great difficulty: 'I am no better and have had so many blows this year I am quite hopeless. ... I do not think I will ever be well again' (*MEW* 204). She seemed to hint, too, that in order to succeed in the terms that she understood in their friendship, she had bravely suppressed her darker secrets, only to have the darkness catch up with her: 'the burden broke me at last' (*MEW* 204). The seventy-year-old Weber, responding to her brief December letter the year before, had registered his disbelief at her sorrowful news that she did not expect to recover from what turned out to be her final breakdown. And he thanked her for the generous shower of letters that she had bestowed on him: '... when I count my many blessings my correspondence with you all these decades is among them. You have been generous with me,' he wrote (Weber, B-Précis 435).

Weber heard the news of her death when he turned on the radio on 24 April 1942: 'The famous Canadian author of *Anne of Green Gables* and other girls' books died this morning.' Weber, who would live until 1956, noted: 'We miss deciphering her letters together, wife and I, and I miss the writing to her' (*MEW* 204).

NOTES

1 Montgomery's earliest extant letters to Weber, the fifteen that she wrote from March 1905 to September 1909, were edited by Weber's friend Wilfrid Eggleston and published as *The Green Gables Letters* in 1960.
2 Smith makes her observations about more formally constructed *autobiographies*, but, as she makes clear, she does not wish to exclude *letters* from her thinking (e.g., *Poetics* 188n.73).
3 Weber clearly had some sense of Montgomery's own isolation even in the midst of a busy family, church, and public life after 1911. In his reflections on their correspondence, he wrote in 1942: '... we exchanged wisdom and epigram, perhaps not so original as we then thought; but so we kept our intellectual souls in clover when the local pickings were scant at either end' ('Letter-Writer' 304).
4 Montgomery met MacMillan face-to-face in 1911, during her honeymoon in Scotland. MacMillan offered Montgomery a particular kind of cultural kinship, though he was not, in her view, 'so academically clever' as Weber (*SJ* 1:297). Selections from Montgomery's letters to MacMillan were published in *My Dear Mr. M.* (1992), edited by Bolger and Epperly.
5 See, for example, Weber's letters in *Ephraim Weber's Letters Home, 1902–1955*. Weber mentioned Montgomery to his friend Leslie Staebler a number of times and referred to their correspondence. He also sent Staebler copies of his 1942 and 1944 *Dalhousie Review* essays on Montgomery.
6 See Tiessen and Tiessen, 'Lucy Maud Montgomery's Ephraim Weber.'
7 Weber, in the context of apparently having sent Leslie Staebler a copy of his first *Dalhousie Review* essay on Montgomery, suggested to Staebler in 1942 that Montgomery's 'wholesome girls' books' might be familiar to 'Mrs. S' and to the Staeblers' daughter (Weber, *Letters Home* 98) – and he excluded Staebler himself from the circle of such readers. Similarly, to his friend Wilfrid Eggleston, Weber observed that it might be Eggleston's wife, Lena, who would be interested in Montgomery's next work of fiction, and not Eggleston himself (though, as it happened, Eggleston was himself an admirer of Montgomery) (unpublished letter to Eggleston, December 1930).

PART 4

WHERE LIFE WRITING MEETS FICTION

The expectation that the name of the author is identical with the first-person narrator in the text, what Philippe Lejeune has termed the autobiographical contract, is an important cornerstone of autobiographical studies. But what happens when that boundary is deliberately blurred? For many writers, including Virginia Woolf, Colette, Anaïs Nin, and L.M. Montgomery, autobiographical writing was a self-consciously literary form of self-expression, as earlier chapters have shown. Conversely, as this final section shows, fiction provided a safe screen of disguises and transpositions for Montgomery to work through intimately personal materials. Part 4 focuses on the crossroads where life writing and fiction meet to produce hybrid genres, including confessional and autobiographical fiction. Confessing her own frustrated desire to find the truth behind the writing of *Anne of Green Gables*, Cecily Devereux probes the memoir and the journals for clues, and concludes that Montgomery herself encouraged in her personal writings a public identification with her fictional characters. Taking an historical approach, Melissa Prycer argues that the fictional representation of consumption was intensely personal for Montgomery, as she confronted the terror of the illness which killed her mother, negotiating its fiction and reality in her novels. From *Anne of Green Gables* to *A Tangled Web*, Montgomery's fiction invites biographical readings that trace the author's projection of autobiographical selves into fictive characters. Anne and Emily, Valancy and Aunt Becky, then, become the public – fictive – costumes of Montgomery's multiple personae, as Mary Rubio and Elizabeth Waterston suggest in the final chapter of this book. For the biographical and historical sleuth, the novels ultimately reveal a complex play on reality and fiction.

10

'See my Journal for the full story': Fictions of Truth in *Anne of Green Gables* and L.M. Montgomery's Journals

Cecily Devereux

In 1941 L.M. Montgomery revoked a clause of the will she had drawn up in 1939 dividing all her household goods and personal effects equally between her two sons, Chester and Stuart Macdonald. In a codicil (fig. 10.1) appended to the revised will, she provided careful details of 180 items that were to be delivered to Chester after her death, provided he was still 'living with his wife Luella Macdonald.' Many of these items are presented with brief accounts of their provenance, as well as an indication of their personal value to Montgomery. She also refers the executors of the will and, presumably, Chester and Stuart to her personal diary: 'See Journal,' Montgomery wrote after several items, and in two cases, 'See my Journal for the full story.' The circumstances of Montgomery's bequest, and the alteration of her will in 1941, are beyond the scope of this chapter, which is not about her life *per se* or her relationships with her sons at all, but about the connections she makes between her life and her fiction through her journals.

What is of relevance to this chapter is the codicil's demonstration of two important points. First, Montgomery wanted her journals to be seen as truthful and accurate sources of information on certain personal aspects of her life. And, second, she wanted her journals to perform a particular posthumous work with regard to her fiction as it related to aspects of her life. One brief example shall suffice. The ninth entry in the codicil reads: 'Framed picture of orchard. This was enlarged from a picture taken by me of our old back orchard in Cavendish in 1900. It figures as the King orchard in the STORY GIRL. My flower garden was beyond the open space. See Journal.' The picture of the orchard (see fig. 10.2) has relevance with respect to Montgomery's personal identity, in particular, her love of nature, while it also evokes her professional work

LIST OF BELONGINGS WHICH I WISH MY SON, CHESTER
CAMERON MACDONALD TO HAVE.

1:- Framed painting of cover design of ANNE'S HOUSE OF DREAMS,
large size. This is the original artist's painting given me by
my publishers, F. Stokes and Co. at Christmas, 1917.

2:- The largest framed picture of my mother, Clara Woolner
Macneill. Taken a few months after her marriage in 1874. Said
to be a very poor picture. See Journal.

3:- Framed picture of Chester at pump with pail. Enlarged from
a snapshot taken by me at old pump in Leaskdale manse back-yard
in 1914.

4:- Framed picture of ANNE. Just the head.

5:- Framed picture of Chester with hat on. Taken in 1914 at the
age of two. Sent be by the nurse, Mrs. Aubin, who was with me
when little Hugh was born.

6:- Small framed picture of KILMENY.

7:- A slender green bottle found in the "blue chest" at Park
Corner, P.E. Island. See my Journal for the full story.

8:- One old brass candlestick ... the odd one. Used in my old
home at Cavendish for many years. Age unknown but is at least
79 years old now, in 1937.

9:- Framed picture of orchard. This was enlarged from a picture
taken by me of our old back orchard in Cavendish in 1900. It
figures as the King Orchard in the STORY GIRL. My flower garden
was beyond the open space. See Journal.

10.1 'See my Journal for the full story' – L.M. Montgomery's codicil to her will.
(L.M. Montgomery Collection, Archival and Special Collections, University of
Guelph Library.)

by presenting the orchard as creative inspiration. Montgomery signals an explicit connection between her fiction and her life, and refers to that connection as a story, a point to which I will return.

Montgomery is referring in her will to what is now well known as the multi-volume journal she began in 1889 at the age of fourteen and maintained until her death in 1942, with only one or two significant interruptions. In 1939 the journal had not been published, with the exception of a few selections mined for the writing of her memoir 'The Alpine Path,' the story of her career, for the Toronto magazine *Everywoman's World* in 1917. Nor had the journal circulated publicly: Montgomery does not ever indicate that she invited or allowed anyone to read her journal during her lifetime. Nonetheless, she clearly intended the journal for publication. In 1919 or possibly in late 1918, she had begun to rewrite her earlier journals, painstakingly copying out thirty years of entries (Turner 93–100). Her objective in the laborious task of transcription was to attain uniformity in the volumes, as she explained in her journal on 2 September 1919 (*SJ* 2:341). Given that by then she was – in Canada and internationally – a literary celebrity whose life had itself become something of a public property, the rewriting is comprehensible as an act of editing the early text, and as an indication that she intended her journal, now already a work of considerable magnitude and great potential interest, to have a public circulation.[1] The 1939 will indicates that all her letters, diaries, and personal papers were to be delivered after her death to her son Stuart, with these instructions:

> I give to my son Ewan Stuart Macdonald the sole right and discretion to arrange for the publication of my diaries in whole or in part if he so chooses and if they have not already been published prior to my death.[2]

Stuart Macdonald did, in fact, arrange for the posthumous publication of the diaries, or at least for their preservation at the University of Guelph and their editing by Mary Rubio and Elizabeth Waterston, although not until the 1980s.

As their title indicates, the *Selected Journals* (1985, 1987, 1992, 1998, 2004) do not represent a complete version of the 1889–1942 diaries, but a series of choices for abridged volumes based on the handwritten volumes bequeathed by Montgomery to her son in 1942 and acquired by the University of Guelph in the early 1980s. Mary Rubio has compellingly recounted the arduous process of bringing these volumes to press, and in particular the difficulties for herself and co-editor Elizabeth Waterston of selecting what material to retain and what to omit for the abridged versions that the publisher deemed necessary. Rubio points out that the editors were initially required by the publisher to 'reduce Montgomery's narrative by about 50 percent' ('"A Dusting Off"' 56). But the handwritten journals of 1942 are themselves not necessarily complete or precise. That is, they are selective with respect to the circumstances and events in Montgomery's life – a conventional matter of journal writing – but they were also subject to ongoing revision during her lifetime with a view to publication.

Since the original diaries appear to have been destroyed, it is impossible to know whether in 1919, and during the years following, Montgomery changed the original writings or excised material as she saw fit at the time, although she claimed to be copying the early volumes exactly (*SJ* 2:341). It is evident, however, that she made many editorial decisions about the journals before her death. In addition to rewriting the early volumes, she altered sections of the journals even after the transcription. Rubio and Waterston, in their introduction to the first published volume of the *Selected Journals*, note that 'several pages of the handwritten volumes were carefully cut out and replacements just as carefully inserted' (*SJ* 1:xxiv). Moreover, in 1919 and later, Montgomery added photographs and other visual supplements to her journals, some of which may confuse their chronology and add new layers of interpretation. Each of the excisions and reconstructions creates a gap in the story that is both a sign of its incompleteness and a space through which it is possible to see Montgomery constructing her life narrative for her public readership, and in which intention is revealed as a crucial element in the way the journals signify.

The Private and the Public Diary

Montgomery's preparation of her journals for public consumption is not in itself unusual. The public nature of private diaries has been discussed by American literary scholar Lynn Z. Bloom, who observes: 'Very often, in either the process of composition over time, or in the revision and editing that some of the most engaging diaries undergo, these superficially private writings become unmistakably public documents, intended for an external readership' (23). In fact, as Felicity Nussbaum has suggested, it may be an aspect of the diary genre – the private and the public diary – that audience is not only implicit but is actively engaged by the author. In the preceding chapter, Paul and Hildi Tiessen have traced Montgomery's sense of audience in both her letters and her journals. Diary writers routinely construct their texts as if they were private, while addressing readers outside of themselves.[3] 'Though the diary is not always strictly secret,' Nussbaum points out,

> it usually *affects* secrecy, and it is often sold today with lock and key. It is a private and personal revelation that cannot be spoken to anyone except the self. It is a confession to the self with only the self as auditor and without the public authority; but, on the other hand, it becomes necessary at the point when the subject begins to believe that it cannot be intelligible to itself without written articulation and representation. (Nussbaum 135)

Thus, it is not simply the act of, or the intention for, publication that shifts the diary into the public sphere: it is the act of writing itself. A diary's textuality ensures that it is always potentially public. A writer can attempt to control access through various strategies of secrecy and physical restriction of access, but the fact of the text exceeds all these efforts, something that is implicit in the flimsiness of the conventional lock and key to which Nussbaum refers. Unless it is destroyed, moreover, the diary remains beyond the possibility of controlled access by the author: it can always be read after death; it can always be reproduced and circulated. A good example is found in this volume in the intensely private diary by Amy Andrew, intended for herself and for her immediate family, but reproduced in excerpts and theorized for a wider readership by Mary McDonald-Rissanen in chapter 5.

Indeed, even before death, the diary can be read and interpreted by readers other than the author. The author, as Nussbaum argues with the example of Boswell's anxiety that his diary should fall into the hands of his enemies (136), cannot help but know that any writing is potentially available to any reader, and is always subject to circulation. Montgomery was well aware of the fundamentally uncontrollable nature of textuality, in terms of circulation and interpretation, and she demonstrated an anxiety not unlike Boswell's in her treatment of her journals and of other documents relating to herself. Montgomery transcribed her early journals and presumably destroyed the early versions, as she indicates she had for her childhood diary. In addition, Montgomery regularly burned letters and papers, keeping only those documents that, it is possible to argue, affirmed particular self-representations, performed specific tasks, or had a perceptible value as textual commodities.

Her transcription of the early volumes beginning in 1919 signals a shift in her perception with respect to the work her private writings could do, and, crucially, with respect to the image of herself they would convey to her public. Montgomery saw her journal performing a particular kind of posthumous work, and it is possible to see this work as the exertion of control – or, at least, of the *desire* for control. She wrote her journals for a public readership, and she continued to adjust the text after she had written it. She also undertook to shape the text that would circulate in publication, and to attempt to limit the ways in which the text would signify. The journals, thus, represent Montgomery's attempt to manage the ways in which her public would see her, and, crucially, how they would read her published fiction in relation to that constructed figure. Carole Gerson has astutely described Montgomery's journals as 'sequels to her life and her published books,' carefully constructed texts in which the 'professional storyteller shaped her own story retrospectively' ('"Dragged"' 56). The journals, in other words, need to be understood in terms of narrativity and of fictionality, for they are, as Gerson observes, stories to be read posthumously in relation to the novels as well as the life.

Shari Benstock has argued that there is always something inherently fictional in autobiographical writing. Autobiography, she suggests,

> reveals gaps, and not only gaps in time and space or between the individual and the social, but also a widening divergence between the manner and matter of its discourse. That is, autobiography reveals the impossibility of its own dream; what begins on the presumption of self-knowledge ends in the creation of a fiction that covers over the premises of its own construction. ('Authorizing' 11)

Georges Gusdorf, in his influential essay 'The Conditions and Limits of Autobiography,' has noted that autobiography is not the simple recapitulation of the past but 'the attempt and the drama of a man struggling to reassemble himself in his own likeness at a certain moment of his history' (43). We should not, according to Gusdorf, assess the autobiographical in simple terms of truth and falsity, but should rather regard the life-text in aesthetic terms, as a work of art (43). We might add to this other kinds of work typically performed by the life-text. When we read a diary (when it has become public), its supposed work of truth and revelation is a crucial element of the symbolic contract. We understand that we are opening a text that is not a novel or a work of fiction, but one that will provide us with exclusive and private information about and by the writer, information that we can use to interpret his or her professional and personal life, as well as his or her writings outside of the autobiographical genres.

The autobiographical text, in other words, serves as what Gusdorf describes as 'the mirror in which the individual reflects his own image' (33). This image may be – will necessarily be – mediated by ideology, as well as by motives of particularized self-representation, performativity, and specific intentionality. The author's motives may include writing for revenge, or writing for legal evidence, for instance, both of which are evident in Montgomery's journal. But the emergent image will be interpretable in relation to the author, in ways that more overtly fictional genres will not be expected to be. Moreover, what is fundamental to autobiography, and what differentiates it from the genres of the journal or the diary – and what ultimately makes it not only a document about a life but a work of art – is the narrative process of distancing and reassembling, in short, the representation of a life as a story (Gusdorf 43). It is worth noting that this is precisely what Montgomery undertakes in her journal, not only raising questions about the diary genre itself and, importantly, about how we read it and use it, but suggesting that she saw her journal as a hybrid between diary and conventional autobiography, a document that would take her readers from her childhood and the beginnings of her career as a writer to the end of her life, within a continuous, constructed narrative, and as a work of art.

There is thus considerable tension in the circulation and interpretation of diaries and journals in that they are carefully constructed, but are also committed to the truth-effects of the genre. What is significant, then, in the case of Montgomery's journals, and what makes them so interesting to the critical discussion of life writing, is her manipulation of the diary genre, and her presentation of her putatively day-to-day records of life as story attached to her fiction in numerous ways, and, crucially, related to it as a self-referential text. She is, in effect, exploiting the paradoxical nature of the genre itself, addressing the reader while appearing to address only herself; making private revelations while editing and preparing the text for publication; presenting a seemingly discontinuous account within a fairly consistent narrative structure and system of representations that includes the sequencing and interconnectedness of events and emergent patterns. These representations also include herself as central character along with the roles of husband, sons, friends, and extended family in relation to herself.

That Montgomery's self-representation has had a considerable effect is obvious in the continued popular desire to maintain the connection she herself established in her journal between her life and her fiction. Since the appearance of the first volume, the *Selected Journals* have been widely read, and, moreover, have emerged as the impetus for, and the crux of, a new and vigorous Montgomery scholarship. Any critical analysis concerned with contextualizing Montgomery's fiction in social and cultural terms – and such analysis has proliferated since the end of the 1980s – has invoked the journals.[4] There is very little recent scholarship on any aspect of Montgomery's writing that does not make at least some reference to the published journals, although copies of the handwritten originals are also publicly accessible. The impact of the journals is also evident outside the area of scholarly study. In popular biographies of Montgomery, such as Janet Lunn's *Maud's House of Dreams* (2002), the journals are suggested as a primary resource in the acknowledgments (152). The journals also function as an important intertext in the *Anne of Green Gables* television adaptations produced by Sullivan Entertainment since 1985 (Hersey 131–44). This inter-implication of the journals with Montgomery's fiction draws attention to what is part of their appeal: their perceived function as a document that explains the ways in which Montgomery's fiction, notably her most famous and best-loved novel, *Anne of Green Gables*, is connected, as she put it in her 1917 memoir, to the incidents and environment of her life (*AP* 52).

These connections between the author and her fictional character are perhaps nowhere more evident than in the construction of the imaginary Avonlea in Prince Edward Island's Cavendish. Here the boundaries between what Nancy Rootland calls Anne's world and Maud's world have increasingly been blurred. As Irene Gammel puts it in her discussion of the life-size figures of Anne and Montgomery in the Royal Atlantic Canadian Wax Museum, 'The boundaries between fiction and reality disappear in this hyperreal simulacrum' (Introduction, in *Making Avonlea* 5). The illusion created at the Green Gables location in the Prince Edward Island National Park, like that at the Wax Museum, has to do with enabling visitors to see both worlds at the same time. The site itself is presented as the house that was the basis for the fictional Green Gables, and thus functions as a literary shrine, with significant areas marked as the territory in which Montgomery devised her story. For example, the Haunted Wood is signposted throughout with photographs and text pertaining to Montgomery's life. In this, as E. Holly Pike has pointed out for other representations of Montgomery, 'her life is associated with her fiction and fictional locales as if there is no distinction between the real and fictional worlds' ('Mass Marketing' 244). But the house is also presented as the place where Anne actually lived: the bedroom in the Green Gables house, the garden, the kitchen, are marked as Anne's territory. Anne is thus invoked – as readers have always wanted to see her – as a 'real' girl, whose presence is indicated with a range of recognizable traces, including her hat and carpet bag.[5]

The narrative that underpins the various sites in Prince Edward Island's 'Anne's Land,' I argue, is ultimately Montgomery's own. That is, the connections between Montgomery and her heroine that make the sites possible are those that have been produced and released to the public through the issuing of her selected journals, and through the sections of the journals that she released during her own lifetime. The importance of the journals to the sites is obvious, as quotations from the journals appear on the signposts along the path through the Haunted Wood. Given this interface between the author and her creation, it seems all the more baffling that the journals are in fact curiously uninformative precisely on the matter of Montgomery and Anne, on the production of the novel, and on the events and circumstances leading up to it. There are significant gaps in the personal writings where we might imagine the connections to have been forged.

'... I never squeaked a word about it ...': *Anne of Green Gables*

I do not think I can have been alone in anticipating, when the *Selected Journals* began to appear in their edited version in 1985, that these volumes would reveal the full story of *Anne of Green Gables*, as Montgomery claims in her will they do for the framed picture of the Cavendish orchard as it signifies in relation to *The Story Girl*. When I took up the first volume, I opened it, not to the beginning, that is, the first entry of September 1889, but to the years immediately preceding the period of the publication of Montgomery's first novel, that is, the years of 1905 to 1907. For me, it was a moment of wanting to find the 'truth' about the writing of *Anne*. What was Montgomery really doing and thinking when she wrote her book? How would she present her responses to what is now understood to have been the multiple rejections of the manuscript? What made her choose the publisher she did? How did she articulate her ambition to write at this time? How much of herself was she putting into her novel? And on what terms? As readers of the *Selected Journals* will already know, what I found, no matter how far back I went from the summer of 1907, when *Anne* was published by L.C. Page Co. in Boston, there was nothing that directly pertained to the writing of the novel.

My first response was to assume that these entries had been deleted. In the list of omissions provided by Rubio and Waterston at the end of volume 1, as at the end of every volume of the *Selected Journals*, there are twenty complete and ten partial entries deleted from the period of January 1905 to the summer of 1907. When I turned to the copies of the handwritten diaries at the University of Guelph, however, I found that there is no more information about *Anne* to be gleaned from the originals than from the published versions. The editors did not, as we might assume they would not, leave out crucial information pertinent to the novel. In fact, Montgomery simply did not write about writing *Anne*, prior to its acceptance at any rate. At least, she did not preserve any of that writing in the journal she bequeathed to her son Stuart for future publication.

The record Montgomery provides of the writing of *Anne of Green Gables* is generated only after the fact of its acceptance, when she first mentions her novel in the journals. On 16 August 1907 she notes that some months earlier, in April, she had 'received a letter from the L.C. Page Co. of Boston accepting the MS of a book and offering to publish it on a royalty basis' (*SJ* 1:330). There are no references prior to this entry to the account of the writing of *Anne* that is now so familiar to most of Montgomery's readers: of her finding a faded entry in one of the notebooks in which she scribbled ideas for her writing that included the idea that would spark the novel's plot: 'Elderly couple apply to orphan asylum for a boy. By mistake a girl is sent them' (*AP* 72; *SJ* 1:330). There is nothing of the process of writing it, nor of typing it out, nor of her hopes for the book. There are no entries that convey her disappointment when the manuscript was repeatedly returned by publishers who had rejected it, as she later wrote that it was. There is nothing of the story that has now become a major part of the Green Gables mythology of Montgomery's putting the manuscript away in a hatbox in a closet after what she indicates in her journal in 1907 were four rejections, and of finding it again the following year, sending it off to the Page Company in Boston, and, in 1907, receiving their acceptance of the book, with a request that she write a sequel. Montgomery simply summarizes this story in the 16 August entry and subsequently circulates it in almost exactly the same form in the official – public – story of the writing of *Anne* in *Everywoman's World* in 1917.

In fact, it is a curiosity of these journals, which deliberately and self-consciously represent Montgomery's life as a writer, that there is so little explicit information in them about the conception and working up of her first published novel until it had been accepted. It is equally remarkable that there is so little about the other circumstances in her life that must have preoccupied her in 1905, when she was writing *Anne*, and in 1906, when she was trying to get it published. During this period, Montgomery was not only writing her book, but she was also involved with Presbyterian minister Ewan Macdonald, to whom she would become engaged in 1906. Macdonald, although he is mentioned as the Cavendish minister and in passing on several occasions, is not introduced as a suitor until 12 October 1906, when Montgomery writes, 'This afternoon Ewan Macdonald called to say good-bye before leaving for Scotland, where he intends to study at Glasgow University. And I am sitting here with his little diamond solitaire on my left hand!' (*SJ* 1:320). Although she does at last recount the engagement here in her journal, Montgomery would not publicize it or speak of it, even to her correspondents George Boyd MacMillan and Ephraim Weber, until 1911, at the time of her marriage to Macdonald.

Rubio and Waterston have documented that the representation of Ewan in the journals has been subject to revision, that in the entry in which Montgomery first described her future husband, 'she removed the page and inserted a replacement' (*SJ* 1:xxiv). It is not clear, however, if this reconfiguring of her first impression of Ewan accounts for the absence of the story of her early relationship with him – or if there is any similar revision undertaken in the account of *Anne*. As far as can be ascertained from the existing documents, Montgomery seems deliberately to have kept both *Anne* and Ewan entirely secret.

At one level, Montgomery's desire to keep secret the completion and fortunes of her work prior to acceptance seems to operate on the same principle she articulated with regard to her very first publication, in 1890. She wrote then, 'I did not dare hope it would be printed, so I never squeaked a word about it to anyone' (*SJ* 1:35). Certainly, she repeats this sentiment to Weber in 1907 about *Anne*: 'I didn't squeak a word about it,' she tells him, 'because I feared desperately I wouldn't find a publisher for it' (*GGL* 51). This reticence is suggestive of a sign of superstition, or of a compositional practice that depended on the separation of the text in process from all other expressions, or even perhaps of the extent to which Montgomery was already addressing her diary to readers other than herself. Yet none of these reasons explains in a satisfactory way Montgomery's absolute silence about her work on the book. It is also difficult to say what might underlie her secrecy with regard to her engagement, unless Montgomery felt that this too could not be recorded until she had got to the end of the full story, and the marriage, like the book, was a *fait accompli*, or a controlled and closed narrative.

What Montgomery did write about during the period of brooding up and producing *Anne* in 1905 was her profound and chronic unhappiness at this time. When her Grandmother Macneill died in 1911, Montgomery grieved deeply, and for the rest of her life she preserved her childhood in her journal in a fond nostalgia, the bitter memories of her early thirties tempered by age and distance. But her resentment as an adult and her persistent sense of having been unfairly reproved, singled out for punishment, and reminded of her dependence upon the kindness of her grandparents are prominent in much of her personal writing during the first decade of the twentieth century. The journals in this period powerfully convey her sense of herself as a virtual prisoner in the homestead in Cavendish, driven back to the kinds of imaginative retreats in books and nature that she suggests had been her refuge as a child living with her grandparents, and still pursuing her ambition to write in the face of growing difficulty in her domestic circumstances. As well as detailing her resentment of her grandparents, Montgomery writes at this time about the death of her mother, her memories of the funeral, and of her sense of loss. Her 1905 journal, for instance, begins with an account of finding a letter written by her mother in her girlhood and culminates in her dramatic cry: 'It is a dreadful thing to lose one's mother in childhood!' (*SJ* 1:300).

Montgomery's account in 1905 of her childhood has influenced the critical interpretation of *Anne of Green Gables*. On the basis of this account, many readers have seen *Anne* to be a sublimated representation of Montgomery's own story. And critics and biographers, drawing upon the journals, have emphasized the connection between Montgomery's unhappiness in these years and the writing of *Anne*. Margaret Atwood's Afterword to the 1992 McClelland and Stewart New Canadian Library edition of *Anne* is a case in point:

> Knowing what we now know about her life, we realize that Anne's story was a mirror-image of her own, and gathers much of its force and poignancy from thwarted wish-fulfilment. Montgomery, too, was virtually an orphan, abandoned by her father after her mother's death to a set of

strict, judgmental grandparents, but she never gained the love she grants so lavishly to Anne. Anne's experience of exclusion was undoubtedly hers; the longing for acceptance must have been hers as well. So was the lyricism; so was the sense of injustice; so was the rebellious rage. (334)

The idea that *Anne* was Montgomery's adult response to her remembered childhood unhappiness is a potent one. In fact, it is difficult not to speculate that Montgomery, in 1905, was investing her novel with the same kind of therapeutic function of writing out that she repeatedly maintains was performed for her by her journals.

What I am ultimately suggesting in this chapter is that in her journal and memoir, Montgomery herself compellingly linked her novel to her own experience. Admittedly, she would write in 1921 to Ephraim Weber, 'People were never right in saying I was "Anne"' (*MEW* 30), while also maintaining that there was much more of herself in Emily. Yet in her 1917 published memoir, the text we now know as *The Alpine Path*, Montgomery situated her early years and the circumstances of her life in the Macneill homestead in significant relation to her first novel:

> I have written at length about the incidents and environment of my childhood because they had a marked influence on the development of my literary gift. A different environment would have given it a different bias. Were it not for those Cavendish years, I do not think *Anne of Green Gables* would ever have been written. (*AP* 52)

It is not entirely clear whether Montgomery is configuring the novel as a document of her life or as a text in which she has inscribed the symptoms of her own condition, as she presents it in her journal at the time of her writing of the novel. In fact, it is possible that she is doing both, with a deliberate ambivalence, in terms of her representation of the novel's bias. As she notes in her journal at the time of *Anne*'s acceptance: 'Many of my own childhood experiences and dreams were worked up into its chapters' (*SJ* 1:331). Montgomery outlined these incidents and experiences in *The Alpine Path*, expanding on an earlier journal entry in which she had traced the connections. Thus she indicates that she had imagined a Haunted Wood in Cavendish (30–1); that there was a prototype for the Snow Queen (33–5) and for a Story Club (57–8); that she had had a Katie Maurice playmate reflected in the glass panels of a cupboard in the Macneill parlour (72); that she responded to poetry as Anne did (46–7). She also outlined the connections between real Cavendish and imaginary Avonlea in both the autobiographical piece (73–4) and her journal (*SJ* 2:438–45).

There are still other explicit convergences between Montgomery and Anne, which appear in the journals and are not noted in the 1917 memoir. For example, in the very first entry of the journals in 1889, Montgomery named a geranium Bonny: 'I like things to have handles even if they are only geraniums' (*SJ* 1:1). This phrase, as Wendy Barry, Margaret Anne Doody, and Mary Doody Jones, editors of *The Annotated Anne of Green Gables*, have noted, would become Anne's in the 1908 novel (*AAGG* 81n8). The editors have also observed that Montgomery refigured her journal observation that the geranium 'blooms as if it meant it' (*SJ* 1:1) in Anne Shirley's comment on the Snow Queen, 'Oh, I don't mean just the tree; of course it's lovely – yes, it's *radiantly* lovely – it blooms as if it meant it –' (44; *AAGG* 76n1). Other similar self-quotations, to use the term coined by the editors, appear in the first published novel.

These explicit connections can be understood at one level to reaffirm what readers can ascertain from Montgomery's other writings: that she herself was virtually an orphan (Atwood 334); that she felt nobody wanted her, even when her father was alive; that she knew what it was to live with much older and unsympathetic guardians; that she found refuge from an unhappy reality in books and nature, as well as with imaginary friends; that she was intelligent and sensitive, with a strong sense of being misunderstood and alienated; that she had wanted to pursue an education and had encountered gender-based obstacles. What these connections thus suggest is that Montgomery saw herself as emotionally and intellectually like Anne, what James Olney describes as a metaphor of self. Autobiography, Olney suggested in 1972, is more than a history of the past, and more than a book currently circulating in the world: 'it is also, intentionally or not, a monument of the self as it is becoming, a metaphor of the self at the summary moment of composition' (35). Metaphor of self aptly describes the ways in which Montgomery represented herself in all her writing through carefully established continuities and connections. In writing about Anne and Emily, she represents an earlier reassembling of the self produced in both the journals and the fiction that Montgomery aligns with the incidents and environment of her own life. In representing both Anne and Emily, Montgomery mapped herself onto each heroine in her journal as a public document, and she constructed her fictional character as a public reflection of herself. Ultimately Montgomery's assembling of her life story in her journals has produced a compelling 'real-life' system within which Montgomery, her imagined heroine, her novel, and the geophysical space of her childhood all signify in relation to one another. The Maud of the journals has become a crucial component of the now trademarked Anne, the story Montgomery tells of herself a crucial factor in the circulation of the narrative of Anne – and there is little other information to fill in the gaps where Montgomery would not squeak a word.

Epilogue

Finally, let us briefly return to Montgomery's codicil discussed at the beginning of this chapter, and to the photo of the orchard (fig. 10.2), which she bequeathed to her son Chester in 1941, just one year before her death in 1942. The codicil refers her son to her journals, presumably, though not exclusively, to the entry of 1 June 1909, the day on which she both began to write *The Story Girl* and recorded her love of the apple-tree orchard: 'It is at such moments that I realize how deeply rooted and strong is my love for this old place – a love of instinct and passion, blent with every fibre of my soul' (*SJ* 1:351). The journal entry and photo anchored Montgomery's self as one that she saw inevitably tied to nature. She continues:

> Today I began work on my new book 'The Story Girl.' The germinal idea has been budding in my brain all winter and this evening I sat me down in my dear white room and began it. But I feel sad that I cannot be sure that I will be long enough in this old house to finish it and it seems to me that I could never write it as it should be written anywhere else – that indefinable, elusive 'bouquet' will be missing if it is written elsewhere. (*SJ* 1:351)

The entry has a nostalgic tone with a focus on imminent loss and departure. Already Montgomery was anticipating and managing future events, already mourning the loss of her Cavendish home, which would occur two years later in 1911, after the death of her grandmother and her departure for Ontario. She sums up her melancholy feelings in a dramatic one-line paragraph: 'It is terrible to love things – and people – as I do!' (*SJ* 1:351). This passage, no doubt, reverberated with her dark mood in 1941, when she drew up the codicil, anticipating and managing her penultimate departure. The photo of the orchard and her interfacing of the photo with *The Story Girl*, the long list of mementoes, of

10.2 'My flower garden was beyond the open space. See Journal' – the orchard in Cavendish. (L.M. Montgomery Collection, Archival and Special Collections, University of Guelph Library.)

book covers, and of personal photos listed in the codicil – these are all part of Montgomery's personal, artistic, and spiritual legacy bequeathed to her eldest son. In expertly controlled layers, truth and fiction converge, suggestively like the tree branches that gently bend to form an interlocking arch in the compositional centre in her photograph of the orchard. In the visual and verbal composition of her life, this picture is perhaps the perfect metaphor for Montgomery's entire life writing – a virtuoso weaving of enduring fictions of truth.

NOTES

1 The year 1919 was a difficult one for Montgomery. She had not recovered from the anxiety and distress of the First World War years when her cousin and dearest friend Frede Campbell MacFarlane died. In 1919 Ewan experienced severe episodes of depression, and Montgomery was engaged in a bitter lawsuit with her publisher L.C. Page at the time of Frede's death in January. The year thus seems to have been a turning point for Montgomery, and a time of reflection and reconsideration of the past. However, she claims to have begun copying out the journals in the winter preceding the fall of 1919 and thus could have begun prior to January. See *SJ* 2:341.

2 A copy of Montgomery's will, from the Ontario Archives, is included in the holdings of the University of Guelph Special Collections.

3 Sidonie Smith and Julia Watson note that Philippe Lejeune, who has written extensively on journals and diaries, does not distinguish between the two terms. See Lejeune, 'Practice of the Private Journal' (1999). They also observe, however, that 'some critics distinguish diary from journal by noting that the journal tends to be more a public record and thus less intimate than the diary' (*Reading Autobiography* 195).

4 Ahmansson's *A Life and Its Mirrors* (1991) was one of the first critical studies to consider Montgomery's fiction in relation to the journals. Since the mid-1980s, however, the journals have figured prominently in Montgomery scholarship generally. See, for instance, the essays collected in Gammel and Epperly, eds, *L.M. Montgomery and Canadian Culture*, and Gammel, ed., *Making Avonlea*.

5 Montgomery's home is reached by walking through the Haunted Wood, across the road, and up Lover's Lane to the Macneill homestead, where the foundation of the house is all that remains for visitors to see.

11

The Hectic Flush: The Fiction and Reality of Consumption in L.M. Montgomery's Life

Melissa Prycer

Tuberculosis! The very thought of it makes my soul cringe with agony.
L.M. Montgomery, January 1916, *SJ*, 2:175

Scarlet fever. Cholera. Diphtheria. Consumption. All were killers in the nineteenth century, diseases to be fought and conquered. But only one – consumption – captured the imagination of both scientists and artists for decades. Even as the clinical mysteries surrounding consumption, now commonly known as pulmonary tuberculosis, began to unravel, many of the artistic representations of the disease lingered. Throughout L.M. Montgomery's fiction, consumptive characters appear. The peculiar history of consumption and a rich romantic literary tradition intersect in the stories of Cecily King in *The Golden Road*, Ruby Gillis in *Anne of the Island*, Douglas Starr in *Emily of New Moon*, and Cissy Gay in *The Blue Castle*. Writing during a critical juncture in the history of consumption, Montgomery gradually changed her characterizations as scientific knowledge increased. Although she does not document specific medical advances, she eventually breaks free of the literary molds that had defined the artistic portrayal of consumption for decades, ultimately portraying an illness through the lens of her own personal experience.

During Montgomery's lifetime, consumption was the leading cause of death throughout the world. The author's connection to the disease was also deeply personal. Her mother, Clara Macneill Montgomery (fig. 11.1), died of the disease in September 1876, leaving behind a young daughter and a grieving husband (Gillen 3). Montgomery never quite recovered from the loss. Throughout her journals, she periodically wondered about her mother, what her life might have been like had she

11.1   Clara Woolner Macneill died of consumption in 1876. (L.M. Montgomery Collection, Archival and Special Collections, University of Guelph Library.)

lived, and how Clara might have looked as she aged. In 1905 Montgomery wrote: 'How often, when smarting under some injustice or writhing under some misunderstanding, have I sobbed to myself, "Oh, if mother had *only* lived!"' (*SJ* 1:300).

Montgomery was more, however, than a motherless child; she was the offspring of a consumptive, and the spectre of that particular disease haunted her memories. During the nineteenth century, the belief that the disease was hereditary left the children of consumptives carrying a unique burden. After Montgomery's children were born in the 1910s, her writings about her mother changed in tone. Evoking the common bonds of motherhood, she wrote: 'I know how she must have loved me. I know what her agony must have been in the long weeks of her illness when she was facing the bitter knowledge that she must leave me' (*SJ* 2:112). Death from consumption occurs slowly, with some patients lingering for years. With such knowledge, Montgomery wondered why Clara had not left some kind of legacy, so that she would know her. Despite her extensive family ties, few people spoke of Montgomery's mother. The few scraps of information that were shared with Montgomery became treasures, as she struggled to form an image of the woman her mother was.

Clara Montgomery had quickly succumbed to the disease, her death accelerated by the mental stress of her husband's failing business and the physical stress of pregnancy and birth. As her daughter imagined it, 'things were very hard for mother. I am afraid she must have been not unwilling to die. But I *know* nothing – I have never heard anything of what she thought or felt after her illness came on. Did she grieve to leave me?' (*SJ* 3:33). Later in the same entry, she noted: 'I would give anything if mother had only thought of writing a letter to *me* before she died and giving it to someone to keep for me until I was grown-up' (*SJ* 3:34). These experiences and memories shaped Montgomery's later fictive portrayal of the disease. For her, this was a personal disease, not just another literary device.

A Good Death

For centuries, doctors had struggled to gain control over the disease. Even as late as 1908 in Canada, as George Jasper Wherrett notes, 'it was true that "Every time the clock struck the hour in the daytime, one Canadian died from tuberculosis and every time it struck the hour during the night, two Canadians died of the same disease"' (15). Consumption had been mythologized and glamorized for centuries, to the point that dying of consumption was viewed as a 'good death' in popular imagination. However, the real suffering of patients bore little resemblance to the popular images. Diagnosis was difficult because the early symptoms were subtle, and it sometimes took years before doctors finally gave a diagnosis of consumption to a patient. The hallmark symptoms included a dramatic loss of weight, night sweats, a low-grade fever, difficulty breathing, and intense coughing. As the disease progressed, it was common to haemorrhage while coughing. In fact, some folklore claimed that an individual did not have the disease until she coughed up half a teacup of blood. Ironically, some of the symptoms helped patients to appear healthy, as medical historian Barbara Bates notes: '... "the deceptive blush" that fever imparted to the cheeks, the "increased lustre of the eye," the "singular hopefulness" of the patient, and the temporary improvements could engender false optimism in both the physician and the patient's family' (17). The bright red blood patients coughed up was the only sure way to tell the approach of death.

In 1882 German physician and researcher Robert Koch discovered the tubercle bacillus, proving that the disease was contagious and disproving a plethora of earlier theories which linked the disease to heredity, general weakness, or moral deficiency. Koch's discovery began a slow but dramatic shift in how the disease was conceptualized in science and art. This shift remains obscured in Montgomery's work for it took decades for the medical community and general public to fully accept Dr Koch's theories. Doctors quickly pointed out that the contagious nature of consumption did not match what was known about bacteria. If the disease was contagious, then how could there be so many households in which only one member was infected? In addition, it was difficult to pinpoint when an individual contracted the disease because the bacteria could lie dormant for years. Since specialists disagreed, no clear consensus about the cause of the disease or its treatment emerged for the public to understand (Bates 16). The non-scientific press met Koch's news with indifference and scepticism (Caldwell 21–2).

Much of the resistance to Koch's discovery rests in the peculiar behaviour of the disease, with which his contemporaries were intimately familiar. Sometimes several members of a family would die of the disease, suggesting that it was hereditary. Consumption also differed from other epidemic diseases in that a person could be exposed to consumption repeatedly without developing it. When the tubercle bacillus entered the body, it 'might be successfully attacked by the defenses of the body (the white blood cells) and be destroyed; the tubercles might become healed; or several tubercles might coalesce and spread, enlarge, and eventually destroy the patient' (Wherrett 16). Since most people were at one time or other exposed to the disease, a common saying throughout the nineteenth century was that 'everyone is sometime or another a little bit consumptive.' Almost anyone with some type of respiratory infection was thought to be consumptive.

Treatment options for consumption varied. Canadian doctors encouraged some patients to travel west, sometimes to Saskatchewan, where the air was considered cleaner and healthier. Sanatoriums, or specialized hospitals where patients were expected to rest to get well, began to be built.[1] Although sanatoriums became common in the United States in the 1880s, the first Canadian sanatorium, the Muskoka Cottage Sanatorium in Gravenhurst, Ontario (fig. 11.2), did not open until 1898. This institution may well have inspired Montgomery's focus on consumption in *The Blue Castle*, the novel set in the Muskoka region, although Gravenhurst is not referred to in the novel. Patients who were unable to afford the sanatorium were cared for at home, as the patient Cissy Gay is in *The Blue Castle*. Families were encouraged to hire trained nurses, and many home medical books contained detailed instructions on how to arrange a patient's room. It was suggested, for example, that the bed should be placed near a window and that there should be very little excess furniture within the room. Some doctors encouraged light and fresh air; others did not. There was no definite answer for treatment, just as there was no definite diagnosis. With the discovery of the first effective drug, streptomycin, in 1944, many debates regarding care faded away.

Consumption as a Literary Metaphor

Given the omnipresence of the disease in the nineteenth century, it comes as no surprise that consumption was a – if not the – prominent literary metaphor of the century. Many Victorian artists and writers, including the Brontë family, Elizabeth Barrett Browning, John Keats, and Robert Louis Stevenson, suffered from consumption. Prominent works such as *La Boheme* (1896), *Jane Eyre* (1847), *Camille* or *La Dame aux Camlias* (1848), and *Uncle Tom's Cabin* (1852) feature consumptive characters. In her influential book *Illness as Metaphor*, American literary critic Susan Sontag writes that 'fantasies inspired by tuberculosis in the

11.2 Convalescing consumption patients at Gravenhurst Sanatorium, Muskoka. (Acc. 2203. S 3597. Archives of Ontario / Archives publiques de l'Ontario.)

last century ... are responses to a disease thought to be intractable and capricious – that is, a disease not understood – in an era in which medicine's central premise is that all diseases can be cured' (Sontag 5). One way to begin to understand is to assign labels to those who had the disease. Without a clear scientific and medical consensus, artists stepped in to fill the void, as several literary types assigned meaning to consumption.

These types may overlap, but most consumptives in literature, including those in Montgomery's fiction, can be put in at least one of the following categories identified by Sontag: 'Too Good to Live,' 'Artistic Genius,' 'Passionate Patient,' and 'Beautiful Invalid.' Often, as they approached death, patients became increasingly spiritual, and family and friends began to look to the patient for some kind of spiritual guidance. The consumptive finally became too pure to live in a sinful world; they had become 'Too Good to Live.' A male consumptive was often described as an 'Artistic Genius'; his ideas became both the cause and the result of the disease, his mind sapping his strength and causing the body to waste. Others believed that because the patient was unable to behave in a typically masculine way, his mind was freed to reach new, creative heights. The 'Passionate Patient's' consumption was caused by an innate passion, whether political, moral, or sexual, which used up a patient's strength. When the passion was sexual, the disease also became a kind of judgment on the individual. A final type emerged for the advanced stage of the disease, as the patient, usually female, became more beautiful. This last type is seen in Montgomery's journal portrait of her dead mother, a portrait both sensual and beautiful (see chapter 4 for the full quotation). Part of this beauty was spiritual and part was physical, contradicting the expected unattractiveness of an invalid. For the 'Beautiful Invalid,' the constant fever brightened the eyes and gave a rosy glow to cheeks, hence, the phrase 'hectic flush.' It became fashionable in the 1840s to dress in dark colours to emphasize paleness, and the extreme shaping of waists with corsets has also been linked to the consumptive ideal of beauty. These four types provide a useful tool for analysing Montgomery's work below.

Though many nineteenth-century notions of consumption lasted well into the twentieth century, the discovery of the tubercle bacillus did lead to a more immediate shift in the terminology used by doctors and patients when describing the disease. In her fiction, Montgomery, however, always used the older term 'consumption' rather than the modern term 'tuberculosis,' which first became widely used in the 1880s

(Rothman 180). This corroborates Montgomery's affinity with the Romantic literary tradition, but even more important, it is evidence of her class consciousness. Throughout Canada during the early part of the twentieth century there was a public health campaign against tuberculosis that shifted the meaning of the disease. By attributing the disease to dirt and filth, which were most prevalent in urban slums (Caldwell 35), this anti-tuberculosis campaign made tuberculosis a sign of genetic or class inferiority. In the minds of many people, tuberculosis and consumption were two very different diseases: the middle and upper classes had consumption, and the poor had tuberculosis. Tuberculosis, a new disease in some eyes, was 'defined as a disease of only some, not all, people, essentially the immigrant and the poor, not the middle classes' (Rothman 181). The terms 'tuberculosis' and 'consumption' are often used interchangeably today, but this was not the case during the Victorian era. By using the word 'consumption' in her fiction, Montgomery shows her allegiance to the Romantic tradition and identifies her patients as middle class.

In Romantic and Victorian literature, consumption 'was used as a device to enlist the sympathies of the reader,' as literary historian Jeffrey Meyers writes: 'It was believed to affect chiefly sensitive natures, and conferred upon them a refined physical charm before making them succumb to a painless, poetical death' (5). Writing fifty years after the height of Romanticism, when science was changing the realities of disease, Montgomery creatively transformed the conventional images of consumption to reflect a medical world in flux. While she does not discuss the medical shift in treatment options from care at home to sanatoriums and surgery, her portrayal of consumptive characters reflects those changes in a subtle way. In doing so, she reveals how those outside the medical community grappled with the changing perceptions of the deadly disease.

Since consumption was an intimately familiar disease, Victorian authors tended to represent it in coded form, through use of euphemisms, confident that readers would easily decode their meaning. Writers avoided the realistic but unpleasant aspects of sanatoriums, surgery, and blood – images which readers would have associated with the campaigns of the anti-tuberculosis leagues and which would have placed the consumptive character into a lower class (Caldwell 224–5). Modern readers may not instantly recognize the euphemistically depicted symptoms, but Montgomery's contemporary audience was well aware of the impending fate of a character with a hectic flush.

Montgomery's Consumptive Heroines

Written as a fictional memoir, Montgomery's 1910 novel, *The Golden Road*, and its prequel, *The Story Girl*, tell the adventures of the King family cousins. *The Golden Road* implies that Cecily King, one of the younger cousins, later dies of the disease. Consumption runs in the family; her aunt had died of it years before. Although the reader never actually sees Cecily sick, throughout both of the King family novels, Cecily is described as pale and weak, a common sign of impending illness. In the chapter 'Prophecies,' Cecily's fortune is the most evasive and vague of all the cousins. Just before the Story Girl tells her fortune, Cecily coughs, and the Story Girl looks at her 'soft, shining eyes, at the cheeks that were often over-rosy after slight exertion, at the little sun-burned hands that were always busy doing faithful work or quiet kindnesses' (*GR* 201). Writing in hindsight, the narrator leaves no doubt that Cecily will die young. Cecily, with her hectic flush, quiet cough, and virtuous character, is constructed as the classic consumptive heroine who is simply too good to live. The audience did not need details to imagine the end of Cecily's story.

Montgomery was more direct in her first extensive treatment of the disease in her 1915 novel, *Anne of the Island*. In the novel, Anne Shirley faces the loss of a childhood friend Ruby Gillis. Before readers are told of Ruby's diagnosis, they are introduced to a physical depiction: 'She was even handsomer than ever; but her blue eyes were too bright and lustrous, and the color of her cheeks was hectically brilliant; besides, she was very thin; the hands that held her hymn-book were almost transparent in their delicacy' (*AIs* 79–80). Readers would recognize the deadly symptoms, yet Ruby and her family are in denial about the disease. When Ruby says, 'But just see my color. I don't look much like an invalid, I'm sure,' she expresses the false hope of getting well that many consumptives had (*AIs* 86). Ruby continues to go out, buys new dresses, and makes plans to teach in the fall. This illusion of health recurs in consumption studies and is part of the mystique of the disease.

Anne of the Island also reflects the great mysteries surrounding the disease. Anne and her friend Diana Barry endure a particularly un-pleasant discussion with Aunt Atossa, a bitter and cynical woman and distant relative of Diana. When Ruby is mentioned, Aunt Atossa declares, 'The doctors say consumption's catching' (*AIs* 83). By using a minor, unreliable, and pessimistic character to make this statement, however, the novel implies that the truthfulness of the doctor's word is to be doubted. The comment is said in passing and is not taken seriously by either Anne or Diana. Despite Koch's important discovery, the old theory of consumption striking particular individuals based on their character remained strong in Avonlea.

In the two previous Anne novels, Ruby Gillis was portrayed as a sweet, though flighty, young woman who was most concerned with beaux. Anne enjoys her company, but she is not quite a kindred spirit, Ruby being rather shallow. Like many consumptive heroines, Ruby develops an increased spirituality as death approaches, but atypically she does not find that spirituality from within herself; instead, she discovers it in her interactions with others. In her last conversation with Anne, Ruby expresses her fears regarding her approaching death:

> Even if what you say about heaven is true – and you can't be sure – it may only be that imagination of yours – it won't be just the same. It can't be. I want to go on living here. I'm so young, Anne. I haven't had my life. I've fought so hard to live – and it isn't any use – I have to die – and leave everything I care for. (*AIs* 107)

While Ruby's doubts certainly ring more true than the common literary type who gratefully accepts death, Montgomery uses Ruby to teach a moral lesson about the folly of being shallow. Anne's private thoughts only reify Ruby's worst fears, as she realizes that 'there had been nothing in her gay, frivolous life, her shallow ideals and aspirations, to fit her for that great change, or make the life to come seem to her anything but alien and unreal and undesirable' (*AIs* 106). When Ruby dies shortly after this conversation, she no longer fears death. Like many consumptives, she has found the comfort of God and spiritual closeness. In most consumptive fiction, it is the healthy people who discover spirituality by speaking with the ill. For Ruby, who is consistently portrayed as shallow, it takes imminent death to find the depths of her soul.

Traumatic Death and the Burden of the White Plague

Unlike Ruby Gillis, Douglas Starr in *Emily of New Moon* (1923) is portrayed as a source of strength throughout his illness. Since the Emily trilogy is Montgomery's most autobiographical novel, as scholars have established, it is no coincidence that Emily Byrd Starr also loses a parent to consumption. In narrating Douglas Starr's final days, Montgomery may have fulfilled her own desires to have the opportunity to say goodbye to a parent dying of consumption. Douglas Starr is a teacher, a lover of books, and a dreamer – a typical 'Artistic Genius.' Subtly separated from the community by both his intelligence and his illness, he and his daughter live a sheltered, isolated life. Emily is aware of his persistent coughing but does not know the meaning of it until housekeeper Ellen Greene tells her that her father only has a few weeks to live. While Ruby Gillis dies of consumption fairly quickly, Douglas Starr suffers for years, as Ellen explains to Emily: 'He's been dying by inches for the last five years. He's kept it from you, but he's been a great sufferer. Folks say his heart broke when your ma died' (*ENM* 9). Folklore credited long-term survival to having a reason to live. Montgomery believed that her mother had given up; she was not enough to will her mother to fight harder. Douglas Starr, in keeping with the popular myths of the time, developed consumption because of the sudden death of his wife, but he is able to fight his decline for his own daughter. He tells Emily of learning the news years earlier, remembering when the doctor told him to give up work: 'If you don't, I give you a year,' the doctor said, 'if you do, and live out-of-doors all you can, I give you three – or possibly four' (*ENM* 16). This was common advice for the time, as fresh, clean air was thought to purify lungs that had been exposed to bad air. He continues: 'Those years and what I've taught you in them are the only legacy I can leave you, Emily' (*ENM* 17). Emily takes this rich bank of memories with her throughout her life, writing often to her father. In her journals, Montgomery consistently mourns not knowing more of her mother's personality. Longing for memories of her mother, she gives that gift to Emily, who also must live as a survivor of the ravages of consumption.

It is Emily's status as a child of a consumptive that illustrates some of the other conceptions regarding the disease. Many believed that certain individuals were prone to the disease, especially if a direct relative had contracted it or if they had a pale complexion. The housekeeper tells Emily in the first chapter: '*You* can't monkey with colds the way some kids can' (*ENM* 4). 'She'll not likely live long enough to bother any one,' says her Aunt Elizabeth Murray later in the novel during a family conclave which will decide Emily's fate: 'She'll probably die of consumption same as her father did' (*ENM* 37–8). Emily, of course, does not develop consumption, but like the nagging persistence of a consumptive's cough which cannot be shaken off, references to her putative delicate health recur throughout the trilogy. Years after her father's death, when it has become obvious that she will not die of the disease, Aunt Ruth tells her: '*I* am responsible for your health now. You must know that consumptives have to avoid night air and draughts' (*EC* 97). Emily argues that fresh air is best, but, of course, Aunt Ruth wins. The cause of her father's death haunts her throughout her life, shaping other people's perceptions of her health, which was not unusual for survivors of consumptives.

An important shift in Montgomery's perception of the disease can be found in *The Blue Castle* (1926), a novel for adults. The dying character of Cissy Gay is not romanticized like Cecily King, Ruby Gillis, and Douglas Starr. Although the disease remains sanitized, Cissy does not become a role model through her disease. When Valancy Sterling, the novel's protagonist, first sees her after many years, she wonders: 'Could this be sweet Cissy – this pitiful little thing that looked like a tired broken flower? ... The contrast was so terrible that Valancy's own eyes filled with tears' (*BC* 85–6). Consumption has dramatically altered Cissy's appearance, and she is not portrayed as having a new kind of beauty. Cissy and Ruby are likely modelled on Montgomery's childhood friend Pensie Macneill, whom she visited in 1906, noting in her journal on 1 January: 'Poor Pensie is dying of consumption and I do not know when I have made a more sorrowful visit' (*SJ* 1:317). Just as with Valancy and Cissy, Anne and Ruby, so the friendship between Maud and Pensie revived in the face of death. Montgomery had observed the realities of consumption first-hand, and the examples in this later novel draw on this experience more than earlier novels did. The fact that Cissy has trouble breathing and sleeping emphasizes how consumption is more than a persistent cough. Montgomery depicts both good days and bad, noting that life does not gracefully slip away for the consumptive patient. As consumption is shown to ravage the body, the romanticism of the disease is lessened.

The community's reaction to news of Cissy's illness further demystifies consumption as romantic literary metaphor. The good people of Deerwood have ostracized Cissy, ostensibly because of her illegitimate child and her alcoholic father, but also because of her illness. By the 1920s, consumptives were routinely isolated from the community, usually in a hospital or sanatorium, because society had accepted the idea that consumption was contagious. As Cissy never leaves her home, she is quarantined, as it were. The Gays have a difficult time finding help: 'disreputable housekeepers' were 'the only kind who could be prevailed on to go to a house where a girl was dying of consumption' (*BC* 78). Anne Shirley was considered a better person for visiting Ruby as she died; Valancy, in contrast, is thought to be insane when she decides to nurse the dying Cissy. Her family reacts with nothing less than horror. Though there are myriad reasons for Valancy's family's strong reaction, the growing social awareness of consumption as a contagious disease is certainly one of them. Consumption is no longer a purifying disease, capable of making any sinner better through suffering. By 1913 Webster had entered in his dictionary the term 'white plague' as an accepted synonym for tuberculosis, suggesting the changing perception of the illness.

By 1926, then, Montgomery was finally ready to strip the disease of some of its romantic myths. According to the myths, consumption in the 'fallen woman' was seen as the physical manifestation of – and appropriate retribution for – her sexual sin. As the heroine comes closer to dying, she repents her sins, awakens to a deep spirituality, and dies redeemed by God – the disease, as it were, saving her. Cissy, in contrast, never repents and repeatedly contradicts the expectations of society for a woman in her position. She chooses not to marry her lover, and Montgomery portrays Cissy as making the right choice. Her consumption results from her grief following the death of her child, not grief because the child was born. Unlike the classic consumptive fallen woman, the disease is not credited with changing or redeeming Cissy. She says as much herself, and Valancy defends her often, reminding Cissy's father that 'she has always been a good little girl' (*BC* 122). The disease has not become the defining part of Cissy's character or virtue. With the creation of Cissy Gay, Montgomery breaks through the traditional literary models of consumption.

Montgomery's treatment of the central illness of the nineteenth and early twentieth centuries reflects the changing perceptions of the disease across time. Since her journals document that Montgomery kept up with medical developments, it may come as a surprise that many of the 'old wives' tales' from the nineteenth century regarding consumption persist in Montgomery's novels of the early twentieth century. Many histories of consumption portray Koch's discovery as simply the first step on an upward line of progress until successful medication was found to treat the disease. Montgomery's books, and others in the same genre, show that medical knowledge did not immediately enter the general community, especially if the doctors were in disagreement.

Many historical accounts of consumption during this period discuss sanatoriums, but sanatoriums are never even hinted at in Montgomery's work. Even though her characters were not poor, most were not rich either. In an age faced with so many conflicting opinions, and in a community where family was vital, it does not seem likely that many of Montgomery's peers would send a relative to a sanatorium to die away from home and family. Incidentally, despite the efforts of several individuals, a civilian sanatorium was never opened on Prince Edward Island (Wherrett 234).[2] The sick were meant to be a part of the home and a part of the family for as long as possible, and the reader sees that in Montgomery's descriptions of Ruby Gillis, Douglas Starr, and Cissy Gay.

Consumption was a common experience in Victorian and Edwardian society, but, more importantly, it was a defining moment of Montgomery's life. The disease was a haunting presence that filled her with dread and terror. On 3 January 1916, almost ten years after she had visited the dying Pensie, Montgomery recorded in her journal: 'the New Year has opened with bitter anxieties and worries. Chester was miserable all December with colds and sick stomach spells. About Christmas one of the glands in his neck swelled and we had the doctor last Friday. He looked grave and said it might possibly be a tubercular gland! ... the worry is killing me' (SJ 2:175). The spectre of losing her first-born to the same dreaded illness that had claimed her mother filled her with nothing less than terror and panic: 'The very thought of it makes my soul cringe with agony' (SJ 2:175). Thus, in this 1916 journal entry, she had come a long way from the early romantic images in which consumption was an illness that only struck certain people or was a judgment on the way one lived. By 1916, decades after Koch's discovery that it was contagious, consumption became like any other disease, and its mystique began to fade – although the terror it was able to inspire before a cure was found lingered. In her fiction, Montgomery was able to write out her preoccupation with this illness, but only in her later work was she able to strip it of its lore and approach the deadly foe in a more realistic fashion. During this period of dynamic change in the history of medicine, L.M. Montgomery wove together the fiction and reality of consumption to create a unique – and ultimately an intimately personal – tale of this historical killer.

NOTES

1 Patients' time within the sanatorium was strictly regimented. They could do nothing but try to get well. Often, reading and other activities were forbidden until patients were considered 'well' enough to have any kind of

mental activity. These privileges could later be taken away if there was any kind of relapse. For more information, see Betty MacDonald's *The Plague and I.*

2 The generosity of Sir Charles Dalton built the Dalton Sanatorium in North Wiltshire, fifteen miles north of Charlottetown. In 1917 it was deeded over to the federal Military Hospitals Commission, under which it was greatly enlarged. However, when it was returned to provincial jurisdiction, the province felt it could not manage such a large facility. The sanatorium was returned to Dalton in 1920, and it was then torn down. Many of the materials were reused in the Charlottetown Hospital (Wherrett 234).

12

Untangling the Web: L.M. Montgomery's Later Journals and Fiction, 1929–1939

Mary Rubio and Elizabeth Waterston

This book began with L.M. Montgomery and Nora Lefurgey taking turns in the collaborative diary, and it ends with two modern scholars working together via computer exchanges as they collaborate in editing the journals of L.M. Montgomery. At the L.M. Montgomery and Life Writing Symposium, the editors of Montgomery's journals presented their new findings in a lively colloquy, which is reproduced in the dialogue-structure of this final chapter.

MR: You don't have to be a biographer to turn to the twenty-one novels and other creative works to see that these imaginative works reveal pressures, evasions, and releases in Montgomery's life not exposed in the journals. Like many complex people, she had depths of personality of which she herself was probably unaware. We know from her journals exactly when she began a major work such as *Emily of New Moon* or *The Blue Castle*; how and where she worked; what daily events speeded or slowed her compositions. What we don't see is her giving any real analysis of that process. We see almost no self-conscious comment about what part of her life each novel reflects. And sometimes she denies a connection between herself and her heroines which is clearly there, as in her first novel, *Anne of Green Gables* (1908). It is fascinating for the biographically minded sleuth to read Montgomery's journals and her creative work simultaneously, while reviewing people's memories and the contemporary facts gleaned from newspapers and history books.[1]

EW: In this conversation, we will focus on two novels written roughly ten years apart which frame the last portion of her writing life: *A Tangled Web* (written 1929–31) and *Anne of Ingleside* (written 1937–9).

The differences between them illuminate changes in Montgomery's later life, as recorded in her journals, and as yet little explored. Each novel also reflects elements in her family and professional affairs not recorded in her daily entries, but known to us now through research and through interviews with people close to her during those last twelve years of her life. We will thus present two examples of the linkage between Montgomery's two kinds of life writing, the journals and the novels. Warning – we don't always agree on meanings of the linkage!

First, *A Tangled Web*, Montgomery's interesting 'adult' novel of 1931. Not my favourite book –

MR: I love it! A new venture. A book for adults. A new mode – irony.

EW: At any rate there are just five references to it in volumes 3 and 4 of the *Selected Journals*. On 3 May 1929 she says she is housecleaning, thinking daffodils, reading George Eliot's novels, and noting in passing some comments on a 'best set of china.' She reveals her regret at not inheriting Grandmother's 'best set' of china. And then the first reference: 'I am now working on an adult story, centering around the old Woolner jug' (*see SJ* 3:396; fig. 12.1).

MR: For Montgomery, 'having the best set' of china would have shown that her ancestors had been refined and prominent, having had good taste for a long time – a mark of caste and class not only to Islanders but also within the emerging social ladder in Toronto. Maud emphasizes that *her* family (like Emily of New Moon's) 'had traditions': she did not want to be thought a parvenu. The jug focused her personal pride and sense of difference from those without a tradition of class and breeding behind them.

Through the Woolners, she had connections with English culture. In the Cavendish community, Lucy Ann Woolner Macneill had been much respected as a fine lady who was disciplined, proper, and dignified. She had 'class.' And through both the Scottish Macneills and Montgomerys, Maud's ancestors had been politically influential in Prince Edward Island.

But more important: Maud was now centring on the passage of time. She was fifty-five and increasingly conscious of the process of ageing. She could identify with an old lady somewhat like her grandmother had been. The 'adult story' will begin with Aunt Becky as a controlling old woman who calls her clan to a levee to hear how her will disposes of a heritage jug. Using their eagerness to inherit as a shield, she unleashes scathing remarks at all of them ...

12.1 Shards of L.M. Montgomery's Woolner jug in the University of Guelph Archives. (Photo by Mary H. Rubio, 2003.)

EW: ... as Grandfather Macneill used to do, and as Montgomery probably often wished she could do. But to judge from the journals, Montgomery – even when cross at her sons, at her husband, and at her community – would rarely have told them the truth about her feelings.

MR: Montgomery did occasionally 'let fly' – people in Norval remember how she shocked a gathering of church women by saying that religion was nothing but a social club. Another time in the journals, she 'puts down' the Georgetown minister's wife at a social gathering. But, in general, she held her tongue – very hard for someone brought up in a Presbyterian household where verbal put-downs and sarcasm were used as a mode of control. She had built up a store of resentment of her own situation that would find relief in Aunt Becky's tirades. The old woman will die early in the book, but she will dominate her family in absentia, especially the young people.

EW: Yet Montgomery's journal of summer 1929 records her sense of the energy and charm of young people. She speaks to many groups, for instance, five hundred students at Guelph's Ontario Agricultural College (May); she listens to jazz (June 6); she enjoys 'darling Stuart,' who washes all the dishes after an outing to the Canadian National Exhibition. Then, in autumn, she makes a memorable visit to Prince Edward Island, including a visit to Herman Leard's grave. She seems to have swung from a focus on age to a focus on youth.

MR: But she has a new view of youth – after all the books about imaginative, idealistic young people. Her boys' teenage years were rough on her and Ewan. When I interviewed Luella Reid [Macdonald], Chester's first wife, she said Ewan and Chester were at odds with each other all the time after Chester started to mature physically in the Norval years. They argued with and irritated each other in a destructive, hurtful way. The atmosphere around them was heavy. Ewan was once quoted by his wife in the journals as saying that he should not have had children (13 Sept. 1919). It appears to me that when Ewan saw how much Chester was like him, he often became irritable. Montgomery does not describe this in the journals, nor does she talk about how much their bickering upset her.

But she is feeling tensions in her personal life: a lack of control, a lack of contentment, a lack of fulfilment, and a lack of respect in the community. Because her temper is taut, and her mood is ironic, she can create an Aunt Becky during 1929–30.

EW: But the journals for that 'spade work summer' also show her enjoying her Norval home and the view of the Hill o' Pines. She laughs with May and Alec Macneill (see fig. 1.5) in Prince Edward Island. On 19 July 1929 she reads *Tish Plays the Game* and 'laughs so much over Tish that the tears streamed down my face' (*SJ* 3:399).

MR: Yes, and for all its creator's underlying bitterness, *A Tangled Web* will be a very humorous book. Yet it suggests the seriousness of the reservoir the novel draws from – though the journal doesn't directly discuss her sense of lack of fulfilment, her ageing, her feeling bypassed. She looks at trees after an ice storm – when trees become beautiful – and says they look like 'disgruntled old spinsters who had indignantly turned their backs on a derisive world' (*SJ* 4:29).

EW: On 1 March 1930 she writes, 'I know I have been hovering on the brink of a nervous breakdown all winter ...' (*SJ* 4:32). (This is long before the troubles in the Norval church.)

All winter the journal recorded onslaughts by the manipulative and possessive young woman named Isobel who lived in a nearby town (see Mary Beth Cavert's essay, chapter 3). Because of Isobel, who develops a passion for Montgomery and makes a pest of herself, Montgomery is ready to do a study of someone manipulating others. And because of Isobel, Maud had a deeper understanding of obsession. She can now create the possessive relationship between two young widows, Virginia and Donna. Here is 'bosom friendship' represented as a debilitating entanglement.

Another up-beat element in the journals of 1 March 1930: as she plots the new novel, she rereads her own books and all reviews of them (mostly flattering): 'Ah, well a-day! ... I have written to please myself' (*SJ* 4:43).

MR: But more than is apparent lies behind this comment: by 1930 some modernist critics are trying to edge her out of a respected and central spot in the Canadian literary canon. Despite the publication of *The Blue Castle* in 1926, she is still being relegated to the children's shelves, where her books have less status, much to her anger. She determines to write another adult book that will surely not go onto the children's shelves – she hopes it will renew her reputation as someone who writes successful books of general interest for a mature audience.

EW: And now, after the period of gestation for *A Tangled Web*, we come to the writing. 17 March 1930: 'Today I began the actual writing of the book I've been doing spade work on for a year. It has no name yet. It centres around the old Woolner jug and is to be a humorous novel for adults' (*SJ* 4:45). And then, a few entries later, on 30 April 1930, she puts in a picture of John Mustard, her old Prince Albert 'beau.' Thinking of him rubs salt in a wound. What effect would that have on the way she plots the book?

MR: She's ready to think again about the mating instinct. She had spurned John Mustard as a suitor in Prince Albert when he was her gawky and awkward teacher. Now he has risen up the clerical ranks and become a very prominent minister in Toronto. Ewan Macdonald, the man Montgomery *did* marry, is barely able to keep his position in a small country parish. Moreover, John Mustard's letters to Ewan show that the Rev. Mustard was a sensitive, considerate man of discretion, a real gentleman. The public record shows that he was adored by his congregation. Meanwhile, Montgomery's marriage is unrewarding and she knows now that Ewan will never be better. Then, in her friend Nora Lefurgey Campbell, she sees a happy marriage, adventure, life with a soulmate and successful man – everything her own marriage isn't. She's also watching her sons, in the grip of their young love affairs. She muses on what attracts people to each other.

EW: *A Tangled Web* emerges as the story of some fifteen young people, all in love. Lovely golden girls, vivid flappers, warm-hearted young widows, will each appear in love – with a scamp, a worthless young man, a restless wanderer, a long-dead soldier, a shell-shocked veteran. Why such choices? Although there are some tyrants, most of the men in this novel are a poor lot – they are weak, impetuous, often silly, and sometimes fatuous, with names like 'Dandy.'

MR: Montgomery is ready to take an ironic view of impetuous romantic love, which she idealized in earlier novels. She thinks again of her attraction to Herman Leard. Every time she goes back into the past, she emerges with a new perspective. She now can recognize the erratic nature of sexual attraction. She sees the power of that same sexual drive in her son Chester, now eighteen years old. She is watching Chester chasing girls, being foolish and impetuous. (Older women in Norval have described how girl-crazy he was.) She is ready to show young love as both an erratic hormonal attraction and a romantic delusion.

A Tangled Web is a story about people like Montgomery herself, who have dreams – romantic dreams – which mislead them. Luella Reid Macdonald told me that Montgomery read old favourites, particularly Sir Walter Scott, obsessively at this time, escaping to ancient time, out of the real world, living more with imaginary Scottish characters than her own contemporaries. *A Tangled Web* suggests that Montgomery recognized this romantic escapism in herself, or at least saw the danger and folly of it in others. The characters in her new book will be called the Darks and the Penhallows.

EW: After two months without references to the book, Montgomery writes on 5 July 1930: 'I cannot write and that unfinished book haunts me' (*SJ* 4:60). She reports attacks of nervous asthma, sleeplessness. Later, on 11 September 1930, she remembered, 'I have never had such a summer for "company" in my whole life' (*SJ* 4:66). Having to put on a good face when she felt 'ragged' had made her more tense.

She needed to finish her book, for the sake of the money, among other reasons. She had had a large settlement from L.C. Page in 1928, but by 1930 her investments had eroded drastically with the collapse of the stock market. Her bank account was depleted. And the boys are now about to go to college. She writes on 18 August 18 1930: 'Am trying desperately to catch up with my new book' (*SJ* 4:63).[2]

MR: The desperation is dissolved when she is actually writing. She uses writing to elevate her mood. She turns her troubles into humour, sees the funny side; turns off the world, takes her grim stuff and recasts it in humour. A young playmate of Stuart in the Leaskdale years remembered her sometimes bouncing up and down and chuckling when she was writing. She concocts an unbelievable plot in *A Tangled Web* and intersplices keen insights with what people are really like (for instance, what they think during a sermon). Clinically, laughter is known to be a mood elevator. Laughter was important for her – in writing and in life – many people remember her wonderful sense of humour. The Darks and the Penhallows in the story remind us of the Cavendish clans, the Macneills, Clarks, and Simpsons. But the names also suggest that if people make funny stories out of frustration and anger and misery, their laughter (or pen) can lead them out of the dark hollows in their lives. The names suggest the seriousness of the reservoir the novel draws from – though the journal doesn't directly mention her sense of the darkness, the growing hollowness of her middle age.

EW: 2 September 1930: 'Yesterday ... in the morning I finished my new book. This summer has been the hardest one I've ever known as far as finding time for literary work goes' (*SJ* 4:65).

Yet the narrative is worked out briskly, confidently, ingeniously, rather like Shakespeare's comedies where lovers get mixed up and then realigned. Like George Eliot, she weaves many stories together, and the conclusions of all the tales are deft, appropriate. For each of the young women, reunion with a better lover; for the old maid, Margaret, happiness and a beloved little boy, without undergoing marriage. So much for romance – and blue castles and houses of dreams.

In the end of the story, the treasured jug smashes – but in the process brings about the final happy ending, releasing the shell-shocked man into memory and reunion with his long-enduring wife. (This is a variant of the *Anne's House of Dreams* ending – she must have wished Ewan could be cured so easily.) The will – Aunt Becky's will that has kept them all on tenterhooks – winds up in the pigsty, eaten by pigs. At the end, like Montgomery watching *Tish Plays the Game*, we laugh to tears. There are no references to revising in the next months. She finished it around September 1930 – then spent four months wrangling with the publishers about the name for the new book.

MR: Where is the life writing, then, in this ironic book?

EW: It seems to me that this book supplements the journals neatly. It gives an emotional correlative for most of the things that were bothering her in 1929–30: things clear enough to her that she can work from them, bathe them in an alchemy of humour, and turn them into clever, funny anecdotes. You see, I have talked myself into liking it, mostly because of its relation to the journal.

MR: As to Montgomery herself, we deduce three states of being in the period of writing *A Tangled Web*:

    1 the minister's wife with a superficial social life, keeping the parishioners happy;

    2 the murky and disturbed private journal-keeper; and

    3 the writer who draws on a sense of humour and irony to elevate her mood, pull out of depression, and at least make half of each day happy.

EW: Ten years later in the *Anne of Ingleside* period, she no longer had parish duties, but she was still keeping her journals. In the journals of 1937–9, she tells us in much greater detail what she is writing – there are some thirty references to *Anne of Ingleside*. Considering that the early journal never recorded her work on *Anne of Green Gables* until the glorious moment of the manuscript's acceptance by Page and Company, the details that she now enters are remarkable. So we should really be able to connect the book with events in her life, and events in the 'real' world: concern over Edward VIII's 1936 love-tossed abdication and her distress over growing statistics on divorce; terror of the growing madness of Hitler; persisting economic depression. In the late 1930s, another war loomed, doubly horrifying to someone of the generation who had endured the sorrows of the First World War. These public facts all appear in the journal.

But *Anne of Ingleside* (1939), unlike *Rilla of Ingleside*, will spend little time on affairs of the world. The novel goes back to the beginning of the century. The story will run from just before the birth of Rilla (Anne's youngest child) to the time when young Rilla can venture out alone in the community.

MR: *Anne of Ingleside* is not directly related to what she writes in her journal, but is a record of what memories she draws up, what emotions consume her. She is writing her life again, in a different way, in a different mood, in a different time.

EW: She also recorded in her journals the books she read, such as Agatha Christie's mysteries and Frederick Philip Grove's novels, and the movies she saw, such as *East Lynne, The Lady Vanishes, Bringing Up Baby, Robin Hood, Myerling, Judge Hardy's Family, Marco Polo, Ali Baba, Snow White.* But again, we see no direct reflection of these in the novel. Except for Frederick Philip Grove's novels, it's all escapist stuff. And yet, she was following a different path of escape in 1938–9.

MR: Ignoring the growing world tensions, she moved back into her own memories of childhood, but reconfigured them. Her journals show that life writing is always filtered through memory and tempered by experience and, in her case, mood. Her memories now select different elements of her childhood, given her present experience of raising children. Not only was the world darkening. She personally felt 'bitter – rebellious – envious' (18 Aug. 1938).

EW: By 1938 Montgomery was engaged in a secret battle with the son she had once adored. In April she had given Chester (see fig. 12.2) a 'bitter letter' threatening to cut off all financial support from him while he finished his law studies at the university. She demanded that he promise to re-establish his marriage to Luella Reid and give up his new love, Ida Birrell, a young Toronto woman who had attracted his roving eye. And she warned Stuart about his choice of friends and girlfriends.

MR: Outside the family, her reputation as a writer was waning, partly thanks to the sour comments of W.A. Deacon, the literary critic for the *Mail and Empire* (it became the *Globe and Mail* in 1938). He attacked Montgomery viciously in his critical book *Poteen* (1926), saying that

12.2   Chester Cameron Macdonald, Luella Reid Macdonald, and baby Luella in front of Norval Presbyterian Church, circa 1934. (L.M. Montgomery Collection, Archival and Special Collections, University of Guelph Library.)

Canadian literature was to stoop no lower than Montgomery's writing. On top of her other troubles, hostile criticism from such a powerful man wounded her – something not mentioned in the journals.

She was angry, too, that her novels were being regarded as children's books, even after *A Tangled Web*. She would no longer try to buck that attitude, but would write a book centred on children.

EW: Her depression deepened drastically. On 5 May 1938 she wrote in her journal, 'I am possessed with a desire to *die*.'

Yet, on the surface, her life seemed easier in 1938. She had settled at last into a home of her own, 'Journey's End.' Her church work and parish duties were ended. She was more involved in the Canadian Women's Press Club, the Canadian Authors' Association, the Book Fair. Her sons were at college and living at home. Ewan Macdonald had joined bowling clubs, played euchre (but continued to be a dismal companion). Enjoying her new Toronto house and new neighbours, Montgomery registered attention to Toronto scenes in *Jane of Lantern Hill* (1937).

MR: But she had now seen a lot of the lives of the Toronto matrons who were her new neighbours – capable women living stultifying lives of tea parties, social pretense, emptiness, trying to impress others. She wanted to escape again. In *Anne of Ingleside*, she returns to Prince Edward Island and to the Glen St Mary community that Anne was moving into at the end of *Anne's House of Dreams*.

EW: Her journal lays out the 'further chronicle' of *Anne of Ingleside* – its journey's end, and its beginning. The first specific references to *Anne of Ingleside* – also suggest writer's block.

On 12 September 1938: 'I sat me down and began to write *Anne of Ingleside*. It is a year and nine months since I wrote a single line of creative work. But I can *still* write. I wrote a chapter. A burden rolled from my spirit. And I was suddenly *back in my own world* with all my dear Avonlea and Glen folks again.'

On 13 September 1938: 'Wrote another chapter today and hated to stop ...'

MR: Her memory of the past, according to her younger son, Stuart, was incredible. He often said to me: 'She lived too much in the past.' Her powers of memory were so tenacious and vivid that she could not escape what she remembered. Most people find that time blurs events from the past – but Montgomery's memory of events and what she had read stayed uncommonly vivid. In the past she recalled good friends when she was happy, and she focused on poisonous ones when she was depressed.

As a writer she experiences something like the movement into a dream life. She slips into other time zones. The past floods forward. Fiction separates her from reality. She had three kinds of dream lives: in memories of the real past; in waking dreams of an imagined life; in the writing of novels.

EW: The opening two chapters find Anne at 'Green Gables' with Diana, Mrs Lynde, and Marilla. The perfect friendship is re-established; Anne and Diana walk – like Montgomery and Nora Lefurgey Campbell – but Diana is overweight (a recurring theme in this book – Montgomery now weighs about the same as Diana, while Nora has remained trim).

After the first two chapters, the story moves from Avonlea to Glen St Mary and to Ingleside, the home that has replaced the old House of Dreams.

Montgomery is now working through an increasingly unhappy period. In her novel, she takes us from scenes with dear Diana and Marilla to a very different situation. From chapter 3 to 14, the story is dominated by Aunt Mary Maria, a marvelously annoying old character, bland, malicious, petty, spiteful, who almost destroys Anne's happiness. Aunt Mary Maria is imposed by Gilbert (as his second cousin, she rouses his clannish sense of obligation).

MR: This Aunt Mary Maria is the visitor from hell. Like Stella Campbell in the old days, like Isobel in the Norval years, she outstays her welcome. She's also like Mrs Lockie from Leaskdale, the woman who was master of the poisonous innuendo (*SJ* 3:94, 129). She's even reminiscent of Aunt Emily Montgomery, with her genius for saying hurtful things (*SJ* 3:143). And, finally, she is a new version of old womanhood. Montgomery is now sixty years old herself.

She is different than Aunt Becky, who enjoyed her own mischief. Aunt Becky's barbs had more the flavour of Scottish flyting: the socially accepted tradition of delivering insults. Aunt Mary Maria is totally different – she's a habitual whiner, self-pitying, and quite unaware of how much her barbs sting.

EW: Is Aunt Mary Maria also a nightmare version of what Montgomery is becoming – ? During the infestation by Aunt Mary Maria, disobedient little Jem is lost, reminiscent of the time Stuart was lost after skating away on the frozen Credit River after they moved to Norval. And in the novel, Walter is sent away from home during the end of Anne's pregnancy with Rilla. The clever woman who takes Walter in is a writer, an authority on childhood. She teases Walter by telling him his mother is dying! Such cruelty! – clever, self-enjoying cruelty, unlike Aunt Mary Maria's. These vignettes are not related to anything in the new journal, but in the old ones. She remembered adults' unwitting cruelty to her. Memories of her boys as little children were probably stirred by her worry about the war, since both boys were now reaching military age. There is a cruel streak in these twelve chapters – the kind of cruelty that is deeply hurtful or outright vicious.

MR: The tone becomes more satiric in chapters 15–17. These lighter chapters are not on Anne's family. Anne turns outward and decides to act as matchmaker for young people she barely knows. This time we are closer to the journals.

Montgomery had played matchmaker for 'The M's' (for her relative Marion Webb and Murray Laird, a young parishioner in Norval). The journals now show her playing match-*preserver* for her daughter-in-law Luella, and match-disrupter *re* the young woman, Ida, for whom Chester felt such romantic passion. Montgomery was also pushing for a match between Stuart and his next door neighbour, Margaret Cowan, and obstructing his interest in a Norval girl. Yet *Anne of Ingleside* shows the folly of matchmaking. (Montgomery herself vowed 'never again' after her 1930s efforts to make a match between Marion Webb and Murray Laird. They eventually did marry, but there were many ups and downs in their courtship.)

EW: As the story goes on, Montgomery is fulsomely – though indirectly – justifying herself as a mother. Jem takes his troubles to his mother – he calls her 'Mother dearwums.' She comforts him about the loss of his pets: 'What else are mothers for, darling?' 'Mother knows everything.' Yet earlier this year, she cries in her journal: 'Motherhood is awful' (15 June 1938). A real disconnect.

In an abrupt departure from the family story, Anne is asked to write an 'obitchery' for a neighbour. She is comically disillusioned in her literary ambition: her work is travestied by a schoolboy's addition to her poem.

MR: Although Montgomery was now spending a lot of time with the Canadian Authors' Association, she suffered the mockery of her work by the male literary establishment. She was not part of the old boy network which was taking over the Canadian Authors' Association – once a meeting place for *both* men and women. She felt out of sympathy with the incoming style of modernist writers. She felt passed by, although *she* believed her work was better and shouldn't be dismissed.

EW: Undaunted, Montgomery begins the second half of the book (half way would be at the end of chapter 24):

21 November 1938: As the winter began in Toronto, Luella, looking 'nice,' brought the children in. There has now been another birth – Cameron – born during the past summer. Montgomery found little Luella, nicknamed 'Pussy,' charming. In *Anne of Ingleside*, Montgomery began to give more attention to the girls in Anne's family. Incidentally, at this time she attended the Brampton Players' production of *Anne of Green Gables*, with emphasis on the love between Anne and Diana.

MR: But the treatment of little girls in this book is very odd. Children in the next chapters are either gullible (Anne's children) or horribly mean and malicious (other children). Montgomery had moved back again into memories of childhood. These were now significantly different from her actual early records of childhood pleasures, and also from the moody memories said to be recorded in the journal of 1904–5 (see *SJ* 1:300), which was recopied in 1919. In fiction, she is reconfiguring her formative years as she writes about them again. This late novel gives a third example of such reconstruction.

EW: She now creates a series of little monsters. First, Di is fooled by Jenny Penny. This begins a sequence of stories about bad friends, in contrast to the love of Diana and Anne. Next, Nan is tortured by Dovie, a fat and jealous little girl, who fools Nan into believing she is not Anne's child.

It's an amazing switch from the whimsical but kindly tone of the earlier novels. The negativism regarding the child's world continues until near the end. In chapter 3, Rilla's pride leads to trouble. In chapters 35–6, Nan's romantic dream is disillusioned; in chapters 37–8, Di finds and unmasks another poisonous friend, Delilah.

MR: Montgomery remembers her own moments of frustration as a child – when teased by Uncle John's children, or when she was mocked for her family pride, just as the young Blythes are mocked. (I would interject that I think Montgomery herself had quite a happy childhood, all considered, but we all remember moments of humiliation.)

She also reveals obliquely her intense worry when believing her sons are misled by bad companions. Her sons' real-life troubles as young adults are transfigured in those of Anne's young children. These stories end with everything fine, but the intensity of evil in some of these fictional children shows Montgomery's depth of disturbance. Childhood is not paradise. The stories grab the reader with a sense of genuine fear. This is a world with Hitler in it.

EW: Two late chapters inserted into the sequence of stories about malicious children offer an interlude. They were probably written at the time she made the journal entry on 4 November 1938: 'I wrote three hours [today] and enjoyed it.' These are the best chapters in the book, the happiest and saddest: a quilting party and a funeral.

MR: The quilting party is a gossip fest for women – note that it is mocked by Gilbert at the outset. But, at the end, he appears promptly and says to Anne: 'Tell me the gossip.' As Patricia Meyer Spacks shows in her book called *Gossip*, men relied on the women for gossip, so as to share in social control.

As for the funeral, a story told at the quilting party, it involves another woman erupting at the end of a life (like Aunt Becky in *A Tangled Web*): Clara Wilson's rising and condemning Peter Kirk at his funeral. The dead patriarch, Peter Kirk, recalls Grandfather Macneill and all the exploitative patriarchs, including harsh ones like Jarback Priest (like 'Peter Kirk,' another symbolic name) in *Emily*, and nonaggressive ones like Ewan Macdonald in his own unconscious cruelty (e.g., his irritation at Montgomery's keeping her own name for her writing, his not reading her books, and his resenting her fame). In the novel, after Peter Kirk's death, the truth emerges: Peter's cruelty to all the women in his life.[3]

EW: About this time, Montgomery wrote in the journal on 30 November, her sixty-fourth birthday: 'Ewan forgot it.' Montgomery observes once in her journals that mentally disturbed people are curiously self-absorbed. But their lack of responsiveness to their partner still hurts that partner.

In these chapters, a real pathology is revealed. When Clara Wilson speaks her mind at the funeral, it is bitter in a way that Aunt Becky's final words were not. Clara Wilson's tale is chilling, frightening, the words of a woman maddened by repressed anger. Even Anne steps in to reflect this is not a child's story, one that Walter should not hear – perhaps this is Montgomery's final jab at those who thought her novels were strictly for children.

Well, these are two excellent chapters – the quilting and the funeral – but it seems that there is little continuity with the Nan and Di stories.

MR: The connection is in Montgomery's emotions. The unity is in her, not in the book. She relegates her own resentment to the women at the funeral, her worry about her sons to the bad young people in a hostile world, her depression to the carping Aunt Mary Maria.

EW: And then a surprising ending: She adds a final section, in chapters 39–41, about Anne's jealousy and sense of abandonment. Christine Stewart, Anne's onetime rival for Gilbert's affection in college days and still a free spirit, has turned up. Christine seems worldly, successful, brilliant in conversation, but in the end is shown up as shallow and inconsequential in her discussion. The final chapter includes reconciliation, revelation, and a happy ending. All suspicions are dispersed at the end. Gilbert was not turning away from Anne – he was busy on a scientific discovery. You have to be very young to like this ending.

MR: It's interesting, however, from the point of view of life writing. If we think of this final novel through the lens of life writing, looking at what's in Montgomery's experience that she chooses to recast in fiction, we can see another version of her frustration and sense that life has passed her by – one deeper than in *A Tangled Web*. In *Anne of Ingleside*, we sense that she feels even more ignored and forgotten by her mentally ill husband. She feels bitter about how the literary world of male modernists has trashed her books.[4] The tone of *Anne of Ingleside* is more sombre. The characters may be the old ones – Anne and Gilbert and their kids – but the tone is quite different. Perhaps the disguise is not entirely successful. She was in depression near the end of her life – earlier she might have found a clearer way of unifying the tone in the story.

EW: Still, depressed or not, she could write on 8 December 1938: 'I finished "Anne of Ingleside" today – my 21st book.' There was still work to do.

13 December 1938: 'Am busy revising "Ingleside." I have felt so well all day. Better than I have felt for ten years.'

1 January 1939: 'I worked all day hard ...'

6 January 1939: 'Today I began revising "Anne of Ingleside." Got three chapters done ...'

18 January 1939: 'On Monday I wrote my article on P. E. Island ... and finished revising *A. of I* Tuesday. I began to type it and typed all day till 9 o'clock in the evening. So I was overtired at night. Today I typed all day again. ...'

21 January 1939: '... have been typing steadily ...'

Then, after revising, before typing, a saddening, revealing entry:
24 January 1939: 'Ewan came up to our room this evening when I
was trying to work and made a terrible scene. I am so sick of these
scenes – twenty years of them. I cried a little and returned to my
work.'

But she persevered.

On 21 March 1939: 'I went downtown after lunch yesterday to take
the completed manuscript of *Anne of Ingleside* to Mr. McClelland ...'

On the same day, another journal entry: 'Hitler has seized Czecho-
slovakia and a new war scare is in the offing.'

MR: In a journal which truly reflected a life's tribulations, one would
expect Montgomery to tell us what Ewan said in the 'terrible scenes'
he makes, especially if he had been creating them for twenty years.
She does not, and never has. We can guess what he may have said,
but it is conjecture. We can guess it was very hurtful. He was jealous
of her writing, and of the fact her income had outstripped his. He
worried incessantly about his own health and thought she should
worry *with* him. Their family life is troubled. But Montgomery's journal does not attempt to tell the entire truth. Montgomery's journals
were written to tell her own story in her way, and, like most writers,
she wants to focus on her hardships and how she overcame them. So
we don't hear what Ewan actually said, and whether it hit the mark, at
least partially – we only hear that she cried a little and continued.

EW: Montgomery writes her own story over and over, just as she writes
Cavendish's and Prince Edward Island's stories again and again. It
has been said that *all* writing is life writing, and we would concur,
based on our study of Montgomery. When she was young and buoyed
up, she gives us the light and funny episodes in *Anne of Green Gables*.
When she is middle-aged, and reflecting on how she became a writer,
she gives us the *Emily* stories. As she ages, she gives us *A Tangled Web*,
where an old woman has her say at the end of her life, with a bite to
the humour. But, by *Anne of Ingleside*, Montgomery is losing the
ability to laugh, and the tone grows bitter. Yet, through it all, she
reconfigures these experiences, and they are always compelling because they are so genuine.

MR: The journals are life writing of a guarded sort, but full of factual
detail from real life. The novels are life writing of a less guarded sort,
but they are about fictional characters, another type of evasion. They
take their shape from Montgomery's emotion. She uses her immense
creativity to reconfigure her childhood stories again and again.

Our conclusion is this: Montgomery's writing comes out of the genuine emotions of real human beings, and her writing still *lives* and resonates because of that. It doesn't matter what the plots are, what the flaws in the novels may be. Her books continue to touch us because they are built out of the most important thing in the world – the tangled web of human emotions.

NOTES

1 The journal entries take on extra interest because there is a rich fund of documentary data that lets us set Montgomery's private record against actualities. Some facts confirm (or add to) her perceptions of events in her family, her church, medicine, politics, business, and the literary establishment. Others call her journal version into question. Mary Rubio has gained a special knowledge of these facts from her research in preparation for her biography, and from her time interviewing people who knew Montgomery before the first journals were published. (After publication of the journals in 1985, 1987, 1992, and 1998, people's memories became assisted by, or tainted with, what they read in the journals.)

2 For more on publishing history, see Gerson, '"Dragged at Anne's Chariot Wheels."'

3 For more on *Anne of Ingleside* and patriarchy, see Jennie Rubio, '"Strewn with Dead Bodies."'

4 For more on modernism's attack on Montgomery, see Gerson, 'Anne of Green Gables Goes to University.'

Works Cited and Consulted

I. L.M. Montgomery's Texts: Published and Unpublished

Against the Odds: Tales of Achievement. Ed. Rea Wilmshurst. Toronto: McClelland
    and Stewart, 1993.
The Alpine Path: The Story of My Career. 1917. Markham, ON: Fitzhenry, 1997.
Anne of Avonlea. 1909. Toronto: McClelland-Bantam, 1992.
Anne of Green Gables. 1908. Toronto: McClelland and Stewart, 1992.
Anne of Ingleside. 1939. Toronto: McClelland-Bantam, 1983.
Anne of the Island. 1915. Toronto: McClelland-Bantam, 1992.
Anne of Windy Poplars. 1936. Toronto: McClelland-Bantam, 1992.
Anne's House of Dreams. 1917. Toronto: McClelland-Bantam, 1992.
The Annotated Anne of Green Gables. Ed. Wendy Barry, Margaret Anne Doody,
    and Mary E. Doody Jones. New York: Oxford UP, 1997.
The Blue Castle. 1926. Toronto: McClelland-Bantam, 1988.
Emily trilogy: *Emily of New Moon.* 1923. *Emily Climbs.* 1925. *Emily's Quest.* 1927.
    Toronto: McClelland and Stewart, 1989.
The Golden Road. 1913. New York: Bantam, 1989.
The Green Gables Letters: From L.M. Montgomery to Ephraim Weber, 1905–1909.
    Ed. Wilfrid Eggleston. Ottawa: Borealis, 1981.
Jane of Lantern Hill. New York: Stokes, 1937.
Kilmeny of the Orchard. 1910. Toronto: McClelland-Bantam, 1987.
L.M. Montgomery's Ephraim Weber: Letters, 1916–1941. Ed. Paul Tiessen and
    Hildi Froese Tiessen. Waterloo, ON: MLR Editions, 2000.
Magic for Marigold. Toronto: McClelland and Stewart, 1929.
Mistress Pat: A Novel of Silver Bush. Toronto: McClelland and Stewart, 1935.
My Dear Mr. M.: Letters to G.B. MacMillan from L.M. Montgomery. Ed. Francis
    W.P. Bolger and Elizabeth R. Epperly. Toronto: Oxford UP, 1992.

The Poetry of Lucy Maud Montgomery. Ed. John Ferns and Kevin McCabe. Markham, ON: Fitzhenry, 1987.

Postcard to Nora Lefurgey Campbell, Sept. 1939. Mary Campbell Collection, Rye, New York.

Rilla of Ingleside. 1921. Toronto: McClelland-Bantam, 1992.

The Selected Journals of L.M. Montgomery. Vol. 1: *1889–1910.* Vol. 2: *1910–1921.* Vol. 3: *1921–1929.* Vol. 4: *1929–1935.* Vol. 5: *1929–1942.* Ed. and introd. Mary Rubio and Elizabeth Waterston. Toronto: Oxford UP, 1985, 1987, 1992, 1998, 2004.

A Tangled Web. 1931. Toronto: McClelland and Stewart, 1973.

Unpublished handwritten journals. L.M. Montgomery Collection, University of Guelph Archives.

Unpublished letters to G.B. MacMillan. National Archives of Canada.

Unpublished scrapbook 12. Public Archives of Prince Edward Island.

Unpublished scrapbooks: CM67.5.11; CM67.5.12; CM67.5.14; CM67.5.15; CM67.5.18; CM67.5.24. Confederation Centre Art Gallery and Museum, Charlottetown, PEI.

Unpublished scrapbooks. X25 MS A002: 2 volumes with red covers: vol. 1, c.1910–13; vol. 2, c.1913–26. X25 MS A003: 1 volume containing reviews, c.1911–36. L.M. Montgomery Collection, University of Guelph Archives.

Unpublished typed journals. L.M. Montgomery Collection, University of Guelph Archives.

II. Archival Materials and Interviews

Anderson, Isabel. 'Erato.' 'Mother Image.' 'To Live.' In 'Poems by Isabel Anderson.' Unpublished MS. Private Collection, Acton, ON. 1, 17, 46.

– *Our Kirk: 1845–1995.* ON: Knox Presbyterian Church, 1995.

Andrew, Amy Darby (née Tanton). 'A Line a Day.' Unpublished diary, 1910–14. Private Collection, Summerside, PEI.

Boswall, Elizabeth. Interviewed by Irene Gammel, Charlottetown, 10 May 2003.

Campbell, Bette. Letter to Mary Beth Cavert, 4 October 1995.

– Letter to Mary Beth Cavert, 14 August 1996.

– Telephone interview by Mary Beth Cavert, 27 August 1995.

Campbell, Edmund, Jr. Letter to his family, 16 May 1977. Private Collection, Haileybury, ON.

– Letter to Mary Beth Cavert, 11 October 1995.

– Telephone interview by Mary Beth Cavert, 14 October 1995.

Campbell, Mary E. 'Gran's Scarf.' Unpublished memoir. Private Collection, Rye, NY.

– Letter to Mary Beth Cavert, 11 October 1995.

– Telephone interview by Mary Beth Cavert, 5 October 1995.

Campbell, Nora Lefurgey. Letters to Mary E. Campbell, undated, 1967–8. Private Collection, Rye, NY.

– Unpublished diary. Private Collection, Haileybury, ON.

Cavendish Literary Society minutes. Public Archives of Prince Edward Island, Accession 2412.

Coles, M. Telephone interview by Mary Beth Cavert, 2 February 2000.

Hansen, P. E-mail letter to Mary Beth Cavert, 10 April 2003.

Laerd, Waldron. Telephone interview by Irene Gammel, 10 May 2003.

MacFarlane, Nancy. Interview by Irene Gammel, Lower Bedeque, 30 July 2002.

– 'Summary of Notes from Jean MacFarlane and the Diary of Montgomery.' Unpublished typescript [n.d.], Private Collection, PEI.

Macneill, Jennie. Telephone interview by Irene Gammel, 15 May 2003.

Weber, Ephraim. Précis of unpublished letters to L.M. Montgomery, 1902–41 (Précis, 1902–14, and B-Précis, 1909–41). Ed. Wilfrid Eggleston [c.1959]. Wilfrid Eggleston Papers, National Archives of Canada.

– Unpublished letters to Wilfrid Eggleston, 1920–54. Wilfrid Eggleston Papers, National Archives of Canada.

III. L.M. Montgomery and Life Writing

Adjutant. *The 116th Battalion in France*. Toronto: E.P.S. Allen, 1921.

Åhmansson, Gabriella. *A Life and Its Mirrors: A Feminist Reading of L.M. Montgomery's Fiction*. Uppsala: Almquist, 1991.

Armstrong, Nancy. *Desire and Domestic Fiction: A Political History of the Novel*. New York: Oxford UP, 1987.

Atwood, Margaret. Afterword. In *Anne of Green Gables*, by L.M. Montgomery, 331–6.

Bates, Barbara. *Bargaining for Life: A Social History of Tuberculosis, 1876–1938*. Philadelphia: U of Pennsylvania P, 1992.

The Bend in the Road: An Invitation to the World and Work of L.M. Montgomery. CD-ROM. L.M. Montgomery Institute, 2000.

Benstock, Shari. 'Authorizing the Autobiographical.' In Benstock, ed., *The Private Self*, 10–33.

– ed. *The Private Self: Theory and Practice of Women's Autobiographical Writings.* Chapel Hill and London: U of North Carolina P, 1988.

Bloom, Lynn Z. '"I write for myself and strangers': Private Diaries as Public Documents.' In Bunkers and Huff, eds, *Inscribing the Daily,* 23–37.

Bolger, Francis W.P. *The Years before 'Anne': The Early Career of Lucy Maud Montgomery.* 1974. Halifax: Nimbus, 1991.

Brady, Laura. 'Collaboration as Conversation: Literary Cases.' In *Authority and Textuality: Current Views of Collaborative Writing.* Ed. James S. Leonard, Christine E. Wharton, Robert Murray Davis, and Jeanette Harris. West Cornwall, CT: Locust Hill P, 1994. 149–68.

Bristow, Joseph, ed. *Wilde Writings: Contextual Conditions.* Toronto: U of Toronto P, 2002.

Brodzki, Bella, and Celeste Schenck, eds. *Life/Lines: Theorizing Women's Autobiography.* Ithaca: Cornell UP, 1988.

Bruss, Elizabeth. *Autobiographical Acts: The Changing Situation of a Literary Genre.* Baltimore: Johns Hopkins UP, 1976.

Bunkers, Suzanne L., ed. *Diaries of Girls and Women: A Midwestern American Sampler.* Madison: U of Wisconsin P, 2001.

Bunkers, Suzanne L., and Cynthia A. Huff, eds. *Inscribing the Daily: Critical Essays on Women's Diaries.* Amherst: U of Massachusetts P, 1996.

Buss, Helen M. 'Decoding L.M. Montgomery's Journals / Encoding a Critical Practice for Women's Private Literature.' *Essays on Canadian Writing* 54 (Winter 1994): 80–100.

– 'A Feminist Revision of New Historicism to Give Fuller Readings of Women's Private Writing.' In Bunkers and Huff, eds, *Inscribing the Daily,* 86– 103.

– *Mapping Our Selves: Canadian Women's Autobiography in English.* Montreal and Kingston: McGill-Queen's UP, 1993.

Byatt, A.S. *Possession: A Romance.* London: Vintage, 1990.

Caldwell, Mark. *The Last Crusade: The War on Consumption, 1862–1954.* New York: Atheneum, 1988.

Cavert, Mary Beth. 'L.M. Montgomery and Friendship.' In McCabe and Heilbron, *The Lucy Maud Montgomery Album,* 281–4.

Clark, Hilary. 'Depression, Shame, and Reparation: The Case of Anne Sexton.' In *Scenes of Shame: Psychoanalysis, Shame, and Writing.* Ed. Joseph Adamson and Hilary Clark. Albany, NY: State U of New York P, 1999. 189–206.

Coleman, Linda S., ed. *Women's Life-Writing: Finding Voice / Building Community.* Bowling Green: Bowling Green State U Popular P, 1997.

Coleridge, Samuel Taylor. 'Dejection: An Ode.' In *The Complete Works of Samuel Taylor Coleridge.* Ed. Ernest Hartley Coleridge. Vol. 1. Oxford: Clarendon, 1912. 362–8.

Collins, Carolyn Strom. 'The Scrapbooks.' In McCabe and Heilbron, *The Lucy Maud Montgomery Album*, 112–17.

Conway, Jill Ker. *When Memory Speaks: Exploring the Art of Autobiography*. New York: Vintage, 1999.

Cooke, Nathalie. '"Mi rage": The Confessional Politics of Canadian Survivor Poetry.' In Gammel, ed., *Confessional Politics*, 65–80.

Cottam, Rachel. "Diaries and Journals: General Survey." In Jolly, ed., *The Encyclopedia of Life Writing*, 267–9.

Culley, Margo. 'Introduction to *A Day at a Time: Diary Literature of American Women from 1764 to 1985*.' In Smith and Watson, eds, *Women, Autobiography, Theory: A Reader*, 217–21.

Deacon, William Arthur. *Poteen: A Pot-Pourri of Canadian Essays*. Ottawa: Graphic, 1926.

de Man, Paul. *The Rhetoric of Romanticism*. New York: Columbia UP, 1984.

Devereux, Cecily. '"Canadian Classic" and "Commodity Export": The Nationalism of "Our" *Anne of Green Gables*.' *Journal of Canadian Studies* 36.1 (2001): 11–28.

Donoghue, Denis. *Ferocious Alphabets*. London: Faber, 1981.

Doody, Margaret Anne. Introduction. In *The Annotated Anne of Green Gables*, by L.M. Montgomery, 9–34.

Drain, Susan. 'Telling and Retelling: L.M. Montgomery's Storied Lives and Living Stories.' *Canadian Children's Literature* 81 (1996): 7–18.

Earle, Rebecca, ed. *Epistolary Selves: Letters and Letter-Writers, 1600–1945*. Aldershot: Ashgate, 1999.

Edwards, Owen Dudley, and Jennifer H. Litster. 'The End of Canadian Innocence: L.M. Montgomery and the First World War.' In Gammel and Epperly, eds, *L.M. Montgomery and Canadian Culture*, 31–46.

Egan, Susanna. *Mirror Talk: Genres of Crisis in Contemporary Autobiography*. Chapel Hill: U of North Carolina P, 1999.

Eliot, T.S. *The Use of Poetry and the Use of Fiction*. London: Faber, 1964.

Epperly, Elizabeth R. 'Approaching the Montgomery Manuscripts.' In Rubio, ed., *Harvesting Thistles*, 74–83.

– *The Fragrance of Sweet-Grass: L.M. Montgomery's Heroines and the Pursuit of Romance*. Toronto: U of Toronto P, 1992.

– 'L.M. Montgomery and the Changing Times.' *Acadiensis* 17.2 (Spring 1988): 177–85.

– 'The Visual Imagination of L.M. Montgomery.' In Gammel, ed., *Making Avonlea*, 84–98.

Faderman, Lillian. *Surpassing the Love of Men: Romantic Friendship and Love between Women from the Renaissance to the Present*. New York: William Morrow and Co., 1981.

Fairclough, Norman. *Language and Power*. London: Longman, 1985.

Felski, Rita. 'On Confession.' In *Beyond Feminist Aesthetics: Feminist Literature and Social Change*. Cambridge: Harvard UP, 1989. 86–121.

Fiamengo, Janice. 'Towards a Theory of Popular Landscape in *Anne of Green Gables*.' In Gammel, ed., *Making Avonlea*, 225–37.

Freud, Sigmund. *Civilization and Its Discontents*. 1929. London: Chatto & Windus, 1992.

Gammel, Irene. 'Mirror Looks: The Visual and Performative Diaries of L.M. Montgomery, Baroness Elsa von Freytag-Loringhoven, and Elvira Bach.' In Smith and Watson, eds, *Interfaces*, 289–313.

– 'Safe Pleasures for Girls: L.M. Montgomery's Erotic Landscapes.' In Gammel, ed., *Making Avonlea*, 114–27.

– ed. and introd. *Confessional Politics: Women's Sexual Self-Representations in Life Writing and Popular Media*. Carbondale: Southern Illinois UP, 1999.

– ed. and introd. *Making Avonlea: L.M. Montgomery and Popular Culture*. Toronto: U of Toronto P, 2002.

Gammel, Irene and Elizabeth Epperly, eds. *L.M. Montgomery and Canadian Culture*. Toronto: U of Toronto P, 1999.

Gerson, Carole. 'Anne of Green Gables Goes to University: L.M. Montgomery and Academic Culture.' In Gammel, ed., *Making Avonlea*, 1–31.

– '"Dragged at Anne's Chariot Wheels": The Triangle of Author, Publisher, and Fictional Character.' In Gammel and Epperly, eds, *L.M. Montgomery and Canadian Culture*, 49–63.

Gillen, Mollie. *The Wheel of Things: A Biography of L.M. Montgomery, Author of 'Anne of Green Gables.'* Halifax: Goodread Biographies, 1983.

Gilmore, Leigh. *Autobiographics: A Feminist Theory of Women's Self-Representation*. Ithaca and London: Cornell UP, 1994.

Gusdorf, Georges. 'The Conditions and Limits of Autobiography.' In *Autobiography: Essays Theoretical and Critical*. Ed. James Olney. Princeton: Princeton UP, 1980. 28–48.

Hales, Dianne. *Depression*. New York: Chelsea, 1989.

Hannah, Don. *The Wooden Hill*. N.p.: Canadian Stage, 1994.

Hardy, Barbara. *Tellers and Listeners: The Narrative Imagination*. London: Athlone P, 1975.

Heilbron, Alexandra. 'Memories of L.M. Montgomery.' *Avonlea Traditions Chronicle* 15 and 18 (1996): 1, 4–7, and 22–4.

– *Remembering Lucy Maud Montgomery*. Toronto: Dundurn, 2001.

Hersey, Eleanor. '"It's all mine": The Modern Woman as Writer in Sullivan's *Anne of Green Gables* Films.' In Gammel, ed., *Making Avonlea*, 131–44.

Higgins, Laura. 'Snapshot Portraits: Finding L.M. Montgomery in Her "Dear Den."' In Rubio, ed., *Harvesting Thistles*, 101–12.

Hinz, Evelyn. 'Mimesis: The Dramatic Lineage of Auto/Biography.' In Kadar, ed., *Essays on Life Writing*, 195–212.

– ed. and introd. *Data and Acta: Aspects of Life-Writing*. Special issue of *Mosaic: A Journal of Interdisciplinary Writing* 20.4 (Fall 1987).

'History' [obituary]. *Acton Free Press*, 12 June 1924.

'History of Erin Township.' http://www.town.erin.on.ca/about/townshiphistory.html. 24 April 2003.

Hogan, Rebecca. 'Engendered Autobiographies: The Diary as a Feminine Form.' In *Autobiography and Question of Gender*. Ed. Shirley Neuman. London: Frank Cass and Co., 1991. 95–107.

Inness, Sherrie A., ed. *Nancy Drew and Company: Gender, Culture, and Girls' Series*. Bowling Green: Bowling Green State U Popular P, 1997.

Jamison, Kay Redfield. *Touched with Fire: Manic-Depressive Illness and the Artistic Temperament*. Toronto: Maxwell Macmillan, 1993.

Jolly, Margaretta, ed. *The Encyclopedia of Life Writing*. 2 vols. London: Fitzroy Dearborn, 2001.

Jones, Amelia. 'Performing the Other as Self: Cindy Sherman and Laura Aguilar Pose the Subject.' In Smith and Watson, eds, *Interfaces*, 69–102.

Kadar, Marlene. 'Coming to Terms: Life Writing – from Genre to Critical Practice.' In Kadar, ed., *Essays on Life Writing*, 3–16.

– ed. *Essays on Life Writing: From Genre to Critical Practice*. Toronto: U of Toronto P, 1992.

Keats, John. 'Ode on Melancholy.' In *John Keats: Complete Poems*. Ed. Jack Stillinger. Cambridge: Harvard UP, 1982. 283–4.

Kornfield, Eve, and Susan Jackson. 'The Female Bildungsroman in Nineteenth-Century America: Parameters of a Vision.' In Reimer, ed., *Such a Simple Little Tale*, 139–52.

Lee, Hermione. *Virginia Woolf*. London: Vintage, 1996.

Lejeune, Philippe. 'The Autobiographical Pact.' In *On Autobiography*. Ed. Paul John Eakin. Minneapolis: U of Minnesota P, 1989. 3–30.

– 'The Practice of the Private Journal: Chronicle of an Investigation (1986–1998).' In *Marginal Voices, Marginal Forms: Diaries in European Literature and History*. Ed. Rachel Langford and Russell West. Amsterdam: Rodopi, 1999. 185–211.

Lunn, Janet. *Maud's House of Dreams: The Life of Lucy Maud Montgomery*. Toronto: Doubleday, 2002.

McCabe, Kevin, comp., and Alexandra Heilbron, ed. *The Lucy Maud Montgomery Album*. Toronto: Fitzhenry, 1999.

MacDonald, Betty Bard. *The Plague and I*. Philadelphia: J.B. Lippicott, 1948.

McGillivray, Allan. *Tales from the Uxbridge Valley: Historical Highlights*. Uxbridge, ON.: Uxbridge Millenium Committee, 2000..

298   Works Cited and Consulted

MacLulich, T.D. 'L.M. Montgomery's Portraits of the Artist: Realism, Idealism, and the Domestic Imagination.' *English Studies in Canada* 11.4 (Dec. 1985): 459–73.

Marcus, Laura. *Auto/biographical Discourses: Theory, Criticism, Practice.* Manchester and New York: Manchester UP, 1994.

Meyers, Jeffrey. *Disease and the Novel, 1880–1960.* New York: St Martin's P, 1985.

Mullally, Sasha. '"Daisy," "Dodgie," and "Lady Jane Grey Dort": L.M. Montgomery and the Automobile.' In Gammel and Epperly, eds, *L.M. Montgomery and Canadian Culture,* 120–30.

Nodelman, Perry. 'Progressive Utopia; or, How to Grow Up without Growing Up.' In Reimer, ed., *Such a Simple Little Tale,* 29–38.

Nussbaum, Felicity A. 'Toward Conceptualizing Diary.' In *Studies in Autobiography.* Ed. James Olney. New York and Oxford: Oxford UP, 1988. 128–40.

Obituary. *Georgetown Independent,* August 1994.

Olney, James. *Metaphors of the Self: The Meaning of Autobiography.* Princeton: Princeton UP, 1972.

Ong, Walter J. 'The Writer's Audience Is Always a Fiction.' *PMLA* 90.1 (1975): 9–21.

Perreault, Jeanne. *Writing Selves: Contemporary Feminist Autography.* Minneapolis: U of Minnesota P, 1995.

'Picturing a Canadian Life: L.M. Montgomery's Personal Scrapbooks and Book Covers.' Virtual Museum of Canada. Launched 30 August 2002. http://lmm.confederationcentre.com.

Pike, E. Holly. 'Mass Marketing, Popular Culture, and the Canadian Celebrity Author.' In Gammel, ed., *Making Avonlea,* 238–51.

– '(Re)Producing Canadian Literature: L.M. Montgomery's Emily Novels.' In Gammel and Epperly, eds, *L.M. Montgomery and Canadian Culture,* 64–76.

Podnieks, Elizabeth. *Daily Modernism: The Literary Diaries of Virginia Woolf, Antonia White, Elizabeth Smart, and Anaïs Nin.* Montreal and Kingston: McGill-Queen's UP, 2000.

– 'Introduction: Private Lives / Public Texts: Women's Diary Literature.' In *Private Lives / Public Texts: Women's Literary Diaries and Journals.* Special issue of *A/B: Auto/Biography Studies* 17.1 (Summer 2002): 1–10.

Poe, K.L. 'The Whole of the Moon: L.M. Montgomery's *Anne of Green Gables* Series.' In Inness, ed., *Nancy Drew and Company,* 15–35.

Pratt, T.K. *Dictionary of Prince Edward Island English.* Toronto: U of Toronto P, 1988.

Raoul, Valerie. 'Women and Diaries: Gender and Genre.' *Mosaic* 22.3 (Summer 1989): 57–65.

Reimer, Mavis, ed. *Such a Simple Little Tale: Critical Responses to L.M. Mont-omery's 'Anne of Green Gables.'* Metuchen: Children's Literature Association and Scarecrow P, 1992.

Ridley, Hilda. *The Story of L.M. Montgomery.* Toronto: Ryerson, 1956.

Rootland, Nancy. *Anne's World, Maud's World: The Sacred Sites of L.M. Mont-gomery.* Halifax: Nimbus, 1996.

Rothman, Sheila. *Living in the Shadow of Death: Tuberculosis and the Social Ex-perience of Illness in American History.* Baltimore: Johns Hopkins UP, 1994.

Rubio, Jennie. '"Strewn with Dead Bodies": Women and Gossip in *Anne of Ingleside.'* In Rubio, ed., *Harvesting Thistles,* 167–77.

Rubio, Mary. '"A Dusting Off": An Anecdotal Account of Editing the L.M. Montgomery Journals.' In *Working in Women's Archives: Researching Women's Private Literature and Archival Documents.* Ed. Helen Buss and Marlene Kadar. Waterloo, ON: Wilfrid Laurier UP, 2001. 51–78.

– 'Satire, Realism and Imagination in *Anne of Green Gables.'* In Sorfleet, ed., *L.M. Montgomery,* 27–36.

– 'Subverting the Trite: L.M. Montgomery's "Room of Her Own."' *Canadian Children's Literature* 65 (1992): 6–39.

– ed. *Harvesting Thistles: The Textual Garden of L.M. Montgomery.* Guelph, ON: Canadian Children's P, 1994.

Rubio, Mary, and Elizabeth Waterston. *Writing a Life: L.M. Montgomery: A Biography of the Author of 'Anne of Green Gables.'* Toronto: ECW, 1995.

Saint-Martin, Lori. 'Sexuality and Textuality Entwined: Sexual Proclamations in Women's Confessional Fiction in Quebec.' In Gammel, ed., *Confessional Politics.* 28–46.

Schwartz, Arthur, and Ruth M. Schwartz. *Depression: Theories and Treatments.* New York: Columbia UP, 1993.

Showalter, Elaine. *The Female Malady: Women, Madness, and English Culture, 1830 -1980.* New York: Pantheon, 1985.

Skidmore, Colleen. '"All That Is Interesting in the Canada's": William Notman's Maple Box Portfolio of Stereographic Views, 1860.' *Journal of Canadian Studies* 32.4 (1997–8): 69–90.

Smith, Sidonie. *A Poetics of Women's Autobiography: Marginality and the Fictions of Self-Representation.* Bloomington and Indianapolis: Indiana UP, 1987.

Smith, Sidonie, and Julia Watson. *Reading Autobiography: A Guide for Interpret-ing Life Narratives.* Minneapolis and London: U of Minnesota P, 2001.

– eds. *Interfaces: Women, Autobiography, Image, Performance.* Ann Arbor: Michi-gan UP, 2003.

– eds. *Women, Autobiography, Theory: A Reader.* Madison: U of Wisconsin P, 1998.

Sontag, Susan. *Illness as Metaphor*. New York: Farrar, Straus and Giroux, 1978.

Sorfleet, John Robert, ed. *L.M. Montgomery: An Assessment*. Guelph, ON: Canadian Children's P, 1976.

Spacks, Patricia Meyer. *Gossip*. Chicago: U of Chicago P, 1985.

Spender, Dale. *Man Made Language*. London: Routledge, 1980.

Stanton, Domna, ed. *The Female Autograph*. New York: New York Literary Forum, 1984.

Steffler, Margaret. '"This has been a day in hell": Montgomery, Popular Literature, Life Writing.' In Gammel, ed., *Making Avonlea*. 72–83.

Thomas, Clara. *All My Sisters: Essays on the Work of Canadian Women Writers*. Ottawa: Tecumseh, 1994.

Tiessen, Hildi Froese, and Paul Gerard Tiessen. 'Lucy Maud Montgomery's Ephraim Weber: "A Slight Degree of Literary Recognition."' *Journal of Mennonite Studies* 11 (1993): 43–54.

Trotter, Bernard F. *A Canadian Twilight and Other Poems of War and Peace*. Toronto: McClelland, Goodchild and Stewart, 1917.

Turner, Margaret E. '"I mean to try, as far as in me lies, to paint my life and deeds truthfully": Autobiographical Process in L.M. Montgomery's Journals.' In Rubio, ed., *Harvesting Thistles*, 93–100.

Van Wart, Alice. '"Life out of Art": Elizabeth Smart's Early Journals.' In Kadar, ed., *Essays on Life Writing*, 21–7.

Waterston, Elizabeth. *Kindling Spirit: L.M. Montgomery's 'Anne of Green Gables.'* Toronto: ECW, 1993.

– 'The Poetry of L.M. Montgomery.' In Gammel and Epperly, eds, *L.M. Montgomery and Canadian Culture*, 77–84.

Weber, Ephraim. *Ephraim Weber's Letters Home, 1902–1955: Letters from Ephraim Weber to Leslie Staebler of Waterloo County*. Ed. Hildi Froese Tiessen and Paul Tiessen. Waterloo, ON: MLR Editions Canada, 1996.

– 'L.M. Montgomery as a Letter-Writer.' *Dalhousie Review* 22 (Oct. 1942): 300–10.

Wherrett, George Jasper. *The Miracle of the Empty Beds: A History of Tuberculosis in Canada*. Toronto: U of Toronto P, 1977.

Wiggins, Genevieve. *L.M. Montgomery*. New York: Twayne, 1992.

Wilde, Oscar. *Plays, Prose Writings and Poems*. London: Everyman Classics, 1975.

Willoughby, John H. *Ellen*. Charlottetown: N.p., 1995.

Wilmshurst, Rea. 'A Montgomery Chronology.' *Avonlea Traditions Chronicle* 10 (1995): 20.

– 'L.M. Montgomery's Use of Quotations and Allusions in the "Anne" Books.' *Canadian Children's Literature* 56 (1989): 15–45.

– 'Quotations and Allusions in L.M. Montgomery's Other Novels.' Unpublished manuscript. Toronto, 1990.

Woolf, Virginia. *The Diary of Virginia Woolf.* Vol. 1. Ed. Anne Olivier Bell. New York: Harcourt, 1977.

Wordsworth, William. 'Resolution and Independence.' In *Wordsworth: Poetical Works.* Ed. Thomas Hutchinson. Oxford: Oxford UP, 1985. 155–7.

Wylie, Betty Jane. *Reading between the Lines: The Diaries of Women.* Toronto: Key Porter, 1995.

Contributors

Joy Alexander is a lecturer in the Graduate School of Education at Queen's University, Belfast. She has an interest in children's literature and has published articles on C.S. Lewis.

Mary Beth Cavert has researched Montgomery's friends for many years and has published her findings in *Kindred Spirits Magazine* and *The Lucy Maud Montgomery Album*. A teacher at Creek Valley Elementary School in Edina, Minnesota, since 1972, she is a member of the L.M. Montgomery Literary Society and co-writes and edits its newsletter, *The Shining Scroll*. She is writing a book on Montgomery's book dedications.

Cecily Devereux is an associate professor in the Department of English at the University of Alberta, specializing in English-Canadian women's literature of the late nineteenth and early twentieth centuries. Her publications on L.M. Montgomery, Sara Jeannette Duncan, Nellie McClung, and Isabella Valancy Crawford have appeared in various scholarly journals. She is the edition of a scholarly editoin of Montgomery's *Anne of Green Gables* (2004).

Elizabeth R. Epperly is professor of English at the University of Prince Edward Island and founder of the L.M. Montgomery Institute (1993). She is the author of *The Fragrance of Sweet-Grass,* co-editor of *My Dear Mr. M.* (with F.W.P. Bolger) and *L.M. Montgomery and Canadian Culture* (with I. Gammel), and lead member of the creative team for the Montgomery CD-ROM *The Bend in the Road*. She has curated four exhibitions on Montgomery, including the Virtual Museum of Canada exhibition 'Picturing a Canadian Life: L.M. Montgomery's Personal Scrapbooks and Book Covers.'

Janice Fiamengo is assistant professor of English at the University of Ottawa with a special interest in early Canadian women writers. She has published essays on Nellie McClung, Sara Jeannette Duncan, and Charlotte Yonge.

Irene Gammel is a professor of English and Canada Research Chair in Modern Literature and Culture at Ryerson University. She is the author or editor of eight books, including *Baroness Elsa: Gender, Dada, and Everyday Modernity – a Cultural Biography* (2002), *Making Avonlea: L.M. Montgomery and Popular Culture* (2002), *L.M. Montgomery and Canadian Culture* (1999, with E. Epperly), and *Confessional Politics: Women's Sexual Self-Representations in Life Writing and Popular Media* (1999). She has served as president of the Canadian Comparative Literature Association.

Jennifer H. Litster teaches American history at the University of Edinburgh. She completed a doctoral dissertation on 'The Scottish Context of L.M. Montgomery' at the University of Edinburgh in 2001 and has contributed articles to *Canadian Children's Literature* and (with Owen Dudley Edwards) to *L.M. Montgomery and Canadian Culture*. She has also written on British children's writer Juliana Horatia Ewing.

Mary McDonald-Rissanen, a native of Prince Edward Island, is a senior lecturer of English at Tampere University, Finland. She is currently researching unpublished women's life writing from the late nineteenth and early twentieth centuries.

Melissa Prycer's lifelong love of L.M. Montgomery's books indirectly led her into the field of history. She received a master's degree in public history from North Carolina State University in Raleigh, North Carolina. She is currently working as a museum educator in Dallas, Texas.

Mary Rubio is co-editor, with Elizabeth Waterston, of *The Selected Journals of L.M. Montgomery* and a co-founder of *CCL: Canadian Children's Literature*. She is the editor of *Harvesting Thistles: The Textual Garden of L.M. Montgomery*, author of the Montgomery profile in *Profiles of Canadian Literature*, Series 7, and co-author (with Elizabeth Waterston) of *Writing a Life: L.M. Montgomery*. Now University Professor Emeritus at the University of Guelph, she is also the author of L.M. Montgomery's forthcoming authoritative biography.

Hildi Froese Tiessen has edited six volumes on cultural issues in Mennonite art and literature. With Paul Tiessen, she has also edited *Ephraim Weber's Letters*

Home, 1902–1955 (1996). She and Paul Tiessen are currently preparing an annotated scholarly edition of L.M. Montgomery's letters to Ephraim Weber from 1916 to 1941. She teaches at Conrad Grebel University College (University of Waterloo), where she was academic dean from 1988 to 1999.

Paul Tiessen has edited books on literature and film, art and photography, most recently *A Darkness That Murmured: Essays on Malcolm Lowry and the Twentieth Century* (2000, with F. Asals). With Hildi Froese Tiessen, he has worked on L.M. Montgomery and Ephraim Weber (cited above). He teaches film studies and English at Wilfrid Laurier University, where he was chair of English from 1988 to 1997.

Elizabeth Waterston is co-editor, with Mary Rubio, of *The Selected Journals of L.M. Montgomery* and a co-founder of *CCL: Canadian Children's Literature.* She has taught at Concordia University, University of Western Ontario, and University of Guelph, where she is now University Professor Emeritus. Her books include *Survey: A Short History of Canadian Literature, Children's Literature in Canada,* and *The Travellers: Canada to 1900.* Most recent publications are *Rapt in Plaid,* which contains a chapter on Montgomery, and *Plaid around the Mountain, a Novel,* with a chapter set in Prince Edward Island in 1804.